New Federalism

About Brookings

The Brookings Institution is a private nonprofit organization devoted to research, education, and publication on important issues of domestic and foreign policy. Its principal purpose is to bring knowledge to bear on the current and emerging policy problems facing the American people.

A board of trustees is responsible for general supervision of the Institution and safeguarding of its independence. The president is the chief administrative officer and bears final responsibility for the decision to publish a manuscript as a Brookings book. In reaching this judgment, the president is advised by the director of the appropriate Brookings research program and a panel of expert readers who report in confidence on the quality of the work. Publication of a work signifies that it is deemed a competent treatment worthy of public consideration but does not imply endorsement of conclusions or recommendations. The Institution itself does not take positions on policy issues.

New Federalism

Intergovernmental Reform from Nixon to Reagan

Timothy Conlan
with an introduction by Samuel H. Beer

The Brookings Institution
Washington, D.C.

130067

Library of Congress Cataloging-in-Publication data

Conlan, Timothy
   New federalism : intergovernmental reform from Nixon to
Reagan / Timothy J. Conlan.
     p.   cm.
   Bibliography: p.
   Includes index.
   ISBN 0-8157-1540-4 (alk. paper). ISBN 0-8157-1539-0
(pbk. : alk. paper)
    1. Federal government—United States. 2. Intergovernmental
fiscal relations—United States. 3. United States—Politics and
government—1969–1974. 4. United States—Politics and gov-
ernment—1981– I. Title.
JK325.C617 1988
321.02'0973—dc19   88-27621
                                            CIP

9 8 7 6 5 4 3 2 1

The paper used in this publication meets the minimum requirements
of the American National Standard for Information Sciences—Per-
manence of Paper for Printed Library Materials, ANSI Z39.48–1984.

Set in Linotron Sabon with Gill Sans display
Composition by Graphic Composition Inc.
  Athens, Georgia
Printing by R.R. Donnelley and Sons, Co.
  Harrisonburg, Virginia
Book design by Ken Sabol

For Marge

Author's Acknowledgements

This book is the culmination of several years of interest in the politics of federalism reform. Chapters 2, 3, and 4 owe a particular debt to Samuel Beer, since they are derived in part from my doctoral dissertation on the politics of Nixon's block grants. In addition, other parts of the book have greatly profited from Beer's stimulating ideas and careful review of the manuscript.

I also benefited enormously from the knowledge and theoretical insights of my former colleagues at the U.S. Advisory Commission on Intergovernmental Relations and the Senate Subcommittee on Intergovernmental Relations, particularly David B. Walker, Margaret Wrightson, and especially, David R. Beam. Each will no doubt recognize many ideas that we discussed over the years, as well as specific improvements in the text stemming from their detailed comments on the manuscript.

I am also grateful to John E. Chubb, Thomas E. Mann, Paul E. Peterson, A. James Reichley, and two anonymous reviewers, for their helpful suggestions. I would also like to thank Venka Macintyre and Caroline Lalire, who edited the manuscript; Richard Aboulafia, who assisted in verifying its factual content; and Lynn Cara Schwalje, who prepared the index.

Finally, I owe a special thanks to my wife, Margaret T. Wieners, who put up with innumerable lost weekends during the writing of this book and demonstrated the perfect mix of patience and impatience along the way which enabled me to bring it to a conclusion.

Earlier versions of parts of this book appeared in "The Politics of Federal Block Grants: From Nixon to Reagan," *Political Science Quarterly* (Summer 1984), pp. 247–70; and "Federalism and Competing Values in the Reagan Administration," *Publius: The Journal of Federalism* (Winter 1986), pp. 29–47.

Contents

Tables

Introduction

I HAVE A COLLEAGUE who likes to kid me about my attachment to federalism. He asks two sorts of teasing questions. One is why I think "ideas" about federalism have any effect on policy. He holds, for instance, that President Reagan's much-touted proposals for federal reform in 1981 were merely instrumental to the overarching drive to cut the federal budget. The real motive was not a regard for federalism as such, but simply conservative hostility to the redistributive policies of the welfare state.

My colleague's second taunt is to question the value of federalism to American government. In his view, it would seem, the chief contribution of the states to our system of government is to introduce further incoherence onto the already chaotic scene of American policymaking. Citing the need to raise productivity, for instance, he claims that the problem can be met not by fifty separate manpower programs, but only by a national policy that reaches into the whole sphere of education and training. Insofar as federalism blocks a national approach to a national problem, it makes policy less coherent and effective than it might otherwise be.

I do not find it easy to answer these questions and welcome the present study as a powerful help. Tim Conlan is concerned with federalism in both respects: federalism as idea and as structure. He examines the explicit proposals for federal reform put forward by Presidents Nixon and Reagan and finds that on balance they have not had much effect. He does not come to this conclusion because he discounts the influence of ideology. He finds that conservatism, in two rather different modes, inspired many of the programs of the two administrations, often with important side effects on the intergovernmental structure. Under Nixon and Reagan, the conservatism of American politics has been expressed, to use the author's terminology, in both an explicit and an implicit federalism. Conlan also takes up the reverse of this relationship, asking what effect federalism has had on our politics. He identifies a very substantial effect and shows how policies have been greatly conditioned by the intergovernmental structure. Looking over the general drift of his argument, one sees that his examination of federalism as idea and structure has led him to consider both the politics of American federalism and the federalism of American politics.

The story Conlan tells is part of a larger historical experience: the attack on the welfare state that had grown up in the United States after World War II. Broadly speaking, a similar development took place in other Western democracies during the same time as attempts to control the economy and to qualify its social effects increasingly aroused criticism and efforts of reform. It will help put Conlan's analysis in perspective if it is looked at in an historical and comparative context, stressing the American background and a comparison with the British experience.

Federalism as Idea

On the first question my skeptical colleague is surely right in essentials. Among the general public, interest in federalism for its own sake as an intergovernmental pattern of authority is slight. This is not to say that individuals may not become deeply attached to patterns of authority. Some citizens of a federal republic may value its intergovernmental structure for its own sake. Quite apart from consequences, they may simply prefer to govern themselves in some matters through a bigger government and in other matters through smaller ones. Overwhelmingly, however, most Americans treat federalism—that is, a territorial allocation of authority secured by constitutional guarantees—as a means to an end, not as an end in itself. The question that moves individuals and groups in the political arena is not which government proposes to act, but what action some government proposes to take. And in general we adopt this sort of pragmatic attitude toward our political institutions. For instance, we value the separation of powers for its consequences, such as its presumed contribution to a regime of individual and political liberty. So also with federalism. It is an instrumental, not a consummatory value.

When President Reagan promised in his first inaugural address to "restore the balance between levels of government," he was being guided by this instrumental view of federalism. He had taken office as the champion of conservative attitudes that had been gathering force around the country for a generation. Though he did not have quite so precise a mandate as he sometimes claimed, he certainly expressed a widespread change in mood. Affirming the old and familiar values of rugged individualism, he sought to cut back the welfare state and to restore the free market—or in the language of political economy, to move social choice away from public choice and toward market choice. In his calculations the reduction of central interventions, such as the grants-in-aid to state and local governments, would serve this purpose. His new federalism was an instrument of his conservative ideology.

To be sure, he also cited constitutional grounds for his program of federal reform. In his view the interventions of the welfare state were illegitimate under the Constitution, not in the strict sense that the courts had declared, that they violate our fundamental law, but in the larger historical and philosophical sense that they offend against the true meaning and intent of the document. As Conlan points out, however, President Reagan was fully able to find constitutional authority for centralizing measures that served his policies. Conceptions of purpose, not authority, controlled his attribution of legitimacy.

There was nothing unprecedented in that. Over the years the broad and ambiguous language of the Constitution has welcomed many "new federalisms." When President Reagan adopted a view of constitutional authority in harmony with his ideology, he was following the example set by political leaders from the earliest days of the Republic. The first administration of George Washington, for instance, was sharply divided by the different visions of the nation's future held by Alexander Hamilton and Thomas Jefferson. This difference of opinion between the champion of central power and the champion of states' rights achieved classic expression in their conflict over the proposed Bank of the United States. Jefferson feared that the bank would corrupt his cherished agrarian order and discovered no authority for it in the Constitution. Hamilton, believing a central bank was necessary to sustain public credit, promote economic development, and, in his graphic phrase, "cement the Union," found in a broad construction of the "necessary and proper" clause ample constitutional authorization. When this question of constitutional interpretation came before the Supreme Court a generation later, John Marshall, speaking for the court, concluded in almost the same words that Hamilton had used that the crucial phrase should be broadly construed.[1] Looking back today and recognizing that the disputed words could bear either construction, but that American government could never have adapted to the needs of a complex modern society under the Jeffersonian view, the reader must be relieved that at that critical moment in the development of our juristic federalism the Hamiltonian vision of national purpose prevailed.

Since the days of Hamilton and Jefferson, the opinions of American political leaders have generally exemplified the instrumental view of federalism, switching back and forth with their policy aims. For most of our history the conservatives have been the centralizers. The Federalists, the Whigs, and the Republicans championed the centralizing and nation-building cause of Hamilton well into the twentieth century. On the other side, the Democratic-Republicans and the Democrats held to the Jeffersonian heritage of "cherishment of the people" and advocacy of states' rights and hostility to central power. The great switch came under the New Deal, when Franklin D. Roosevelt took up the pursuit of Jeffersonian ends by Hamiltonian means, and the ancient friends of central power adopted that opposition to federal intervention which is still one of their leading traits. From the 1930s these contrasting attitudes toward central government have constituted one of the most consistent lines of cleavage between the two parties in both houses of Congress and among the public.

This recent conflict over federal power sprang from and reflected differing attitudes toward the development of the welfare state under the New Deal. At first it seemed as if the new public philosophy of liberalism sponsored by Roosevelt would simply bypass the states in favor of direct federal intervention in the fields of policy being brought into the public sector. This was the method of the main initiatives of the New Deal, such as social security, the Wagner Act, the Fair Labor Standards Act, TVA, and securities regulation. In terms of administrative effectiveness, such direct federal action might well have been the wisest course, since conceivably it could have mitigated the confusion over accountability that arises when the federal government tries to carry out its purposes by means of state and local governments. As it turned out, however, "partnership" and "sharing" between levels of government, as embodied in "cooperative federalism," carried the day, especially with the immense growth of federal grant programs under the Great Society in the 1960s. Because federal programs were implemented in this way, the intergovernmental system became a major target of opponents of the welfare state. Necessarily, attempts to reduce or rationalize the welfare state became attempts at federal reform. In this instrumental context, federalism became a hot issue.

In their efforts to reshape or to reverse the welfare state, the conservative administrations of Eisenhower, Nixon, and Reagan attempted three major schemes of comprehensive federal reform. Broadly they can be characterized as follows:

—reallocation (sorting out): certain functions along with the resources to finance them would be decentralized to state and local governments (Eisenhower);

—consolidation (blocking): resources would remain centralized, but would be used to finance decentralized functions (Nixon); and

—devolution (turnbacks): functions would be discontinued and in that sense decentralized, but would not get federal financial assistance (Reagan).

In principle, reallocation makes the most sense. Ideally, it would lead to a system of dual federalism in which each level of government had separate functions that were financed and controlled by the constituency enjoying the benefits. The growing interdependence of behavior and sentiment in the country as a whole makes this separation of functions more and more difficult. Under President Eisenhower, however, the Kestnbaum Commission, after a searching examination of the burgeoning system of intergovernmental grants, formulated criteria that presumed to identify conditions justifying either national or state action.[2]

Even if functions could be thus sorted out, however, the further problem remained of transferring to the states from the federal side the tax resources necessary to enable each state to pay for the full support of the programs transferred to it. The resulting difficulty of getting financial balance across jurisdictions made it impossible to mobilize a strong coalition in support of the Eisenhower effort. The Joint Federal-State Action Committee set up to carry out the Kestnbaum recommendations did make a few intelligent, though limited, proposals.[3] But the governors did not support them, Congress did not act on them, and the whole effort toward reallocation accomplished nothing except that its very failure confirmed the existing system. Eisenhower conservatism not only gave cooperative federalism the measured and expert approval of the Kestnbaum Report but also substantially expanded it in such fields as health and highways.

Nixonian conservatism even more markedly than the Eisenhower variety accepted a large and expanding welfare state. Indeed, in the late 1960s and early 1970s federal domestic spending took that sudden leap upward which led observers to speak of budgets being "out of control" and governments "going bankrupt."[4] As Conlan shows, the Nixon plan of federal reform was a kind of "rationalizing politics." It was, however, by no means a mere tidying up operation, but was expressly proposed as an alternative to the philosophy of the Great Society. For though this Nixonian welfare state would be expansive, it would also be radically decentralized. Spokesmen cited its aim as "revitalizing state and local governments."[5] This aim was reflected in the conservative rationale for the centerpiece of the reform, the massive scheme of general revenue sharing. While the liberal argument for the measure was economic and social, its object being to give aid to communities according to their relative needs and fiscal capacities, the Nixonian proposal was political in conception and sought to reward communities that showed their capacity for self-government by high tax effort and substantial spending on public goods of their own choosing. Yet, though the effort was local, the "unmet needs" it was directed at were conceived to be national. As Conlan points out, the intergovernmental elements in Nixon's program fitted in with the "centralizing and national dimensions" of his general policy toward the welfare state; and William Safire spoke of Nixon's "national localism." In contrast with Rooseveltian liberalism, one might say, Nixon pursued Hamiltonian ends by Jeffersonian means.

Nixon's plans for reform of federalism and the welfare state were comprehensive and coherent. But, as Conlan concludes, they failed politically. Liberal pressures in Congress forced the compromises that reduced general revenue sharing to an almost unrecognizable hybrid. The grandiose block grant strategy of special revenue sharing was largely rejected, and the radical proposal for a new federal role in welfare, the family assistance plan, was sunk by congressional crosscurrents.

In matters of federal reform, the conservatism of Ronald Reagan veered sharply away from the conservatism of Richard Nixon and Dwight Eisenhower. While defining his ideological stance in his first inaugural address, President Reagan struck the authentic conservative note. He promised not some bold new initiative, but rather to "reverse the growth of government" and to restore "the balance between levels of government." Since that balance has been continually in flux during our history, one may legitimately ask, "Restoration to what date?" One could push the search for contrast back in time, hypothesizing, as has been often alleged, that the Reagan administration sought to repeal the New Deal and restore the conservatism of Herbert Hoover. Reagan's sharp but short-lived assault on the social security system early in his first year suggests that such was his preference. The prompt and continued resistance of Congress and public opinion made any such attempt politically unrealistic.

Clearly Reagan's conservatism was opposed not only to the centralized welfare state of Lyndon Johnson but also to the decentralized welfare state of Richard Nixon. The bias of his cuts was directed mainly at grants to state and local governments. Reagan vehemently rejected general revenue sharing and any form of negative income tax, such as Nixon's family assistance plan. He tolerated block grants, but only as a half-way house to the elimination of all forms of federal aid—which he called "my dream." [6] He found himself politically obliged to offer a temporary transfer of tax resources to subnational governments, but other aspects of his tax policy would weaken the capacity of these governments to continue the programs being reduced or eliminated by the federal government. He liked the little Leviathans at the state level no better than the big Leviathan in Washington. Decentralization, he expected, would hold down state and local spending by interstate competition and by the closer control of taxpayers.

In pursuit of these objectives, Reagan's explicit federalism, as embodied in proposals of 1981 and 1982, was not as well thought out as Nixon's and enjoyed even less success. In 1981 his fiscal program triumphed, but not his federal reforms. He did get a number of his block grant proposals, but the principal achievement was the big cuts made in other parts of the budget, especially the grants to subnational governments. In 1982 the "single bold stroke," consisting of an elaborate scheme of trade-offs and turnbacks, was rejected by the governors and was not even considered by Congress. Again it was the implicit federalism of his tax and budget policies that had the greatest effect on the intergovernmental balance.

By 1983 it was clear that there was no longer hope for comprehensive federal reform. As Conlan shows, from then on it was not grand schemes of reform that changed the federal intergovernmental structure, but the indirect effects of what Paul E. Peterson has called a "new politics of budget deficits." The thirty-year effort of conservatives for comprehensive federal reform, starting with the appointment of the Kestnbaum Commission, had come to naught.

Federalism as Structure

How account for these failures of comprehensive federal reform? Conlan lays stress on the "fragmentation" of American politics in recent decades. His most impressive examples are taken from the Nixon years. That administration's greatest success was the passage of general revenue sharing. This reversal of the categorical thrust of the Great Society programs held the promise of a major reshaping of the federal structure and the welfare state. That promise was not fulfilled for two reasons. When Nixon tried to extend his design to a wider program of block grants, he was unable to mobilize the political forces that had given him general revenue sharing, but was obliged to attempt, with only modest success, a new coalition for each proposal. Even more revealing of the political grounds of the failure, the general revenue sharing coalition itself was hardly a model of coherent governance. The compromises that assembling this coalition forced on Nixon's original rationale produced a kind of distributive localism that simply spread the money around among the 38,000 recipient governments.

Distributive politics is one of the oldest afflictions of American government. Whether in the classic pork barrel appropriation or the more recent "social pork barrel" denounced by David Stockman, it means that government does not "judge claims," but merely gives in to them, with results having little regard for the long run or for the common interest.[7] Machiavelli and Montesquieu held that this tendency toward confusion and incoherence was inherent in popular government in the extended republic. In the nineteenth century one of our friendliest foreign critics, James Bryce, concluded that federalism made matters even worse. By dispersing authority between state and nation and among the several states, he argued, the federal structure, along with other constitutional devices for dividing power, weakened the ability of the public opinion to engender and sustain comprehensive views of the welfare of the nation as a whole. Therefore, when a great national question, such as slavery, arose, "it was the function of no one authority in particular to discover a remedy, as it would have been the function of a cabinet in Europe."[8]

Under the impact of cooperative federalism, this interaction of structure and opinion took a new and specific form. As Conlan shows, the categorical programs called into existence a wide array of specialized lobbies. They were of two sorts: the professional and bureaucratic complex, that is, for each program a core of government officials with scientific or professional qualifications, working closely with interested legislators and spokesmen for the beneficiary group; and the intergovernmental lobby, consisting of governors, mayors, county supervisors, city managers, and other officeholders, mainly elective, exercising general responsibilities in state and local governments. Neither of these two types of political group was in a position to formulate and advocate an overall view of the national needs. Their impact was to further fragment the political process. Yet, though the two types were in a sense opposed, both also wanted "more" and so were a sustaining force in the undisciplined growth of domestic spending on federal grants in the 1960s and 1970s.

To sum up Conlan's analysis: the new structure given to American federalism in the 1960s set in motion forces that considerably altered the political process. These new forces shaped the ground for Nixon's attempts at federal reform, producing in 1972, for instance, the conflict between the champions of the existing system of categorical programs and the advocates of general revenue sharing. As Conlan observes, in that struggle the latter group, the intergovernmental lobby, was the key to success. Yet the same general array of political actors restricted the success of Nixon's further efforts. The new federalism of the Great Society, in short, led to the political process that defeated the proposals of Nixon and Reagan to bring into existence a still newer new federalism.

So perhaps this past generation of the American experiment has once again proved Bryce right? In other words, the new federalisms on top of the old have exacerbated the confusion of policymaking in the United States, including the efforts for comprehensive federal reform.

One can make a rough test of this proposition by considering the positive implication of Bryce's comment, namely, that a unitary system under cabinet government would produce more coherent results. This test is facilitated by the fact that Britain under Prime Minister Margaret Thatcher has been governed by a conservative ideology very similar to that acclaimed and practiced by President Reagan.[9] Like Reagan, Thatcher has sought to bring about a major rollback of the welfare state; the Brycean hypothesis would therefore be that Thatcher's efforts have been more successful than Reagan's. And surely when one contemplates the tidy British system of government from the center and from the top, one is likely to assume that Thatcher would be less diverted by the pressures of distributive politics and so more consistently successful in pursuit of her reactionary goals.

One must immediately grant that in some respects its concentration of power does enable the British system to achieve results that would be unthinkable in the United States. The leading instance is Thatcher's anti-inflationary policy, which produced and sustained for several years a level of unemployment higher in numbers, though not in percent, than occurred in the Great Depression.[10] Similar measures in the United States brought on a severe slump, which, being reflected in the congressional elections of 1982, inexorably required by our constitutional calendar, broke the powerful conservative majority that had sustained Reagan during his first two years in office.

Government from the center and from the top, however, does not make the British system immune to pressure. On the contrary, it may make British government peculiarly vulnerable. After all, under that system of concentrated power, governmental and political, leaders can deliver on the promises they have made in the heat of electoral competition. In the 1960s and 1970s these pressures of competitive electoral bidding were one important reason why the ratio of domestic public spending to national product showed the same sharp surge in Britain as in the United States.[11] In reaction, a conservative government came to power in Westminster as in Washington and at about the same time. Like Richard Nixon, moreover, Edward Heath sought not to roll back the welfare state, but to make it work, promising in the manner of "rationalizing politics" to "run this country's affairs efficiently and realistically" so as to "revitalise our Welfare State."[12] The parallel continued when the succeeding Labour government of 1974–79, like the Carter administration, was obliged by economic crisis to make a sharp turn to the right and in 1979 was succeeded by a far more radical conservatism than Heath's in the person of Margaret Thatcher. Rejecting the paternalism that has made traditional conservatism usually a follower and sometimes a leader of the welfare state, Thatcher displayed a profound sympathy with Reagan's ideology of rugged individualism.

A look at social spending takes one closer to the issue that had precipitated the conservative reaction in both countries. The comparative record has been examined in detail by a number of scholars. When only the extent to which social spending has been cut back is considered, observers of the right, left, and center, as Paul Pierson reports, are in striking agreement that in both countries "the assault on the welfare state has largely failed." It appears, as he suggests, that "the main programs of the welfare state are too entrenched, too fervently supported by recipients and administrators alike to allow more than a modest adjustment in the secular trend towards higher levels of social expenditure." On the other hand, as Pierson cautions, since this analysis considers only short-term cutbacks, it is misleading as a guide to long-term trends. Looked at in this light, the efforts of Reagan and Thatcher, he says, have probably achieved more than observers have generally acknowledged.[13]

In Britain, though the assault on health care failed, as did any attempt to cut spending on the aged poor, Thatcher has achieved substantial success in cutting back future expenditure on housing and pensions. But in the United States also, Reagan's politics of deficits, consisting of tax cuts, indexing tax brackets, and increases in spending on defense and interest on the federal debt, has put severe pressure on all social spending for the foreseeable future. In carrying out the aims of a common conservative ideology, the record of the two governments is a not dissimilar mix of success and failure, whether measured by short-run or probable long-run outcomes. With regard to social spending, the tidy politics of Britain has produced results no more coherent than has the fragmented politics of America.

In the United States, when one evaluates where matters of intergovernmental reform stand at present, one sees that the huge rise in social spending that took place under cooperative federalism has been halted, but not significantly reversed. One measure would be the trend of federal aid as a percent of state and local outlays. Taking into account estimates for 1987 and 1988, the coeditor of the authoritative journal on federalism has calculated that this figure, standing at 20.8 percent under Reagan, has been reduced well below the 25.9 percent of the Carter years, but only slightly below the 21.4 percent of the Nixon and Ford administrations, while remaining well above the 15.6 percent under Kennedy and Johnson. Commenting on this record, the author identifies "the singular failure" of Reagan's new federalism as "its inability to dislodge in any fundamental way the basic post New Deal safety-net function of the federal government, which spans social insurance, public welfare, environmental protection, and individual rights." He grants that there have been "reductions in funding, changes in rules, and adjustments in regulations and administrative procedures," but finds "no massive toll-back or 'turn-back' to the states." [14]

Conclusion

A look back over these conservative attempts to reform the federal structure may discourage those who hope, in the spirit of the Fathers of our country, that the form of our government will be controlled by "reflection and choice" and not merely by historical circumstance. One of the lessons of the experience reviewed by Tim Conlan is to show how hard it is to remodel the federal system according to explicit, coherent criteria. Such criteria, setting out a rationale for the allocation of functions and powers between levels of government, have been developed by various authors on the grounds of political, economic, and social theory.[15] Each of the conservative efforts of reform—by reallocation, by consolidation, and by devolution—was informed by its distinctive criteria. The failure of these comprehensive efforts, therefore, may suggest that the actual balance of power and function will reflect not a systematic scheme, but rather the side effects of substantive policies and policy-making.

Cooperative federalism came into existence in this way. To be sure, it did institutionalize a new pattern of authority, shared but sharply more centralized. That pattern, however, was not dictated by a plan of structural reform set out in a book or a report or a party platform. It resulted rather from the perception widely shared by a coalition of groups and leaders that certain problems were both urgent and national and for that reason required the exercise of new forms of power. The new federalism of New Deal and Great Society liberalism arose from new conceptions of purpose, not from a new conception of authority.

Likewise, such changes as the implicit federalism of Ronald Reagan has imposed on the intergovernmental system have largely resulted from his successes in substantive fields of economic and fiscal policy. The failure of his grander schemes of explicit federalism should not be allowed to obscure these real, though modest, achievements in federal reform. Reagan's conception of the welfare state implies a certain kind of federal system and in that sense the changes he brought about in that system are the product of reflection and choice and not merely of the pressures of historical circumstance.

One of the more striking developments in our federal system during the Reagan administration, however, was surely not intended in the president's brand of conservatism. I am referring to that "new era of state government activism" cited by Conlan, who finds it so marked that he speaks of a "state renaissance." Again in our history, it seems, states have shown that capacity for "experimentation in legislation and administration" pointed out by Bryce in 1893 as a leading feature of our federalism,[16] and emphasized in later years by Justices Oliver Wendell Holmes and Louis Brandeis in oft-quoted utterances. Far from interstate competition and local control restraining government action, as expected by Reaganite conservatives, state after state, Conlan observes, has "aggressively addressed issues of educational reform, economic development, and welfare dependency." Nor does this activity reflect merely narrow, parochial concerns. In all these spheres the new measures have a powerful effect on the common life of the nation as a whole. One may well be reminded of President Nixon's grand design of meeting national needs by state and local action. History has a way of tripping up the reformer not only by often defeating his reforms but also by sometimes fulfilling them in unexpected ways and under unlikely auspices.

SAMUEL H. BEER

I

Federalism Reform and the Modern State

Since taking office, one of my first priorities has been to repair the machinery of government and to put it in shape for the 1970s. . . . The purpose of all these reforms is . . . to make government more effective as well as more efficient; and to bring an end to its chronic failure to deliver the services it promises.

Richard Nixon, 1969 Television Address on Federalism

Government is not the solution to our problem. Government is the problem.

Ronald Reagan, First Inaugural Address

WITH THESE WORDS two presidents summarized their basic philosophies of governance as a prelude to launching major reforms of the federal system. One sought more effective and efficient government, the other a reduction of governmental initiative at every level. Both prescribed intergovernmental changes to address what they perceived as fundamental questions about the government's role in society.

At a minimum, their reform initiatives have underscored the continuing importance of federalism and intergovernmental relations in the American system of government, particularly given the dramatic changes in federal-state-local relations since the 1960s. Indeed, the design, operation, and performance of most federal domestic programs cannot be understood outside this intergovernmental context. Thus it is no accident that, not two, but four of our last five presidents have placed issues of federalism at the very center of their domestic policy agendas.

These presidential prescriptions for federalism reform have varied greatly—from the centralizing Creative Federalism of Lyndon Johnson at one extreme to the antinational New Federalism of Ronald Reagan at the other. Because Johnson and Reagan anchor the opposing poles of contemporary intergovernmental policy, contrasts between them are frequently drawn. On the other hand, the more subtle but substantial differences between the New Federalism initiatives of Nixon and Reagan are less commonly recognized. Analysis of these two agendas for federalism reform can be particularly informative because it "controls" for many factors that complicate comparisons with the 1960s.

Both New Federalisms were responses to perceived policy failures of the past; both advanced decentralization as a goal for responding to these failures; both shared certain instruments of reform, such as block grants; and both were launched in an era of divided party government. Yet these two initiatives were remarkably different in their policy objectives, philosophical assumptions, political coalitions, and policy outcomes.

These differences reflect not only the changing domestic priorities of recent Republican presidents, but also important developments in the evolution of modern conservative thought. In the brief period from Nixon to Reagan, the primary objective of conservative policymakers moved from rationalizing and decentralizing an activist government to rolling back the modern welfare state itself.

Equally important are the changes that have occurred in the dynamics of the national policymaking process during this period. The Nixon years were characterized by a degree of political fragmentation unusual even by American standards. The traditional pluralism of American government was magnified by an extraordinary proliferation of new interests, new decisionmaking centers, and new opportunities and incentives for independent political behavior. In contrast, the Reagan administration has generated a far more interdependent policymaking process, marked by heightened partisanship and budgetary stringency. Decisions affecting one part of the agenda can no longer be made in isolation from the others.

Underlying these political developments are broader changes in the interaction between government and society. Under conservative and liberal administrations alike, government has ceased to be merely the passive instrument of external social and political forces and has become an active and autonomous originator of change. In short, this book does more than simply document an important chapter in the history of American federalism. It argues that the intergovernmental reform initiatives of these two presidents address important questions about conservative ideology and the nature of contemporary politics and government.

New Federalism under Nixon and Reagan

Nixon's New Federalism sought to rationalize the intergovernmental system by restructuring the roles and responsibilities of governments at all levels. The strategy devised for this purpose consisted of four main elements. The first was a broad array of management reforms designed to improve program coordination, efficiency, and planning. The second was a series of block grants that were to consolidate individual federal aid programs into comprehensive grants. In part, block grants were intended to further the administrative goals of improved coordination, planning, and funding reliability, but they were also expected to simplify program operations, increase state and local policymaking flexibility and accountability, and reduce bureaucratic influence in favor of elected officials. Third, Nixon proposed to expand upon the block grant principle of flexibility with general revenue sharing, which would provide "no-strings" federal aid to state and local governments. Revenue sharing sought to use the dynamic and progressive federal income tax to increase overall levels of public sector spending by providing larger grants to the most active states and localities and to those with the greatest needs. Fourth, the Nixon administration endeavored to nationalize public sector responsibilities in those areas in which the federal government was deemed to be more efficient or effective, such as welfare, direct entitlements, and many areas of social regulation.

Although Reagan's New Federalism has employed some of the same instruments and strategies, it has done so in different combinations and in pursuit of different ends. For example, the primary purpose of management reforms in the Reagan administration has been to reduce the power, influence, and morale of the national bureaucracy, rather than to improve intergovernmental management and effectiveness. Block grants, also a popular mechanism in the arsenal of Reagan federalism, have been proposed as a stepping stone to the ultimate elimination of federal involvement in the affected program areas, rather than as a means of rationalizing an accepted federal role in a given field. However, the Reagan administration has opposed general revenue sharing in principle. Although the administration initially tolerated the program for political reasons, it achieved the termination of revenue sharing once this became politically feasible.

As was true with Nixon, major portions of the Reagan administration's intergovernmental agenda—such as the budget cuts and block grants enacted as a package in 1981—were subsumed within its budgetary, tax, and regulatory policies. But this is also where differences between the two administrations' aims have been most apparent. Whereas the Nixon administration supported or accommodated fiscal and regulatory policies that substantially increased the size and influence of the federal government, the Reagan administration's nondefense policies have reduced the federal government's fiscal profile and sharply circumscribed its role in a variety of domestic functions. Even the exceptions to this rule have been informative. Consider the Reagan administration's sweeping federalism initiative of 1982, the central item on the president's domestic agenda that year. It called for federalizing funding for the medicaid program, but only in exchange for ending federal participation in food stamps and aid for families with dependent children (AFDC)—the two cornerstones of federal welfare policy and programs in which the Nixon administration had sought to increase federal responsibility. Reagan's proposal to centralize one income-maintenance program and totally decentralize two related programs indicated a sharp departure from the administrative rationality that had characterized Nixon's agenda. It was acknowledged to be a fiscally pragmatic trade-off intended to decrease federal influence over welfare policy. Apart from this one instance, Reagan has consistently favored national over subnational authority only in those areas in which federal policies were more deferential to private markets or could be used to advance the conservative social policy agenda.

The Significance and Origins of New Federalism

Why have recent Republican presidents placed so much emphasis on federalism reform in their domestic agendas? An obvious reason is that intergovernmental relations have become an indispensable component of contemporary domestic policies. But why New Federalism? The answer has three related dimensions: administrative, partisan, and philosophical.

The reformist thrust of this renewed federalism was in part a managerial response to the administrative dysfunctions and implementation failures stemming from the Great Society. Although not confined to any single party or ideology, the criticisms of federal program structures and their management were reinforced by long-standing party differences over the proper size and role of the federal government. Disputes involving governmental centralization and decentralization have arguably been the most powerful and consistent set of issues dividing political parties in the United States since the 1930s.[1] In turn, this dispute resonates with philosophical themes that date back to the founding of the Republic. New Federalism, in this sense, is the contemporay expression of debates that began before the Constitution was ratified and that formed the basis of the first political party system. Under Ronald Reagan, issues of federalism reform were broadened even further as they were merged with a related but larger debate over the legitimate scope and definition of the public sector itself.

Administrative Roots

The administrative problems to which Richard Nixon and, to some extent, Ronald Reagan responded were the product of a more nationally integrated form of government that had evolved over the previous fifty years. This had occurred in two basic stages.

Before the 1930s the responsibility for most public services and spending rested with state and local governments. Although the federal role had gradually increased after the Civil War, particularly as a result of the regulatory expansions of the Progressive Era, it was not until the 1930s and 1940s that the scope of federal activities was dramatically expanded in response to the twin crises of depression and global war. By midcentury, the federal government had acquired major new responsibilities for economic planning and regulation, social insurance, unemployment and family assistance, and military defense on a continuing and historic scale. The tenor of the change was captured by V. O. Key:

> The federal government underwent a radical transformation after . . . 1932. It had been a remote authority with a limited range of activity. It operated the postal system, improved rivers and harbors, maintained armed forces on a scale fearsome only to banana republics, and performed other functions of which the average citizen was hardly aware. Within a brief time, it became an institution that affected intimately the lives and fortunes of most, if not all, citizens.[2]

Initially, these developments helped produce an unusual degree of political parity between the federal government and the states. Whereas domestic federal spending had equaled only 20 percent of state and local spending from own-source funds in 1929, by 1949 it totaled 108 percent of state and local own-source spending. Throughout the 1950s the two remained approximately equal.[3]

Then in the 1960s the intergovernmental system began to evolve at an accelerated pace. The ensuing changes in the scope, content, and structure of federal assistance programs not only made the system far more complex, but also upset the temporary balance of intergovernmental power. Sweeping changes were ushered in by the Great Society:

—The federal government became involved in virtually all existing fields of governmental activity—including many that had traditionally been highly local in character (for example, elementary and secondary education, local law enforcement, libraries, and fire protection). In addition, new public functions were established, such as adult employment training, air pollution control, health planning, and community antipoverty programs.

—The locus of policy initiation and leadership shifted toward the national level.

—The numbers of new federal grant programs, especially highly specific and often unpredictable project grants, nearly tripled between 1960 and 1968, from 132 to 379.

—Federal aid dollars more than tripled, from $7 billion in 1960 to $24 billion in 1970.

—State and local government financial dependence on federal funding increased by 35 percent. Federal aid increased from 17 percent of state and local own-source revenues in 1960 to 23 percent in 1970.

—More and more federal grants bypassed states and went directly to a multiplicity of local governments. Within states, as well, the percentage of state agencies receiving federal aid grew substantially.

—New, more coercive and expensive types of federal regulations affecting states and localites proliferated.

—Federal programs relied much more on the "service strategy," which fostered the use of professionals to deliver services to targeted clients at the local level, rather than on the less bureaucratized approach of cash assistance prevalent in the 1930s.[4]

This transformation to federal preeminence produced numerous positive outcomes. It forced many backward state and local governments to modernize, and it increased fiscal reliance on the relatively more progressive federal income tax. It reduced levels of poverty and brought increased public services to many who had never known them. Most important, it provided a fiscal and administrative structure for turning the hitherto empty promises of equal protection and civil rights for many black Americans into meaningful constitutional protections and greater opportunities.

At the same time, the 1960s' transformation of intergovernmental relationships was plagued by serious administrative problems. These generated seemingly unnecessary conflicts and prevented the attainment of many other policy objectives. Paralleling the growth in federal programs, functions, and policy activism was a rising chorus of complaints from citizens, scholars, and elected officials about governmental fragmentation, inadequate coordination, growing intergovernmental conflict, and federal intrusiveness. In a comprehensive evaluation of the federal aid system in the late 1960s, the U.S. Advisory Commission on Intergovernmental Relations (ACIR) concluded that many of these difficulties were the result of "excessive categorization of grants," "increasing variety and inconsistency in matching ratios," "multiplication and inconsistency of planning requirements," and the "trend toward bypassing the States."[5] Similar opinions were voiced by other management-oriented organizations, from the General Accounting Office to the Bureau of the Budget.

The Budget Bureau was particularly concerned that administrative overload was undermining the federal government's own program goals: "The complexity and fragmentation of Federal grant programs . . . itself creates major problems of administration for both the Federal government and local governments and inhibits the development of a unified approach to the solution of community problems."[6] Such difficulties led Lyndon Johnson's own budget director to question the limits of federal activism. Shortly after leaving office, Charles L. Schultze wrote: "The ability of a central staff in Washington to judge the quality and practicality of the thousands of local plans submitted under federal program requirements and to control their performance is severely limited. . . . I believe that greater decentralization in the government's social programs should and will be made."[7]

Objections at the state and local levels were equally vociferous. The ACIR's landmark report on the state of federalism in 1967 took thirteen pages just to summarize state and local government complaints. Holding hearings to investigate such problems in 1966, Senator Edmund S. Muskie (Democrat of Maine) concluded that "the picture . . . is one of too much tension and conflict rather than coordination all along the line of administration."[8]

These administrative dysfunctions were a major target of Richard Nixon's New Federalism agenda. As the opening quotation of this chapter makes clear, both Nixon's rhetoric and thinking about federalism contained a powerful current of managerialism. As chapter 2 describes in more detail, many of the Nixon administration's initiatives were designed to improve intergovernmental administration, from new procedures used to standardize federal aid requirements across programs to proposed agency and program reorganizations to enhanced coordination and planning.

Nonetheless, many administrative problems in federal assistance persisted and in some ways grew worse as the 1970s wore on. The number of narrowly defined categorical grants continued to increase, state and local fiscal dependency on federal aid grew an additional 50 percent, and new, more intrusive, regulations proliferated. Thus by 1980 the ACIR concluded that intergovernmental relations had become even "more unmanageable" than in the 1960s.[9] As a result, management issues remained a legitimate concern and motivating factor in the design of Reagan's New Federalism, although, in contrast to the Nixon years, they were now clearly a secondary concern. As President Reagan remarked in a 1981 speech to state legislators, "the Federal Government is overloaded . . . having assumed more responsibilities than it can properly manage."[10]

Partisan Dimensions

The New Federalism initiatives of Nixon and Reagan involved more than arcane features of program administration. They also tapped one of the central cleavages of American party politics since the New Deal, when Franklin Roosevelt—with his vigorous use of federal authority and his expansion of the fiscal, personnel, and administrative apparatus of the national government—refashioned existing party alignments and established a new foundation for partisan competition in America. Put simply, Roosevelt's platform—and certainly his rhetoric—can be condensed into two main points: that government can help solve society's economic problems and that the federal government should take the lead in doing so. The success of this formula transformed the Democratic party from the party of parochialism, suspicious of any new exertion of national power, into the party of national vigor.[11] This was a profound reversal of historic partisan roles. Indeed, the Republican party had favored more energetic national policies since its founding before the Civil War. During the 1930s, however, it fell back on a program of laissez-faire and opposed further federal intervention in the economy. In the process, the Republicans gradually attracted many of the more provincial elements of society that rejected the newly acquired nationalism of the Democrats.

For more than thirty years, public opinion analysts argued that fundamental party lines were drawn around issues involving the proper size and scope of the government's role in society and the economy.[12] These issues not only shaped party loyalties among the general public; they elicited strong differences among partisan elites that continued even after most citizens had accepted an activist role for the federal government.[13]

Though persistent, this partisan cleavage acquired renewed salience in the late 1960s. The Great Society programs gave the federal government a new and powerful role extending far beyond that accepted in the 1930s. The Great Society supplemented the New Deal's legacy of social insurance and economic regulation with a large dose of what opponents called social engineering, the melding and application of professional services and social science technology to solve society's problems. As Samuel Beer has demonstrated, the strongest elements of this "service strategy" were concentrated in the federal education, training, and social service programs that constituted the core of the Great Society. All used trained professionals to diagnose problems and prescribe their solutions.[14] In these years, activist federal policies came to touch on some of the most emotional of social and regional issues: racial integration in housing and education, migrant labor in agriculture, affirmative action, sex discrimination, local educational reform, community and neighborhood development, and urban and rural poverty.

Amidst the prosperity of the 1960s, these policies created deep cultural cleavages that overshadowed issues that had favored the Democratic party. Not only was popular support for federal activism less secure in these areas, but the Democratic coalition was splintered by these issues.[15] Even traditional Democratic constituencies were disaffected by many federal policies: big city mayors by federally sponsored community organizations, southern Democrats by racial integration, and blue-collar workers by the cultural liberalism of professional elites.[16]

Hence, beginning under Nixon, the decentralization long celebrated by Republican party platforms and now the central goal of New Federalism touched a responsive chord among a broader segment of American society. This was something that Republicans could and did exploit. New Federalism complemented vigorous efforts in both the Nixon and Reagan administrations to court blue-collar and white southern voters by promising to curb the power and energy of decisionmakers in Washington. After his reelection in 1972, Nixon blamed the nation's problems on a "breakdown in . . . the leadership class in this country . . . the Georgetown cocktail set." He repeated his determination to "diffuse the power throughout the country."[17] Likewise, Ronald Reagan swept into office denouncing the "puzzle palaces on the Potomac" and reiterating his twenty-year crusade against "disciples of 'big government knows best' [who] don't think private citizens should be messing around with their government." [18]

Philosophical Roots

These contemporary disagreements about intergovernmental roles in the United States have their roots in a debate over the virtues and limitations of localistic democracy that is as old as the Republic itself. In fact, the central question here has concerned philosophers and statesmen for centuries.

It has been argued since Aristotle that genuine democracy can flourish only in small political entities. This notion arises ultimately from the physical constraints on a direct democracy, which must be able to accommodate an assembly of its citizens. Even allowing for representation, many have maintained that the association between democratic vigor and community size is a strong one. It is thought that, in a small community, citizens are apt to be more familiar with the issues and will perceive that they have a greater stake and more influence in public affairs.

Thus Montesquieu argued in the mid-eighteenth century that "it is natural for a republic to have only a small territory." His arguments were well known to leading American colonists at the time of the Revolution, and antifederalist opponents of the federal Constitution used them to justify their own passionate views. Men like Patrick Henry, Luther Martin, and Richard Henry Lee were against the creation of a stronger national government because they thought that it would be a threat to individual liberty and to the survival of the states.

These arguments were ultimately rejected by those attending the Constitutional Convention and by the states that ratified the Constitution. Yet the practical and philosophical merits of small versus large governments and the proper balance of power and authority between the federal government and the states have remained concerns throughout American history. In one form or another, they have contributed to the philosophical differences between political parties—not only since the New Deal, but in every party system since Jefferson and Hamilton organized the Federalist and Jeffersonian-Republican protoparties in the 1790s. [19] As a policy matter, these issues seem to receive the greatest attention after periods of extraordinary federal activism or policy failures, often as a provincial response to threats of sweeping social or economic change and a movement toward mass democracy.

With their New Federalism initiatives, both Nixon and Reagan revived these old questions. Both extolled the merits of the local democratic process and its policy decisions and have contrasted these with the failures of national policies and the national policymaking process. As Nixon argued in his 1971 State of the Union address,

> The time has now come in America to reverse the flow of power and resources from the states and communities to Washington. . . . The further away government is from the people, the stronger government becomes and the weaker people become . . . Local government is the government closest to the people; it is most responsive to the individual person. It is peoples' government in a far more intimate way than the government in Washington can ever be.[20]

Likewise, Reagan has argued that "by centralizing responsibility for social programs in Washington, liberal experimenters destroyed the sense of community that sustains local institutions." He has sought instead to restore America as "an archipelago of prospering communities" and thus "return the citizen to his rightful place in the scheme of our democracy, and that place is close to his government." [21]

New Federalism and the Evolution of Conservative Thought

There are, in short, at least three answers to the question, "Why New Federalism?" A coherent program of decentralization was a plausible policy response to real and contemporary problems of governmental management and performance. It also provided a solution that reinforced natural partisan predispositions and was grounded in a long philosophical tradition.

Yet, as stated at the beginning of this chapter, the New Federalism programs of Nixon and Reagan, and the political reactions to them, were as different as they were alike. Those differences reveal much about the nature of contemporary American politics—both about the framework of ideas that organize the political agenda and give rise to specific policies and about the structure of political interests and institutions that constitute the policymaking system.

At the philosophical level, although Nixon and Reagan shared a belief that the federal government had grown too large and influential and that local decisionmaking is generally preferable to national, they differed fundamentally in their beliefs about the desirable ends of decentralization and the role of the public sector. Although actions do not always follow rhetoric and every administration's policies are diverse and evolving, the policies of their administrations proved consistent, on the whole, with their philosophies.

Nixon was deeply suspicious of the federal bureaucracy and the national policymaking system, which he thought was dominated by "iron triangles" of congressional committees, federal agencies, and interest groups. His New Federalism policies were designed in part to disrupt this system. Overall, however, Nixon viewed his federalism strategy as a means of improving and strengthening government, especially at the state and local levels. It was not a path toward dismantling it. Time and again he argued that the American people were "fed up with government that doesn't deliver" and that New Federalism reforms were needed to "close the gap between promise and performance." [22] Improved governmental efficiency and management were part of his solution, to "make government run better at less cost." [23] Since the main problem in the system was thought to be an overextended federal government, he also prescribed decentralization. Yet if the goal of improved performance required nationalizing certain shared or local functions—such as welfare or environmental regulation—in order to rationalize the financing and delivery of public services, Nixon accepted that conclusion.

Nixon's New Federalism reforms were therefore presented as a program for strengthening government and making it more active and creative. As Nixon declared at the start of his second term, "Fat government is weak, weak in handling the problems." He also maintained that "the reforms we are instituting . . . will diffuse power throughout the country . . . and will make government leaner but in a sense will make it stronger." [24] Programs like revenue sharing and block grants were designed to reward and promote governmental activism and problem solving at state and local levels, and to give such governments "a new sense of responsibility." As President Nixon put it, "If we put more power in more places, we can make government more creative in more places." [25] At the same time, the federal government's role could be strengthened in its own areas of special competence. For example, its efficient revenue-raising apparatus could be used to help stimulate and fund local creativity and to establish and finance a national minimum benefit level for public assistance.

Reagan, in contrast, has viewed New Federalism as part of a broader strategy to reduce the role of government in society at every level. The major focus of his retrenchment program, of course, has been the federal government, and his rhetoric on this score has often been extreme. "We need relief from the oppression of big government," he told an assembly of state legislators in 1981, and went on to lay out his proposal for restoring balance to the federal system. Unlike Nixon, he made no mention of rationalizing roles and responsibilities and encouraging the renaissance of state and local creativity and activism. Instead, balance was to be achieved by purely negative means—by enhancing state and local governments in relative terms, by pruning their resources less drastically than at the federal level. "We're strengthening federalism by cutting back on the activities of the Federal government," he told the legislators.[26] He argued, in short, that a reduced role for the federal government would by itself mean an enhanced role for state and local governments.

Far from encouraging states and localities to step in to fill the void left by federal tax and budget cuts, the Reagan administration focused many of its most severe budget cuts on programs that subsidized activism at the state and local levels. In one of the most pointed and ironic contrasts with his Republican predecessor, Reagan even urged that general revenue sharing—which had been the programmatic heart of Nixon's New Federalism—be eliminated. Reagan subsequently denounced state efforts to raise the taxes needed to replace these budget cuts and to assume new responsibilities—despite earlier assurances that his revenue policies were designed to create "tax room" for states.[27] Furthermore, as chapter 10 details, his administration has used federal law and federal regulation vigorously to challenge state and local initiatives considered intrusive in the private marketplace or in conflict with Reagan's social and economic policies. In this way, the Reagan administration gave concrete expression to the emerging theory of "competitive federalism" being developed by conservative "public choice" economists—a theory that applauds interjurisdictional competition in a federal system as a means of restraining governmental activism.[28]

Reagan's positive vision, though heavily localistic, lacks a strong role for government of any kind. His quest for community entails "an end to giantism, for a return to the human scale." This is not the scale of local government, but "the scale of the local fraternal lodge, the church organization, the block club, the farm bureau"—in short, the scale of the private association.[29] It is this vision of private communal action that spurred the administration to emphasize "voluntarism, the mobilization of private groupings to deal with our social ills." Ronald Reagan's strategy was precisely what he detailed in his first economic message to Congress: "we leave to private initiative all the functions that individuals can perform privately," and only reluctantly turn to states and localities to address public needs, with federal action as a last resort.

The Politics of Federalism under Nixon and Reagan

Nixon and Reagan also differed in their political strategies, which in turn elicited different political responses. Nixon tried various lines of attack to gain enactment of his New Federalism policies, but he met with mixed and limited success. These ranged from conciliatory proposals for modest incremental program changes to presentations of sweeping blueprints for comprehensive intergovernmental reform that led to bitter confrontation with Congress. Ultimately, however, the political responses to Nixon's New Federalism were defined by the fragmented character of the policy process in the 1970s. Even seemingly similar or related issues drew varying reactions, depending on the prevailing interests and attitudes in any given policy arena. Although pluralism and institutional fragmentation had long characterized American politics, they were greatly exacerbated in the late 1960s and the 1970s by the extreme decentralization of authority in Congress, the growth of congressional entrepreneurship, the declining role of political parties, the professionally based autonomy of proliferating governmental agencies and programs, and the growing numbers and relative influence of individual interest groups. As a result, unique political coalitions had to be constructed for each issue in Nixon's agenda—a process described by one analyst as "building coalitions in the sand." [30]

Ironically, Nixon had proposed an unusually coherent and balanced program for federalism reform. But he faced a highly fragmented and complicated political system—especially in Congress—that made coherent policymaking unusually difficult. Nixon both encountered, and through the politics of confrontation and the weaknesses of Watergate, helped to create, a highly individualistic Congress that was approaching at least a temporary zenith in its influence vis-à-vis the executive. In the wake of the congressional reforms of the 1960s and 1970s, this was the heyday of independent congressional entrepreneurship and "subcommittee government." [31]

Fragmentation in Congress was reinforced by the atomization of the broader political environment. By the early 1970s political parties in the United States were approaching a nadir in their traditional influence. They had lost their near-monopoly role in nominating, financing, and electing candidates; their firm grip on public loyalties was weakening; and they had barely begun to adapt to the candidate-servicing role that was being successfully developed by independent campaign consultants, the mass media, and other functional competitors. Although the obituary was premature, David Broder's judgment that "the party's over" accurately captured the conventional wisdom and considerable reality at the time.[32]

The increasing fragmentation of the political community was also due in part to the proliferation of new interest groups. By one estimate, approximately one-quarter of all the organizations represented in Washington in 1980 had been established in the fifteen-year period from 1960 to 1975; the fastest growing were the new citizens' and social welfare groups.[33] Many of these groups owed their existence directly or indirectly to governmental action, either in the form of direct subsidies or opportunities for organizing new categories of government clients and service providers.[34]

This situation greatly influenced the reform policies of the Nixon administration. That is to say, Nixon's New Federalism agenda was shaped to a remarkable degree by earlier governmental actions. From consolidating and coordinating proliferating categorical grants, to sorting out governmental responsibilities, to controlling escalating health care costs, the Nixon administration sought to respond to and rationalize the dysfunctions of previous federal policies. So, too, were politics in this period increasingly shaped by the organizational consequences of prior programs and governmental actions. The development of new interest groups often followed rather than inspired the development of new programs in the 1960s. Even the decline of parties had important roots in the New Deal's social insurance policies. Both developments encouraged more independent, entrepreneurial behavior in Congress as members sought to adapt to the demands of a more fluid electoral environment and make use of the new policymaking opportunities provided by the policy breakthroughs of the 1960s.

In contrast, Ronald Reagan won a series of comprehensive policy victories early in his administration by using strongly confrontational tactics and organizing a stable winning coalition based on partisan and ideological loyalties. Levels of party unity and support on key votes in Congress reached relative and in some cases historic highs during Reagan's tenure, after sinking to postwar lows under Nixon. Although Reagan's record of congressional success fell steadily after his first year in office as his winning coalition eroded, his administration's early budgetary, tax, and defense victories both structured and altered the subsequent policymaking environment.

Above all, Reagan's domestic policies have elicited far more interdependent patterns of policymaking than was the case under Richard Nixon. For example, budgetary decisions now dominate the legislative agenda as never before, as symbolized by the evolving and continuing constraints of the Gramm-Rudman-Hollings deficit reduction process. Spending priorities are increasingly addressed in omnibus budget reconciliation packages and massively comprehensive "continuing resolutions." Opportunities for independent, entrepreneurial program initiatives—particularly if they increase the federal deficit—have been severely restricted and the nature of the programs that succeed has been altered. This restricted and increasingly zero-sum policy agenda has been evident in each successive year of the Reagan presidency.

In short, a study of the politics of the Nixon and Reagan federalism agendas can shed considerable light on the way in which political thought and culture are evolving in the United States, as well as on important political developments that have taken place under these presidents—from the rise of an activist, decentralized Congress to the growth of budgetary constraints on issue entrepreneurship. Underlying all these changes is a common dynamic—that government itself now helps to shape its own agenda and political environment. How it does so is a complex process.

Past policies provide the substance and contours of contemporary policy debates. The ensuing government programs, often created with considerable autonomy, give rise to new associations of program clients, providers, and beneficiaries. In this and other ways, the programs alter the structure of incentives for political decisionmakers.[35] This situation, in turn, may prompt an organized reaction against seemingly "uncontrolled" government growth. This book examines these processes over a twenty-year span of intergovernmental reform. It is fundamentally a study of the important changes in American politics and in the dynamics of the policy process during these years.

Part I
Nixon

2

Origins and Objectives of Nixon's New Federalism

TRADITIONALLY, public policies have been interpreted as governmental responses to outside pressures and demands. Such pressures may come in the form of events and crises that require the attention of policymakers, or in the form of external demands for government action generated by public opinion, interest groups, or political parties.

As the public sector has grown larger, more active, and more complex, however, an increasing number of public policy initiatives have been emanating from the government itself. In many of these cases, government officials are responding directly to the perceived failures or consequences of prior programs and public actions. Lawrence Brown calls such initiatives "rationalizing policies" and defines them as the product of "a government-led search for solutions to government's problems." [1]

Rationalizing policies were at the heart of Richard Nixon's domestic agenda. Throughout his six years in office, Nixon made repeated efforts to reform and streamline the plethora of federal assistance programs to states and localities, to improve program efficiency, to decentralize decisionmaking, and to restrain—but not halt—the unbridled growth of public programs. Many means were employed to gain these ends, notably, grant consolidation, general revenue sharing, and an assortment of intergovernmental management initiatives.

Although the Nixon administration's policy objectives remained relatively constant, its strategy for achieving them did not. Initially, the administration relied on block grants and revenue sharing to implement its broad plan for management-oriented reforms in intergovernmental relations. These initiatives grew out of the tradition of incremental administrative reforms that extended back to the Truman and Eisenhower administrations.

Dissatisfied with his lack of progress with this incremental strategy during his first two years, however, Nixon adopted a far more ideological and confrontational approach in 1971. First, the president revised his earlier suggestions for general revenue sharing and a nationally funded income maintenance program. Then he proposed to consolidate 129 existing categorical programs—which accounted for nearly one-third of all federal aid expenditures—into six broad and extremely flexible block grants called special revenue sharing (SRS). Finally, instead of attempting to fashion a professional consensus as before, he launched an aggressive new strategy aimed at forging a conservative coalition that would enact these massive changes in federal aid structures in one bold sweep. When this high-risk strategy fell short, he sought to coerce Congress into accepting special revenue sharing by impounding congressional appropriations for categorical programs and attempting to implement consolidation unilaterally through administrative actions. When this tactic also failed, individual officials in the administration—enjoying new autonomy as the Watergate scandal increasingly preoccupied White House attention—returned to a more incremental style of policymaking and helped build a consensus for grant reform within specific areas of government policy.

Despite these great swings in political strategy, the Nixon administration remained committed to rationalizing governmental intervention across the broad range of public functions and governmental levels. It never intended to reverse the course of governmental activism or to halt the growth of government expenditures in a consistent or comprehensive manner. Rather, it partly shared and partly accommodated itself to the prevailing political culture of modern liberalism that had established the tone and context for political debate in the early 1970s. Thus it sought to channel governmental activity into certain areas and to favor specific types of intervention. In so doing, it hoped to modify and manage the rate of governmental growth at the federal level.

In other words, the Nixon administration sought both to decentralize federal involvement in some traditional state and local fields—namely community development, education, and manpower training—and to centralize most of the costs of income maintenance, on the grounds that a more uniform, effective, and equitable welfare system could best be achieved through greater nationalization. Through grant consolidation, the Nixon administration hoped to streamline intergovernmental program management and, at times, to alter the political dynamics of policymaking and program expansion at both the national and local levels.

However, the administration also proved willing and at times eager to encourage and fund locally determined governmental activism in many areas where it opposed more direct national involvement. The objective, in the words of one high administration official, was to establish "a positive Republican alternative to running things out of Washington . . . something to be *for*." [2] Thus the administration proposed and fought for a multibillion dollar program of general revenue sharing, and it acceded to substantial spending increases to obtain congressional approval of its community development and job-training block grants. It also presided over the greatest expansion in federal regulatory authority and entitlement spending since the 1930s. It sought, in short, to reform the increasingly complex intergovernmental relations of the modern welfare state, but it did not attempt to halt federal funding or to undermine such activities when they were consistent with better management or local government priorities. In this respect, the Nixon administration differed greatly from its Republican successor and marked the culmination of years of attempts at governmental reform.

Nixon and the Managerial Reform Tradition

When Richard Nixon was inaugurated in 1969, many government officials and public administrators were concerned there was a need to streamline the intergovernmental aid system. Although reform efforts had begun as early as the Truman and Eisenhower administrations, the rapid growth in federal programs and administrative complexity during the early 1960s forged a broad consensus for change among generalist officials with broad functional responsibilities. Backed by growing political demands from beleaguered state and local government officials, such sentiments inspired a stream of intergovernmental reform initiatives by the Johnson administration. However, serious differences existed over how reform might best be accomplished. In particular, three distinct but complementary approaches were espoused: intergovernmental management reforms, block grants, and general revenue sharing. All were used aggressively by the Nixon administration, which also added a fourth component: welfare reform.

Intergovernmental Management Reforms

Management reforms, the most modest of the above group, consisted primarily of grant simplification, which left existing categorical program structures essentially unchanged but called for new administrative processes and organizational structures to help coordinate them. This approach was extremely flexible and could be directed at any level of pro-grammatic activity—federal, state, regional, local, or neighborhood. It was generally favored by those who sought to effect rapid, often purely administrative changes and who viewed more far-reaching program changes as politically and bureaucratically impractical.

Management reform was heavily emphasized during the Johnson ad-ministration, virtually from the beginning. Even the community action program—which formed the very core of the "war on poverty" effort—was initially viewed by high administration officials as a relatively low-cost administrative mechanism for coordinating existing federal pro-grams at the local level.[3] Similarly, improved program coordination was the principal goal of many other prominent initiatives of the Johnson administration, such as

—multistate regional planning introduced through the Appalachian Regional Commission, the nationwide system of Title V economic devel-opment planning commissions, and the Budget Bureau's efforts to stan-dardize federal administrative regions;

—the "A-85" process of intergovernmental consultation;

—the Intergovernmental Cooperation Act of 1968, which helped lay the legislative groundwork for expanded program coordination;

—the cooperative area manpower planning system for coordinating state and local job training efforts;

—the model cities program for coordinating and targeting commu-nity development and social service resources in poor urban neighbor-hoods; and

—the concentrated employment program for developing comprehen-sive manpower and social service programs in selected poor communi-ties.[4]

The Nixon administration built upon and expanded this framework of managerial efforts. In 1969, as part of its general policy to decentralize service delivery, the administration formalized the earlier Budget Bureau proposal for standardized administrative regions, providing each with its own Federal Regional Council to improve interdepartmental coordina-tion and intergovernmental liaison. The Nixon administration also sought to simplify and standardize federal grant applications and pro-gram administration through the Federal Assistance Review process and related management circulars. In 1969 it issued Office of Management and Budget circular "A-95," which established formal mechanisms for coordinating federal programs at the state and substate regional levels, thus implementing the coordinating legislation enacted under the John-son administration. The Nixon administration also helped enact the

Joint Funding Simplification Act of 1974, which allowed state and local governments to combine and expedite applications for several related federal assistance programs. Furthermore, in an attempt to permit greater local government control over the model cities program, the Nixon administration experimented with a program of "planned variations," which become one of the models for the block grant in community development.

In general, these rather arcane managerial reforms enjoyed considerable support throughout the public administration and intergovernmental policy communities. By most accounts, however, their impact was modest and even disappointing. Although most of these reforms proved useful in certain circumstances, advocates of more substantial changes in the intergovernmental system pushed for two additional types of reform: grant consolidation and general aid to state and local governments.

Block Grants in the Professional Stream

Block grants entailed the legislative consolidation of numerous overlapping or related programs under a few large grants, each covering a broad functional area. Within these broadly defined spheres, state and local governments receiving grants were to have wide latitude in deciding precisely how the monies should be spent.

This approach to federal aid reform was first advanced in the 1940s and early 1950s. Scholars and public administrators argued that categorical grant programs had sprung up in a piecemeal and uncoordinated way and that they neglected some vital services and overstimulated others, distorted state and local budgets, and ignored or exacerbated differentials in service levels among the states. As Paul Studenski wrote in 1949, "The most immediate need is for the consolidation of the multiple and separately apportioned grant programs into unified grants, on an equalization basis, covering each major grant field."[5] Likewise, the first Hoover Commission identified five significant flaws in categorical assistance programs and concluded: "A system of grants should be established based upon broad categories—such as highways, education, public assistance, and public health—as contrasted with the present system of extensive fragmentation."[6]

Encouraged by the recommendations of the Hoover Commission, the Truman administration advocated block grant legislation in the fields of public health and welfare. Both proposals met with defeat in Congress, for reasons other than the grant consolidation provisions. During the 1950s the Eisenhower administration advanced an even broader set of grant reform proposals. In 1954 President Eisenhower endorsed grant consolidation for several public health and social service functions, but nothing was enacted. He also established the Kestnbaum Commission in 1953 to undertake a comprehensive review of federal aid and intergovernmental relations as a whole. This was followed by the Joint Federal-State Action Committee in 1957, whose mission was to simplify and sort out federal-state responsibilities. However, this committee could agree to return only two modest federal programs to the states, and these proposals received little congressional attention.

These failures underscored the political obstacles to grant consolidation and reform in the 1950s. Opposition came in part from those who perceived a threat to their existing funding sources. But the repeated failures also reflected a lack of consensus on grant reform among public administrators. Throughout the 1950s the categorical grant system remained modest in size and complexity, and many administrative experts were unconvinced of the need for comprehensive grant reform.[7]

Block Grants in the 1960s

Professional dissension about reform strategies subsided in the 1960s, as the growing size and complexity of the federal aid system generated a host of intergovernmental problems. By the late 1960s, many prominent students of intergovernmental relations had come to regard block grants as the leading remedy for these problems,[8] and they were strongly supported by state and local government interest groups, whose members were experiencing firsthand the political and administrative problems tied to federal grants.

The administrative problems were of particular concern. By 1970 there were seventeen separately authorized federal programs for employment and training alone, and they were administered by thirteen different agencies and bureaus.[9] Even program supporters did not think it was possible to effectively manage a network of training programs administered through 30,000 separate contracts with 10,000 local governments and community organizations. "The proliferation of programs made the need for administrative rationalization increasingly clear," concluded Sar Levitan and Joyce Zickler. "Each program had different authorizations, guidelines, clienteles, and delivery mechanisms."[10]

As a result, stories of mismanagement were legion. One Labor Department administrator illustrated "the limits of federal control" by recounting her experience at the conclusion of a grant cycle when a group of manpower officials met to allocate remaining program funds: "One year, when we finished matching requests for funds on the night before the deadline, we discovered we had millions left over. Here it was, three in the morning and we were trading surplus funds for soda and pizza. I got millions in Job Corps money for a piece of pepperoni." [11]

Local officials also grew increasingly concerned about the managerial and political problems stemming from this proliferating array of categorical grants. During congressional testimony, the mayor of Oakland, California, complained that there were twenty-two separate manpower projects operating in his city, yet few needy individuals were receiving job training appropriate to the local labor market. His efforts to remedy the situation had quickly failed because each separately authorized federal program "tended to resist coordination, and unfortunately local government was all but ignored." [12] A community development official in another city painted the problem of inadequate coordination more graphically: "Our city is a battleground among federal Cabinet agencies." [13] The mayor of Omaha even suggested that city employees had become more concerned with the administration of federal programs than with the locally determined needs of their own community. "Are we going to wake up some morning and find that only 25% of city employees are working on city business?" he asked. [14]

As predicted by the model of rationalizing politics, however, some of the most influential voices advocating block grants in the 1960s came from within the federal government itself. Organizations like the Advisory Commission on Intergovernmental Relations, the General Accounting Office, and the Budget Bureau—whose responsibilities gave them a broad perspective on the growing dysfunctions across the grant system as a whole—all expressed strong support for block grants as a tool for comprehensive reform of the federal aid system.

Even more important were the views of high officials in the Johnson administration. Walter Heller, former chairman of the President's Council of Economic Advisers and a well-known proponent of general revenue sharing, endorsed grant consolidation in 1967, arguing that "we must move toward broader categories [of aid] that will give states and localities more freedom of choice." [15] In testimony before Congress, President Johnson's budget director, Charles L. Schultze, also endorsed the block grant concept as a means of making "further progress . . . in overcoming the problem of excessive categorization and fractionating of Federal aid." [16]

The Johnson administration did more than preach the merits of grant consolidation, however. In the public health field, President Johnson proposed and obtained enactment of the Partnership for Health Act in 1966.

This long-sought consolidation, which combined nine public health formula grants into a single block grant program, had been recommended
since the days of the first Hoover Commission. By 1966 the concept was
supported by most members of the public health community, and the
president's proposal faced little opposition in Congress. Although he had
recommended a categorical program structure in law enforcement, President Johnson also signed into law a congressionally inspired block
grant—the Law Enforcement Assistance Act of 1968. In the closing
weeks of the administration, additional block grants were under consideration in the Budget Bureau for such broad purposes as "reducing economic dependency," "children and youth" services, and "improving our
physical environment." [17] The level of refinement in some of these proposals illustrates the degree of organizational capacity and institutional
support for grant consolidation that existed within the federal government before the inauguration of the Nixon administration.

Nixon and Block Grants

Originally President Nixon hewed closely to this tradition of grant
consolidation. In one of his first speeches on the subject, he endorsed
block grants as a means of remedying "the confusion, arbitrariness and
rigidity of the present system." [18] Early in his administration he proposed
legislation to establish a streamlined process for congressional consideration of grant consolidation proposals, similar to the one used in executive reorganizations.

The president's first proposal for a job training block grant in 1969
reflected similar managerial concerns and differed sharply from the later
"no-strings" consolidation approach used in special revenue sharing. Developed by policy professionals in the Labor Department, the proposed
Manpower Training Act featured a range of management-oriented provisions, including management incentive grants, a regional planning focus, and a phased consolidation of programs to help states gradually
build the capacity to administer the program. The administration also
deferred to policy specialists in community development and elected to
retain the model cities program while experimenting with adding block
grant features to it. Through the planned variations program, it increased
mayoral involvement, expanded program activities, and reduced federal
paperwork in sixteen selected cities.

Indeed, the administration nearly won congressional approval of a
management-oriented employment training block grant in 1970. A compromise proposal, combining manpower block grant features with a

temporary public service jobs program, passed the House of Representatives that year with the president's support. The Senate, however, refused to accept the consolidation of many members' favored categorical programs, and Congress failed to pass a bill that the president would accept. Frustrated with the lack of progress on this bill and other managerial reform attempts, Nixon abruptly altered his grant reform strategy in January 1971 with his sweeping proposal for six highly decentralized special revenue sharing block grants.

Revenue Sharing and the Mainstream

The third approach to grant reform, general revenue sharing (GRS), was proposed as a replacement of or supplement to existing categorical grants. Revenue sharing was to provide a source of virtually unrestricted federal funds to state and local governments, to be spent in almost any manner deemed appropriate. Because of this no-strings approach, the GRS concept was strongly favored by state and local governments and their organizations in Washington.

The concept also appealed to many economists. They viewed it as an efficient means of equalizing interstate variations in fiscal capacity, of reducing the "fiscal drag" expected from projected federal budget surpluses during the 1960s, and of harnessing the relatively progressive federal income tax apparatus to provide needed revenues for what appeared in the 1960s to be fiscally starved state and local governments.[19] Overall, proponents of revenue sharing tended to focus on the problem of inadequate state and local revenues, and to trust such governments to make wise or appropriate spending decisions if only this fiscal inadequacy could be overcome.

As the 1950s and 1960s progressed, the revenue sharing concept received growing support in both political parties. The first major revenue sharing bill was introduced in 1958 by Congressman Melvin R. Laird, a mainstream conservative Republican from Wisconsin. A more important boost came in the early years of the Johnson administration. The chairman of the Council of Economic Advisers, Walter Heller, endorsed revenue sharing along with grant consolidation, and he sought to gain the president's backing for it during the 1964 campaign. A White House task force established to study the idea endorsed it in the fall of 1964, but the president ultimately rejected the concept for complex personal and political reasons.[20] When Heller left the White House staff soon thereafter, he escalated his efforts on behalf of revenue sharing. In an influential series of lectures at Harvard and in a subsequent book, he argued vigorously that

> revenue sharing, or similar general-purpose grants, could provide the missing fiscal link . . . a dependable flow of Federal funds in a form that would enlarge, not restrict, the options of state and local decision makers. . . . [Such grants] combine the sound conservative principle of preserving the decentralization of power and intellectual diversity that are essential to a workable federalism with the compassionate liberal principle of promoting equality of opportunity among different income groups and regions of the United States.[21]

By 1968 the revenue sharing concept was supported by both parties' candidates for president, although significant differences existed in program content and emphasis. By this time, too, most state and local government officials in both parties had placed GRS at the top of their legislative agendas and were prepared to fight for such a program. Scholars also supported the revenue sharing concept in large numbers, and many viewed it as the most attractive strategy yet proposed for reforming the intergovernmental system.[22]

Revenue Sharing and the New Federalism

The push for revenue sharing gained new momentum with the election of Richard Nixon. In the president's first major address on domestic policy in 1969, revenue sharing was one of the three main pillars of the New Federalism. Although the president's proposals were billed as "the first major reversal of the trend toward ever more centralization of government in Washington," they had, in the words of one participant, "a quite progressive cast."[23]

Specifically, Nixon's first revenue sharing bill adopted an *entitlement* approach to intergovernmental assistance. It proposed that 1 percent of personal taxable income eventually be allocated to state and local governments, phased in gradually to minimize the immediate effect on the federal budget. Equally significant, the program's formula was designed to reward active and innovative state and local governments rather than simply siphon funds away from Washington. Grants were to be distributed to states partly on the basis of "tax effort," the level of tax burden that states were willing to impose on themselves. Thus in congressional testimony, administration officials explained that one of the "ultimate purposes" of the president's revenue sharing proposal was to "provide both the encouragement and the necessary resources for local and State officials to exercise leadership in solving their own problems" and "to restore strength and vigor to local and State governments." [24]

Despite the high priority given to revenue sharing by President Nixon and the growing support for the concept throughout the intergovernmental community, Congress failed to advance the proposed legislation during Nixon's first two years in office. This was due in part to the fact that the president was preoccupied with foreign policy matters and issues like welfare reform. More important, however, was the fact that the bill itself had powerful opponents. Although local governments vigorously endorsed the revenue sharing concept, they were unhappy with the distribution of funds to them under the administration's plan. Supporters of existing categorical programs viewed revenue sharing as a dangerous threat to their own funding, and they were strongly backed by congressional committee chairmen who saw unrestricted federal aid as a challenge to their own authority and prerogatives to establish federal priorities. In addition, many fiscal conservatives were opposed to the program's price tag, and they too viewed unrestricted aid as fiscally irresponsible.

Nationalizing Welfare: The Family Assistance Plan

To those accustomed to viewing Nixon's federalism initiatives simply as an attempt to dismantle the federal government and to undermine the welfare state, no element of the New Federalism was more surprising than the family assistance plan (FAP). This proposal, which was part of the original New Federalism package unveiled in 1969, would have abolished the aid to families with dependent children (AFDC) program and established a federal minimum income payment of $1,600 annually for a family of four. It would have substantially increased government support for families in many poor states and enlarged the total welfare budget of the federal government. Combined with other elements of the New Federalism, FAP was part of a strategy for "sorting out" intergovernmental functions, which consisted of enlarging the federal government's role in income maintenance—a policy area with broad national ramifications—while decentralizing several areas of predominantly state and local interest.

Like block grants and general revenue sharing, the concept of a guaranteed national income had a heritage of bipartisan support. The concept was first seriously proposed by the conservative economist Milton Friedman in 1962. Calling his proposal a "negative income tax," Friedman proposed replacing the existing welfare structure with a system of graduated income supplements that would vary in size with earnings. Friedman believed that the primary fault of the welfare system lay in its financial disincentives, which discouraged recipients from accepting low-paying jobs and ending welfare dependency. At the bottom of the employment ladder, welfare payments could be larger than earnings, and they were eliminated on a dollar-for-dollar basis as wages were received. Thus Friedman proposed a system of graduated welfare payments that would decline as earned income rose, but would always provide greater combined income with employment than without it. Such a system, he argued, would preserve the incentives to find and retain a job.[25]

Despite its conservative origins, the negative income tax found its major political champion inside the Johnson administration—at the very core of the Great Society. Sargent Shriver, the first director of the Office of Economic Opportunity (OEO), endorsed the concept in 1965. Although President Johnson never agreed to adopt it on a large scale, OEO funded a multiyear project to experiment with such a program in 1967.

Two years later, this concept was sold to Richard Nixon by Richard P. Nathan, assistant director of the Office of Management and Budget (OMB), and White House domestic adviser Daniel Patrick Moynihan. Over the strenuous objections of more conservative members of his administration, the president made the multibillion dollar family assistance plan, with its national income floor, the second pillar of his New Federalism.

As described in chapter 5, this proposal enjoyed mixed success in Congress. It passed the House in 1970 but was stymied in the Senate. There it was caught in a difficult bind between southern conservatives, who worried about the plan's effects on low-wage workers in the South, and northern liberals and welfare rights proponents, who saw the minimum payment as too low.

Political Dimensions of the New Federalism

By 1971, then, virtually the entire New Federalism agenda, except for a few modest management initiatives, was bogged down in Congress. No block grants had been enacted. The House had refused even to hold hearings on general revenue sharing. And the family assistance plan had died an unceremonious death in the Senate.

Developing a New Strategy

This congressional inertia spurred a dramatic change in administration strategy that broke the ties with the managerial reform tradition and heightened the salience of the political aims of the New Federalism. A bold New Federalism initiative was made the centerpiece of Nixon's 1971 domestic agenda. In his State of the Union address, the president proposed a revised family assistance plan, which raised the federal minimum floor for a family of four by one-half, to $2,400. A revamped, $5 billion general revenue sharing plan was unveiled. Most dramatically, President Nixon proposed six highly decentralized block grants that consolidated 129 programs in the fields of urban community development, rural development, job training, law enforcement, education, and transportation. Combined with GRS, the $11.3 billion price tag for these six special revenue sharing initiatives totaled 45 percent of all federal aid in 1972 and consolidated more than one quarter of all intergovernmental programs.

This sweeping new initiative, and the legislative strategy developed to advance it, focused new attention on the political objectives of New Federalism. Nixon's reform proposals always were intended to redistribute power in the intergovernmental system, as well as to improve governmental management. In his first address on federalism in 1969—in which he announced proposals for general revenue sharing, an employment training block grant, and welfare reform—Nixon stated:

> My purpose . . . is . . . to . . . present a new . . . drastically different approach . . . to the way the responsibilities are shared between the State and Federal Governments. . . . These proposals . . . represent the first major reversal of the trend toward ever more centralization of government in Washington. . . . It is time for a New Federalism in which power, funds, and responsibility will flow from Washington to the States and to the people.[26]

The objective was to use grant consolidation to alter the ground rules of federal aid politics, undercutting the influence of Washington-centered interest groups and their congressional and bureaucratic allies who promoted and benefited from individual categorical grants. As Richard Nathan, then assistant OMB director and chief architect of the Nixon administration New Federalism proposals, observed in a subsequent interview, the administration hoped that individual program clienteles would reduce their lobbying efforts once the payoff was diluted in a consolidated grant: "There were people in the administration who . . . understood that once there was a broad based grant, it would weaken the individual claims for more money." Elsewhere Nathan has added that "the idea was to weaken the federal bureaucracy." [27] Even the historic family assistance plan was sold to Nixon partly as a way to bypass human services bureaucracies and to "get rid of social workers." [28]

Despite these political objectives, the primary motivation for this sweeping new initiative was dissatisfaction with the tactics of the past, not a fundamental change in goals. Management reforms continued. In fact, the federalism thrust shared top billing on the president's agenda with a historic restructuring of cabinet departments that reduced their number from twelve to eight. An expanded national welfare role was retained. The revenue sharing formula retained incentives for state and local activism.

At the same time, top White House officials concluded that emphasizing continuities with past reforms would not succeed. They believed that established Washington power centers—interest groups, bureaucrats, and members of Congress—had stymied change and had to be challenged more directly and aggressively. As Nathan wrote in early 1971 with regard to block grants: "It has become increasingly clear that a new strategy is needed . . . [The old] approach is one which emphasized the consolidation of individual grants and would have us work within the system to take successive incremental steps to streamline Federal aids. The problem, simply put, is that this approach doesn't work." [29] Likewise, administration documents reveal that John D. Ehrlichman, then President Nixon's chief domestic adviser, believed that the initial grant consolidation efforts and GRS had failed in Congress because they were "too small." Ehrlichman felt the proposals weren't dramatic enough, that "they didn't grab the point." [30] Consequently, a search was launched in 1970 for an alternative approach to the reform of federal grant programs.

A Megagrant Rejected

As early as July 1970, the president decided to focus the search on some type of tax sharing or expanded revenue sharing approach to federal aid. However, the real work did not begin until November. The first alternative explored at that time was a gigantic general revenue sharing program, with funds derived from terminating a wide variety of federal grant and nongrant programs. At one point, reports Paul Dommel, the White House considered eliminating "all categorical grants," although this idea "did not last long." [31] Nonetheless, work on selecting a group of programs to be merged into a giant revenue sharing package continued into December.

This revenue sharing proposal differed from the subsequent special revenue sharing approach. OMB and Treasury officials developed economic criteria for selecting candidate programs for merger and termination. Programs whose effects were deemed to "spill over" into a number of states or other jurisdictions, like contagious disease control, were deemed inappropriate for merger into an unrestricted grant program. Many direct income transfers and grants for human and social services were also excluded as "long term investments in human capital." [32] On the other hand, a broad range of grant and nongrant expenditures with "primarily local benefits" were included in the GRS initiative.

Accordingly, forty-one diverse federal programs were identified as candidates for revenue sharing, including the Army Corps of Engineers, the Agricultural Extension Service, the Tennessee Valley Authority (TVA), urban renewal, model cities, and the tax subsidy for state and local government bonds. Altogether, these programs had outlays of approximately $9.25 billion in 1972 (see table 2-1). In contrast, many programs that would later be marked for consolidation into SRS plans were excluded by these criteria, including Title 1 of the Elementary and Secondary Education Act, manpower training programs, and vocational education. In all, over $15 billion in federal grant programs were excluded from the GRS package.

Just one month before the State of the Union address, this massive revenue sharing plan was suddenly abandoned as too impractical and impolitic. "We shot that down," said Nathan of OMB, "that plan was Ehrlichman's and Harper's. They didn't have much idea of what they were doing, or an understanding of the politics of it." [33] Nevertheless, the White House continued to insist on a dramatic proposal, and OMB director George P. Shultz agreed. "I favor a bold approach," he told the president in mid-December, "cutting into the categorical programs to the maximum extent possible." [34] But he successfully pushed for a series of virtually unrestricted block grants instead of the gigantic revenue sharing plan because block grants will "offend the interest group less." These arguments carried the day, and in the few remaining weeks before January 22, 1971, the broad outlines of the president's proposal were quickly thrown together.

Despite their high visibility and new strategy, the revised proposals met with mixed success. The specific politics of each component of Nixon's New Federalism—block grants, revenue sharing, and welfare re-

TABLE 2-1. Programs Proposed for Inclusion in Revenue Sharing
by the Office of Management and Budget, 1970
Millions of dollars

Program	Outlays
Appalachian Regional Commission	288
Economic Development Administration	240
Regional Action Planning Commissions	9
Highway beauty	30
Forest highways	23
Public lands highways	8
State and community highway safety	70
Cooperative State Research Service	60
Extension Service	156
Farmers Cooperative Service	2
Rural electrification	292
FHA sewer and water grants	58
Forest Service grants	22
Forest Service permanent	120
Bureau of Land Management permanent	93
Sport fish permanent	57
Land and water conservation fund	90
Anadromous fish	3
Bureau of Reclamation	358
Bonneville Power Administration	129
Southwest Power Administration	8
Southeast Power Administration	1
Alaska Power Administration	1
Corps of Engineers—civil works	1,350
Tennessee Valley Authority	685
Waste treatment facility grants	702
Minor categoricals (books and libraries)	287
Medical facilities construction grants	218
Regional medical program grants	70
Community mental health staffing grants	50
Partnership for health grant	125
Maternal and child health formula grants	117
Air pollution abatement control grants	25
Social services (excludes administrative costs for public assistance)	760
Model cities	210
OEO direct operations (excludes R&D, Indian, and migrant programs)	575
Urban renewal	1,300
Water and sewer	170
Open space	70
Planning	50
Tax subsidy	400
TOTAL	9,282

SOURCE: OMB, Revenue Sharing Working Group, "Initial Report," Washington, D.C., December 1, 1970.

form—are reviewed in subsequent chapters. Suffice it to say that the overriding factor shaping the political fortunes of Nixon's New Federalism was simply this: neither Congress nor the broader political system of the 1970s was prepared to deal coherently with the complex and comprehensive reforms that the president was proposing. Both his early efforts to encourage and persuade and his later efforts to cajole and compel Congress to accept his plans faltered in an environment of fragmented politics.

3

The Fragmented Politics of Block Grants

I F ONE WERE to choose a single term that best characterized the national policymaking process in the 1970s, it would probably be "fragmented." The splintering of power that occurred in this decade pervaded the political system: it could be seen in the rise of "subcommittee government" in Congress, the proliferation of interest groups and political action committees in Washington, and the decline of party loyalties in the electorate and party voting in Congress. Nowhere was the fragmentation more evident than in the politics of federalism reform.

By 1971 Nixon's ambitious New Federalism program was at the top of the domestic policy agenda. Its mix of block grants, revenue sharing, and welfare reform constituted an unusually coherent response to the complex, interrelated problems plaguing the public sector. Even in the best of circumstances no president could expect an independent and pluralistic Congress to accept such a package in toto. Given the Democrats' control of Congress and the ideological overtones of decentralization, a vigorous partisan conflict appeared likely. Yet once in the congressional arena, the New Federalism proposals were confronted by a multitude of idiosyncratic coalitions rather than a disciplined legion of steadfast opponents. Each reform was treated independently, according to the predominant forces and political sentiments in the particular policy arena.

Consider what happened to Nixon's block grant proposals, which aimed to consolidate one-third of all federal programs into six loosely defined megagrants called special revenue sharing. Despite talk at the time of an "imperial" presidency, two of these special revenue sharing initiatives were dismissed summarily by Congress in response to the preferences of interest groups and legislative specialists most familiar with the affected programs. Two were debated and rejected. Only two block grants were passed in modified form, and these enactments owed their

TABLE 3-1. Proposed Program Consolidations and
Spending Authorizations in Special Revenue Sharing Plan, 1971

Amounts in billions of dollars

Program	Amount in first full year	Number of programs folded in
Education	3.0	33
Transportation	2.6	26
Urban community development	2.1	12
Manpower training	2.0	17
Rural community development	1.1	39
Law enforcement	0.5	2
TOTAL	11.3	129

SOURCE: U.S. Advisory Commission on Intergovernmental Relations, *Special Revenue Sharing: An Analysis of the Administration's Grant Consoidation Proposals*, M-70 (GPO, 1971), p. 6.

success more to the consensus among community development and manpower training officials favoring grant consolidation than to presidential leadership. The fate of Nixon's block grants illustrates not only the fortunes of the New Federalism, but also the predominant patterns of policymaking in the fragmented political system of the early 1970s.

Block Grant Failures

In 1971 President Nixon announced his plan to consolidate 129 existing categorical programs into six special revenue sharing programs in the fields of transportation, education, rural development, law enforcement, community development, and employment training (see table 3-1). The negative response in Congress to the first four proposals stemmed from the unanimous opposition of interest groups and program specialists in the affected policy areas.

One of these areas was transportation. The president of the American Trucking Association expressed "revulsion" at portions of the administration's plan, calling it a "large scale raid on the federal Highway Trust Fund." [1] Many others involved with highways and airports were also opposed, including state highway officials, who feared losing some of their control over highway programs to the governors. Even some officials within the Nixon administration had reservations about the proposal. In a later interview then assistant OMB director Richard Nathan reported that he "never thought transportation [revenue sharing] made sense." It was one of the "least-studied" proposals before its introduction to Congress, he said, and could be considered one of the "throwaways" in the president's package. [2]

Given the lukewarm support from the administration and the hostile reception from powerful interest groups, it is hardly surprising that the program found little support in Congress. Even Republicans in both the House and Senate refused to introduce the transportation bill, and so hearings were never held on it in either chamber of Congress. Transportation Department officials identified yet another cause of opposition within Congress: its desire to retain control over porkbarrel projects. As the under secretary of transportation observed: "Our categorical programs are nearer and dearer to Congressmen's hearts than any other. They are the porkiest of the pork, and Congress guards them very jealously." [3]

Similarly, before the rural development revenue sharing proposal was even sent to Capitol Hill, parts of the plan came under attack from important members of both parties. Leading Republicans like Senate Minority Leader Hugh Scott of Pennsylvania and Senator John Sherman Cooper of Kentucky, ranking member of the Senate Public Works Committee, argued that the Appalachian Regional Commission would be virtually eliminated if it was consolidated into a broadly based proposal for rural revenue sharing. Supporters of the Agricultural Extension Service mobilized to thwart consolidation of their program as well. As in the case of transportation, the public interest groups were indifferent or opposed to the president's proposal. The National League of Cities and U.S. Conference of Mayors testified against the proposal at Senate hearings because it placed authority for administering rural development programs in the Agriculture Department rather than the normally more sympathetic Department of Housing and Urban Development (HUD). They were also opposed to the idea of distributing funds to the states rather than directly to municipalities.

Consequently rural revenue sharing was hardly even considered by the House Agriculture Committee, whose chairman, W. R. Poage (Democrat of Texas), in particular, reinforced the views of dissenting constituency groups. On both personal and institutional grounds Poage staunchly rejected the very concept of block grants as antithetical to the principles of fiscal conservatism and to the interests of Congress. Rather than accept the concept of program consolidation and simplification, the House Agriculture Committee recommended that the government increase funding in existing rural development programs and establish new grant programs for planning, pollution control, and land use.

The Senate Agriculture Committee also rejected the idea of program consolidation, although a coalition of liberal and conservative Democrats did propose that a supplemental rural development "block grant" be appended to existing categoricals as a means of increasing federal spending for rural areas. This supplemental block grant was opposed unsuccessfully by a combination of liberal opponents of block grants led by Senator Adlai E. Stevenson III (Democrat of Illinois), and by Republican fiscal conservatives like Senators Carl T. Curtis of Nebraska and Milton R. Young of North Dakota. Although the supplemental block grant was adopted by the Senate, it was deleted in the House-Senate conference on the Rural Development Act of 1972.

The Nixon administration's education revenue sharing (ERS) proposals elicited yet another negative response from interest groups and Congress. The liberal chairman of the House Education and Labor Committee complained that special revenue sharing allowed little federal control over education funds and likened it to "throwing money down ratholes."[4] Others feared that ERS was simply an indirect method of reducing the education budget. A congressional staffer observed in an interview that "people didn't believe they'd spend the money under ERS. They thought it was just a new attempt to subvert the programs." Education interest groups echoed these reactions. The federal relations director of a major education organization remarked frankly in an interview that "our reaction was literally 'screw them.' We weren't going to give it the light of day." "The whole education community was up in arms at the proposal," said another interest group representative. So strong were the negative reactions that even many Republicans who supported education block grants in the 1960s—such as Congressman Albert H. Quie of Minnesota—expressed reservations about the president's revenue sharing approach. "You do not want a flat block grant in education," he stated in an interview. "Pressure is so strong for increased pay from teachers' unions."[5]

Given such massive resistance, it is not surprising that ERS was dismally received in Congress. The hearings held in late 1971 were little more than an empty forum for the administration's lonely soliloquy on behalf of ERS, followed by a chorus of dissent by education interests. However, the administration was unwilling to give up on ERS as quickly as it had on transportation and rural development. After his landslide reelection victory in 1972, President Nixon sent Congress a similar proposal in 1973, this time labeling it the Better Schools Act.

Despite the new title and the administration's threats not to consider alternatives, Congress and the education community remained opposed to ERS. It was only the fear of a presidential veto that led Congress to enact a minor compromise consolidation of seven modest programs in 1974 as a price for keeping major education programs intact. With this small symbolic victory, the president declared success and announced that this was "an important first step" toward the creation of a genuine education block grant.[6]

Theoretical Perspectives on Block Grant Opposition

As the reactions of influential Republicans in Congress like Quie and Scott suggest, many potential supporters of block grants were opposed to or ambivalent about some of President Nixon's proposals. Even staunch conservatives were often divided on these measures. Some saw congressional control over spending slipping away in such loosely drawn programs, while others sought to protect their own pet programs from consolidation. Potential advocates outside of Congress, too, failed to support these plans. Members of the intergovernmental lobby—like the National Governors' Conference chairman Arch Moore, a Republican from West Virginia, and spokespersons for the National League of Cities—saw rural development revenue sharing as a threat to other, more important, interests. Nor did governors and state education officials do much to promote education revenue sharing for fear that it might create political problems at the state level.

These patterns of opposition and neglect were consistent with prevailing theories of congressional behavior in the policymaking process in the 1970s. The most influential contemporary works on behavior in the modern decentralized Congress suggest that rational, election-seeking members will strongly favor categorical grants over consolidated block grants. Such conclusions are reinforced by the familiar logic of the "iron triangle" model of policymaking, which stresses the difficulties of enacting comprehensive legislation that upsets the policy preferences of and established relationships among program specialists in discrete policy subsystems.

The implications of the incentive model of congressional behavior for intergovernmental grants-in-aid have been most thoroughly explored by David Mayhew. Members of Congress, writes Mayhew, strive above all for reelection. The means by which they tailor their behavior to this goal consist of political "advertising" and "credit claiming":

Congressmen find it electorally useful to engage in . . . *advertising,* defined here as any effort to disseminate one's name among constituents in such a fashion as to create a favorable image. . . . [And] *credit claiming,* defined here as acting so as to generate a belief . . . that one is personally responsible for causing the government . . . to do something. . . . The staple way of doing this is to traffic in what might be called "particularized benefits."[7]

An important policy consequence of such behavior, writes Mayhew, is a congressional preference for categorical grants. Narrow categorical grants permit congressmen to obtain particularized benefits corresponding to the needs of their own constituency, and members can do so in such a way that they can be identified with a program for advertising purposes, for example, through the announcement of grant awards. As Mayhew argues,

> The only benefits intrinsically worth anything . . . are ones that can be packaged. . . . Across policy areas generally, the programmatic mainstay of congressmen is the categorical grant. In fact the categorical grant is for modern Democratic Congresses what rivers and harbors and the tariff were for pre–New Deal Republican Congresses. It supplies goods in small manipulable packets.[8]

Starting from similar premises, Morris Fiorina has identified another factor that motivates congressmen to support categorical grants. It has to do with legislative casework, which is an added means by which congressmen appeal to their constituents. Members assume an ombudsman role with the bureaucracy, Fiorina asserts, helping voters deal with governmental problems:

> Congressmen . . . earn electoral credits by establishing various federal programs. . . . At the next stage, aggrieved and/or hopeful constituents petition their congressman to intervene in the complex . . . decision processes of the bureaucracy. The cycle closes when the congressman lends a sympathetic ear, piously denounces the evils of bureaucracy, intervenes in the latter's decisions, and rides a grateful electorate to ever more impressive electoral showings. Congressmen take credit coming and going.[9]

Because of the specific and complex character of categorical grants, they are more effective at creating such dysfunctions and enhancing bureaucratic accountability to Congress than are block grants, which are more general in nature and are administered by means of set formulas. As Fiorina observed, "We have heard talk about more flexible, less centralized policies [but] . . . we should expect . . . little action. . . . To lessen federal control over the daily operation of the country is to lessen incumbent congressmen's chances of reelection.[10]

In short, block grants pose a threat to the self-interests of congressmen as understood through such incentive theories, because they diminish opportunities for advertising, credit claiming, and casework. Block grants do this not only by consolidating many separate pieces of what some have labeled the "social pork barrel," but also by devolving significant decisionmaking authority to state and local governments, which can then take credit for their own projects because they are more or less beyond the reach of Congress.

Contemporary models of the public policy process are equally pessimistic about the prospects for enacting block grants. The most commonly accepted model suggests that specialized subunits of government play a preeminent role in the formation of public policy. These policy subsystems consist of congressional subcommittees, executive bureaus, and affiliated interest groups, arranged in interlocking "iron triangles" of influence and expertise. They are said to shape the bulk of federal policy, to which Congress as a whole and the president by and large defer. Former White House aide Douglass Cater described them this way:

> In one important area of policy after another, substantial efforts to exercise power are waged by alliances cutting across the two branches of government and including key operatives from the outside. In effect, they constitute subgovernments of Washington comprising the expert, the interested, and the engaged. . . . The subgovernment's tendency is to strive to become self-sustaining in control of power in its own sphere.[11]

Categorical grants are generally consistent with the dynamics of policy subsystems because they are narrowly defined and therefore program decisions can be made within the subsystem. The interests of each partner can be served in the process. Benefits can be targeted to specific clienteles. Congressmen can tailor programs to their individual constituencies or to the interests of individual groups associated with a subcommittee. And each agency's penchant for a stable and predictable program environment can be satisfied.

Block grants, in contrast, challenge the strength of the triangles on all three sides. By consolidating individually funded programs into a single authorization that spans a broad functional area, block grants eliminate the guarantee of benefits to specific clienteles. Similarly members of Congress lose control over programs as more players take part in the decisions and as the authority to allocate resources is decentralized to subnational governments. Executive agencies experience a similar loss of program control and face the specter of program elimination or reduced budgets or employment as functions are reorganized and devolved.

This subsystem model has been rightly criticized by Hugh Heclo and others for exaggerating and oversimplifying certain aspects of policymaking. Heclo argues that most policy arenas are porous and much more open to interested and informed outside opinion than the enclosed and autonomous "subgovernment" model suggests.[12] Even so the implications for grant consolidation remain relatively unchanged. Genuine and sustained policy influence continues to depend on unevenly distributed incentives for participation in policy debates—incentives that favor concentrated attention by the interest groups, agencies, and members of Congress most deeply affected by a given policy decision. Such incentives are not deterministic; they may be overcome by the power of new ideas, new participants, and new circumstances. But they do establish certain predispositions toward particular outcomes and the views of particular actors.

The response to education revenue sharing reflected the workings of an active subsystem in education. Major education groups met "two or three times a week" to compare notes on administration activities, funding, politics, and other common interests. In the process groups received considerable assistance from allies within the Office of Education. As one lobbyist recalled, "I never knew what my mail would bring. I would receive something from the HEW mail and see the schedule of a secret meeting. . . . These people [in the agency] were unsung heroes. They were providing us with all sorts of inside information. When a meeting took place, it was almost as if we were present." Congressional staff members also reported seeing "those [reform] proposals before the Commissioner [of Education] did." Such staffers considered themselves allies of the bureaucrats who were suspicious of ERS. "Most of the career people considered it as a means to abolish their jobs, if not in the short run then in the long run," said one.[13]

Block Grant Enactments and Their Implications for Policymaking

Despite the sharply negative response to most of Nixon's block grant proposals and the pessimistic implications of the policy models discussed above, not all the special revenue sharing proposals met with failure.

Two major block grants, albeit significantly modified forms of what the president originally proposed, were enacted during the Ninety-third Congress: the Comprehensive Employment and Training Act of 1973 (CETA) and the Community Development Block Grant (CDBG) program of 1974.

On the surface the success of these enactments appears to be inconsistent with the results predicted by the policy models just described. The politics of these block grants does suggest that such models underestimate the importance of ideas and a normative commitment to making "good policy" within the legislative process.[14] Equally important, however, these programs were the product of the complex and decentralized policymaking process of the 1970s and as such are largely consistent with the implications of the rational choice and subsystem models.

Specifically, these block grant enactments reflected the unique alignment of interests and earlier experience with particular programs in the areas of employment and community development (CD). Both CDBG and CETA enjoyed considerable support from professionals and powerful interest groups that developed independently of President Nixon's federalism initiative. To be sure, many members of Congress—especially Senate liberals—remained protective of the individual grants that they had sponsored. The enacted block grants were modified to reflect these programmatic loyalties and the congressional interest in greater program oversight and control. Yet many other members of key congressional committees from both sides of the aisle supported grant consolidation for political and policy reasons. Besides responding to the active lobbying by local government officials and the president, many shared the professional consensus that consolidation would improve program performance in these two fields. In some respects the most interesting question concerning these two programs is not why they were enacted, but why it took so long, given all the important sources of support for grant reform in these policy arenas.

Factors Promoting Enactment

Block grants were enacted in these two areas not only because of the Nixon administration's strong support, but also because of two other critical factors: the troubled history of categorical grants and the alignment of interests in the subsystems involved. This view was reinforced by the alignment of interests within the two policy subsystems. In community development, for example, the principal clientele of the affected programs was the nation's mayors, who would also be the principal beneficiaries of an urban block grant. Subsystem support was less unanimous in job training, where state and local government officials shared influence with organized labor. However, the involvement of local governments and their strong ties with major legislative leaders promoted the passage of a modified block grant in this area.

A TROUBLED CATEGORICAL HERITAGE. By 1970, many people familiar with both community development and job training programs had become disenchanted with the existing categorical programs and were beginning to support the concept of grant consolidation and decentralization. These sentiments were shared not only by officials in the Nixon administration, but by many program administrators, grant recipients, academic experts, and members of Congress. Their dissatisfaction became increasingly evident in both trade and scholarly writings about these programs, in conversations with administrators and participants in the programs, and in the actions of relevant interest groups and public officials. More important, it was expressed in a series of policy initiatives gradually moving in the direction of block grants that began even before the Nixon administration launched its proposals.

The evolution toward grant reform was particularly evident in manpower training. Apart from venerable programs for vocational education and unemployment compensation, most employment and training programs were recent products of the 1960s. That decade witnessed a series of public concerns with problems like "structural unemployment," automation, and persistent poverty—which led to a sudden proliferation of new employment and training programs. By 1969 fourteen federal agencies were involved in operating seventeen separate job training programs administered through thousands of individual contracts with local governments and nonprofit agencies. Although their goals and clients frequently overlapped, each had its own administrative structure, funded different sponsors at the local level, and used a range of job enhancement techniques.[15]

As a result of this complexity Congress and the federal agencies often had little clear understanding of how individual programs were being implemented or how they related to one another, despite sometimes strenuous and even intrusive efforts to find out. Locally the situation created problems for both program administration and service delivery. As Garth Mangum observed:

> The different sources of funds posed serious, if not insurmountable, obstacles to development of integrated local manpower programs. . . .

The eligibility rules, application procedures, allocation formulas, expiration dates, and contracting arrangements varied as widely as funding sources.[16]

Political problems compounded the administrative ones. Many mayors became embroiled in sometimes bitter disputes over what they perceived to be the politicization of job training and other new social programs administered by local community groups. They began demanding more control over these programs.[17] Other mayors were frustrated by their inability to coordinate conflicting federal programs or to focus them on local priorities.

At the federal level these political problems were exacerbated by the emerging science of program evaluation. Newly refined and developed evaluation techniques like cost-benefit analysis produced little concrete evidence of positive program results that might have made people more tolerant of administrative difficulties. On the contrary, many programs could demonstrate few lasting benefits at all, much less cost-effective results.[18] Complaints about the conservative bias of program evaluation and the need for patience when launching new programs, however accurate, did little to overcome the negative tone of the reports and the effects of political and administrative dysfunctions.

Beginning in 1967, the Johnson administration sought to redress this situation through administrative means. It made two separate attempts to improve the coordination and performance of job training programs within the framework of existing categorical structures. Under the cooperative area manpower planning system (CAMPS) and the concentrated employment program (CEP) existing programs were supplemented with new planning and administrative bodies intended to bring disparate program administrators and services together. Unfortunately these structures had little authority to influence categorical funding decisions and often degenerated into little more than "make-work projects."[19] Politically, however, the newly introduced planning and consultation processes helped to draw more elected officials directly into manpower policy issues and to mobilize a constituency for reform.

Thus when President Nixon was inaugurated in 1969, growing numbers of job training professionals both inside and outside government had concluded that the legislative consolidation of narrowly specified training programs and decentralization of program control offered the best hope of improving program performance and adapting manpower services to local labor market conditions. One prominent group of employment professionals on the National Manpower Policy Task Force declared:

> There is a pressing need to overhaul these categorical and disjointed efforts. . . . Consolidation . . . is an important first step in improving [their] effectiveness. . . . Governmental roles must take into account the inherent limits of the federal government . . . and the increasing steps taken by state and local governments to improve their capabilities.[20]

Through the National League of Cities and U.S. Conference of Mayors, local elected officials also expressed their support for a job training block grant, emphasizing the "urgent need for the coordination of local manpower programs."[21] Despite their attachment to categorical grants, even members of Congress began to enunciate support for grant reform in this area. Although they differed in the programs they included and the degree of decentralization, two bills consolidating job training programs were introduced in Congress in 1969 by members of the House Education and Labor Committee.

As indicated earlier, this emerging policy consensus was evident in the Nixon administration's initial block grant proposal of 1969. The Manpower Training Act of 1969 was developed primarily by specialists at the Labor Department, and its features reflected that fact. Not only did it consolidate almost all of the principal training programs of the 1960s into a single block grant to state governments, it was rife with "good management" features shaped by careerists rather than political officials. These included incentives for effective state administration and for regional cooperation, innovations like a computerized job bank and countercyclical funding during economic downturns, and a multiyear phase-in of decentralization to promote state and local "capacity building" and a smooth administrative transition.

Similar support for reform was building in community development, largely because of dissatisfaction with the two most prominent programs in this area, urban renewal and model cities. Established in 1949, urban renewal was the oldest and largest federal program for community development and it was the first to turn sour. Urban renewal was intended to enhance urban housing and economic development by eliminating "slums and blight." Although the program was initially popular with civic leaders and businessmen, it met with growing opposition in disrupted communities during the 1950s and 1960s. Eventually, the program became a liability to the political leaders associated with it. Liberals at the grass-roots level condemned the program for destroying low-income housing on behalf of downtown businesses, and some derisively dubbed the program "Negro removal." Conservatives, on the other hand, condemned the program for waste and inefficiency. One conservative critic called it a "thundering failure . . . a regressive program." Its results were "negligible," wrote Martin Anderson, while its costs were "high." [22] Local officials criticized the program for its complexity and sought ways to obtain the desired federal funds under less convoluted and politically risky conditions.

In part the model cities program of 1966 was designed to address some of the problems in urban renewal and other rigid (though less controversial) categorical programs. It was intended to enhance coordination at the national and local levels and to provide a source of flexible funding to cities under the auspices of the mayor. As Frieden and Kaplan observed, some early supporters of the program "saw it as a step in the direction of block grants." Although the program became popular with many mayors as a source of new funds, the hoped-for breadth and flexibility were diminished during the enactment process when Congress "redefined the program to make it another grant-in-aid to the cities, not the unifier of all other federal aid programs." [23]

Once in operation, the program became immersed in bitter conflicts between mayors and local neighborhood groups. Partly to deal with these conflicts, planning and citizen participation requirements mounted, and the program drifted even farther from the goal of flexible funding. As in urban renewal, federal paperwork requirements soon became a major source of local complaints.

By the late 1960s there was broad agreement on the need to restructure community development programs in favor of more flexible federal assistance. As a lobbyist for local urban renewal agencies commented in an interview, "The old programs were done, discredited. Something had to take their place." [24]

Initial reform attempts centered on the model cities program. After briefly considering phasing the program out as a symbol of the Great Society's failings, the Nixon administration concluded that the original goals of the program were consistent with Republican philosophy, and in 1969 and 1970 took steps to enlarge local discretion and coordination under the program. Most important were the experiments called "planned variations," which were carried out in twenty model cities and were designed to grant additional authority to local chief executives, reduce federal regulations, and expand the program beyond model neighborhoods to entire cities. Such changes, announced Housing Secretary George Romney, would "go a long way" toward testing the feasibility of block grants.[25] Local government officials supported these developments and urged even stronger action. By 1970 organizations representing the nation's mayors were "aggressively pushing for block grant authority."[26]

These sentiments stimulated considerable interest in reform on Capitol Hill even before the president unveiled his special revenue sharing plan. In fact, congressional efforts were proceeding so rapidly that the Nixon administration was reported to be "in danger of losing legislative initiative in housing and urban programs."[27] Staff members of the Senate Housing Subcommittee had begun earnest consultations with mayoral and community development groups on legislation to consolidate and streamline CD programs. In the House, members of the Subcommittee on Housing released a report in late 1970 denouncing the "piecemeal" scope, "delay," and "excessive red tape" of existing programs.[28] The subcommittee report recommended altering the programs to provide "maximum flexibility for local elected officials . . . within broad national guidelines" and began work on block grant legislation.

SUBSYSTEM INFLUENCE.   The alignment of major interests within the two policy systems also had a considerable effect on the enactment of block grants, particularly in community development, where the principal clients and beneficiaries of existing programs were the nation's mayors. In contrast to block grants in education and rural development, which would have transferred authority from influential clienteles to generalist elected officials, the CD block grant gave mayors additional power to pursue their principal goals for urban policy.

Although housing agency officials and local community groups were also active in the CD subsystem, the mayors had the most influence in the policy community during the late 1960s, especially among members of the House Banking and Urban Affairs Committee. Although some mayors had been directly involved in urban renewal programs from the beginning, others became increasingly involved as CD programs grew more controversial during the 1960s. Indeed, this trend was consciously accelerated by federal policies like model cities and planned variations, which were intended to increase mayoral involvement in CD programs in order to promote greater coordination and policy commitment at the local level. Mayoral influence in Washington was heightened during this period by what proved to be a temporary merger of the two major urban interest groups—the National League of Cities and the U.S. Conference of Mayors. The resulting effect on policy was such that the staff director of the House Housing Subcommittee traced his committee's block grant proposal not to the Nixon administration, but to "a series of dinners I had with (the deputy mayor of New York). As we sat and talked about what mayors needed most . . . we arrived at the concept of a block grant." [29]

The legislative subsystem was more complex in employment and training, and partly as a result the final legislation was somewhat less responsive to the preferences of state and local governments. As their name implies, the House and Senate Labor committees had jurisdiction over a wide range of labor-management issues and, particularly on the Democratic side, had developed close ties with organized labor. In addition, many members, especially in the Senate, had close political and working relationships with a variety of minority and community groups representing the clients of specialized job training programs. Thus while state and local government officials became increasingly involved in training programs during the 1960s, they had to share influence in the policy community with the beneficiaries and protectors of specific categorical programs.

As in CD, state and especially local government involvement in training programs was deliberately encouraged by federal policies. Indeed, some came to view the CAMPS process as the Nixon administration's way of building a constituency for a manpower block grant, a "part of the legislative strategy," according to one county official.[30] Moreover, Labor Department grants funded seminars for mayors on manpower planning and the creation of permanent manpower planning staffs reporting to elected officials. One ranking Labor Department official likened the process to creating an uncontrolled political monster:

> Probably the strongest interest groups have been the PIGs [public interest groups], and that was sort of creating our own Frankenstein. We had used them in the voluntary CAMPS program. We'd give them funds to hire planning staffs, and this built up a strong infrastructure. We also had policy assistance contracts with the various PIGs to provide a mechanism for educating and sensitizing officials on the new initiative. But yes, we were creating a constituency and an adversary group prior to CETA.[31]

Factors Inhibiting Enactment

All in all, it is not surprising that CETA and CDBG were eventually enacted. They were major legislative objectives of the Nixon administra-

TABLE 3-2. Events Leading to the Enactment of the
Community Development Block Grant Program, 1966–74

Date	Event
1966	Model cities program established to coordinate urban programs
1970	Planned variations program instituted by Nixon administration to improve model cities
	Mayors urge reform of urban program in national municipal policy
	House Subcommittee on Housing creates study panels to explore block grants and other program reforms
	Outlines of HUD proposal for an urban block grant developed
1971	Community development revenue sharing legislation formulated by Nixon administration
1972	Senate passes a community development block grant in omnibus housing bill
	Omnibus housing and urban development bill, including a community development block grant, is blocked by House Rules Committee
1973	President Nixon proposes the better communities act, special revenue sharing bill
	President impounds housing and community development funds
1974	Senate passes housing and community development bill, including block grant title opposed by administration
	House passes compromise community development block grant in omnibus housing and community development bill
	President Ford signs community development block grant legislation

tion and they enjoyed considerable support in Congress and among the
principal interest groups affected. Moreover, the block grant concept in
these two fields was endorsed by many policy professionals as an appropriate remedy to implementation problems and perceived policy failures
in existing programs. In short, unlike the block grant proposals in education or transportation, those in CD and job training were not dismissed by the established policy community as an inappropriate or
threatening transformation imposed by a hostile and untrustworthy administration.

Why then did it take so long to enact these two block grants? More
than four years elapsed from the time that the job training block grant
was first proposed in 1969 to the final signing of CETA in late 1973; and
CDBG was finally signed into law by Gerald Ford in August 1974, a few
days after President Nixon resigned from office.

These delays were not just the result of opposition to block grants. In
fact, major grant reform legislation in both areas was almost passed
much sooner (see legislative chronologies in tables 3-2 and 3-3). A manpower training block grant could have been signed into law in 1970 if
President Nixon had then been willing to accept (as eventually he was)

TABLE 3-3. Events Leading to the Enactment of the
Comprehensive Employment and Training Act, 1962–73

Date	Event
1962	Enactment of the Manpower Development and Training Act (MDTA)
1964	Enactment of the Economic Opportunity Act (EOA)
1967	Incremental efforts begin to reform categorical job training programs: concentrated employment program (CEP) and coordinated area manpower planning system (CAMPS)
1969	Academic specialists on National Manpower Policy Task Force endorse reform Congressman William Steiger introduces a state-oriented block grant: Comprehensive Manpower Act (H.R. 10908) Congressman James O'Hara introduces a nationally oriented consolidation bill: Manpower Act (H.R. 11620) Nixon administration proposes a job training block grant bill: Manpower Training Act (S. 2838)
1970	Senate passes omnibus manpower bill with public employment, categorical, and block grant provisions: Employment and Training Opportunities Act (S. 2867) House passes compromise manpower reform bill with modest public employment title: Comprehensive Manpower Act (H.R. 19519) President Nixon vetoes conference bill patterned after Senate legislation
1971	President Nixon proposes manpower revenue sharing legislation (H.R. 6181) Each amendment to substitute a revenue sharing–like block grant for temporary public employment program fails on the House floor Emergency Employment Act signed by President Nixon
1973	Nixon administration attempts to implement manpower revenue sharing through administrative means Senate passes separate block grant and public employment programs in a conciliatory gesture House passes compromise proposal linking public employment and block grant programs President Nixon signs the Comprehensive Employment and Training Act

the creation of a federally funded public service employment program and the retention of more categorical grants than the administration would have liked. Similarly a community development block grant was almost enacted in 1972 as part of an omnibus housing and community development bill. The grant was kept from final consideration by the full House in the waning days of the Ninety-second Congress mainly because of other elements in this large and complex bill.

These two near misses point up the difficulties of enacting comprehensive reform legislation in Congress. As a rule, it is easier to obstruct legislation than to pass it, even when such measures enjoy support from key groups and individuals. It is not sufficient to build a supportive coalition for a policy concept. Majority support must be garnered for each important provision of the proposed legislation, although supporters may disagree among themselves over key details of the structure, funding, and operation of the program.

The conflicts over block grants in the Nixon years can be classified into two main types: policy differences and contests for power. Policy differences arose over which programs were to be consolidated, what residual level of federal control should be retained, which recipients should be automatically eligible for funding, what overall funding levels would be appropriate, and what spillover effects emerged from related programs. Power contests had to do with partisan differences between the Democratic Congress and Republican administration, personality disputes in Congress, and turf battles within the administration, among congressional committees, and between state and local governments. Of course, policy disputes do not occur in a political vacuum. Although these two conflict types can be treated as distinct entities for purposes of discussion, they often overlapped, as was evident in the often bitter disputes among state and local jurisdictions over program formulas and operating authority.

POLICY DIFFERENCES.   In the main, the proponents of block grants disagreed on the following points: (1) which specific categorical grants should be consolidated into the new program; (2) what degree of residual federal control should be retained over the recipients' use of more flexible funds; and (3) which levels of government should be eligible for automatic formula grants and what level of funding should be provided. Reaching majority agreement on each of these points proved to be a difficult task.

1. In community development a serious dispute arose over the programs to be consolidated into the block grant even before the special revenue sharing legislation could be introduced in Congress. Congressman William B. Widnall of New Jersey, ranking Republican on the House Banking Committee, led an insurrection against the administration's plan to include the water and sewer program in the bill. Water and sewers was the third largest CD program in existence, and White House officials believed the programmatic rationale for removing it was "very weak." [32] But Widnall argued successfully that including it made no political or policy sense. He had sponsored the program in 1965 to address the needs of rapidly expanding suburban communities. Now a Republican administration proposed to fold it in with larger programs aimed at distressed urban areas and to distribute most of the funds to big city

Democratic mayors. Water and sewers was removed from the bill, and Widnall introduced it in the House.

Similar problems emerged over the proposal to include model cities appropriations, which up to then were distributed through discretionary grants to a select number of cities. Under any conceivable block grant formula, those communities with large model cities grants would lose funds, and the prospects of this financial loss canceled out the reputed advantages of a block grant. For three years they fought a rear guard action against including model cities, threatening to take any action necessary "short of kidnapping Patty Hearst." [33] By 1974, however, the prospects for future funding of model cities had so diminished that most activity had been redirected to securing the most favorable "hold harmless" provisions, to smooth the transition to new funding levels.

Significant as they were, these disputes over which programs to consolidate in CD were modest compared with the battles fought over this issue in employment and training. The differences are obvious in the results. Both model cities and water/sewer were eventually included in the final CD block grant, whereas CETA was enacted as a "hybrid" block grant. One part of the program was a genuine consolidated grant, but other parts created or preserved separate authorizations for public service employment, the Job Corps, and special programs for Native Americans, migrant workers, and certain categories of young people.

As in the case of the water/sewer program, many of the key legislators who resisted consolidation identified with the programs slated for merger. This was especially true in the Senate. The chairman of the Senate Labor and Human Resources Committee, Gaylord Nelson (Democrat of Wisconsin), was a former governor and was sympathetic to the block grant concept. Yet he was fiercely protective of the "green thumb" program that he had sponsored in 1965 to provide employment opportunities for older workers. Similarly, Jacob Javits of New York, the ranking Republican on the committee, was protective of the "special impact" program for jobless inner city youths. Other members had favored programs for other categories of disadvantaged workers, particularly in training operations like the Job Corps or Opportunity Industrialization centers. Outside groups such as labor unions fought strenuously to protect apprenticeship training programs operated by union locals. All were motivated by a common fear: that assured funding for their particular program would evaporate once program decisions were turned over to state and local governments.

Thus job training was not exempt from the categorical incentives that were such powerful factors in the policy fields where block grants were not enacted. But the desire to preserve old or established priorities was not the only factor working against the manpower block grant. Equally important, members of Congress were interested in establishing a historic new responsibility for the federal government—that of ensuring full employment through public service jobs. Faced with rising unemployment and a decade of disappointing experience with multiple job training programs, a growing number of legislators had come to the conclusion by 1970 that the federal government must do more than train the disadvantaged for nonexistent private sector jobs. It must offer the unemployed jobs in the public sector in order to expand opportunities for productive employment and to strengthen incentives for job training.

Whereas manpower reformers and the Nixon administration focused their efforts on consolidating grants, many leading Democrats in Congress made public service jobs their number one priority. However, the president became irreconcilably opposed to public employment. Although legislative specialists in Congress devised a broad range of compromises, it took four years to break the stalemate. For example, in 1970 the House passed a bill, with the administration's backing, to consolidate most manpower programs into a single block grant and to establish a modest public jobs program for training participants. This compromise fell apart, however, when the House-Senate conference committee adopted provisions from the Senate's legislation that limited the block grant's scope, preserved separate spending authority for most categorical programs, and reduced restraints on the public employment program. This proposal proved unacceptable to the president, and, in a major blow to Senate leaders, he vetoed it.

The dispute between the Nixon administration and Congress over job training and employment legislation continued for another three years. In the wake of the rapid climb in unemployment in early 1970, the president reluctantly agreed to a temporary public jobs bill in 1971, but he opposed renewing it in 1973. After months of wrangling, Congress and the president finally came to an agreement on legislation that was not unlike the basic outlines of the bill passed three years earlier. It was a hybrid block grant with "something for everybody": the president got his block grant; categorical sponsors preserved a range of special programs outside of the consolidated grant, and public jobs supporters won the renewal of public service jobs. It was the ultimate compromise.

2. The fact that legislators were wary of proposals that might limit their authority was equally evident in their arguments with the administration over the degree of control that the federal government should retain over recipients' use of block grant funds. Indeed, the mechanisms

of legislative oversight and the degree of residual federal authority became the main topic of debate in congressional deliberations over an
urban block grant, almost from the moment that the president's plan for
community development revenue sharing (CDRS) was introduced.

Under this plan, "automatic" grants were to be provided for eligible
communities, and there was to be virtually no federal planning or reporting requirements or standards governing the use of funds. As long as
federal aid was expended on projects encompassed by a comprehensive
list of eligible activities (including a wide range of social services), funds
could be used in virtually any manner a community desired.

Such lax controls struck even many block grant advocates in Congress
as unacceptable. While granting further flexibility, most congressional
adherents sought to ensure that depressed neighborhoods would receive
some, if not most, of the benefits of the program, that certain traditional
activities like slum clearance would be continued, and that communities
would report their activities and remain accountable to Congress for
their use of federal funds. As George Gross, chief counsel of the House
Housing Subcommittee and a leading advocate of block grants, ex-
claimed: "Revenue sharing was never seriously considered. The *idea* of
just sending out money and saying, 'just use it for whatever you want so
long as it's legal!' "[34]

Many Republicans, like Senator Robert Taft, Jr., of Ohio, also dismissed the president's approach, believing that "strong federal direc-
tives" were a "necessity for fulfillment of the federal responsibility to the
taxpayers." Taft argued that "community development is one of the least
suitable . . . programs . . . for a totally 'hands off' revenue sharing approach" because it deals with "problems of economic and racial integration that have proved so difficult for localities to tackle." [35]

Even local government officials supported stronger federal restrictions
than those contained in CDRS. Although they wanted a simpler, more
flexible program, they saw the need for performance standards, some
restrictions on eligible activities, periodic applications, and reporting requirements. In part, this position reflected a shrewd reading of congressional sentiment that could not be ignored, but it also sprang from the
mayors' recognition that some federal requirements offered them political protection when making unpopular decisions. According to one
League of Cities aide, "Some mayors feared [CDRS] would be a political
nightmare—to be held responsible but not have enough money to do
anything."

Federal control was also a concern in job training, particularly among opponents of the block grant concept, who saw no way to reconcile national policy objectives (and their own control over categorical programs) with the decentralized structure of the block grant. As one community activist declared in hearings over manpower reform: "Block grants to state and local governmental entities [are] an open invitation to socially irresponsible political leaders to act even more irresponsibly." [36]

Also distressed were senior members of the Senate Manpower Subcommittee, who sought to reconcile the conflicting desires for greater decentralization within a framework of federal control. As Senator Javits remarked during the first Senate hearing on manpower reform: "The thing that bedevils us here is the fundamental question of government relations. . . . Suppose we get crossed up. . . . We know that for all practical purposes a State or locality could ruin a program. . . . [We must] retain the ability to go in and do what needs to be done." [37]

In both fields these basic concerns were finally dealt with through carefully crafted compromises and artful ambiguity. In community development elaborate and complex planning and application procedures—often hundreds of pages long under urban renewal and model cities—were greatly streamlined, consolidated, and simplified. A brief application outlining each city's needs, objectives, planned activities, and expected costs was required, but the major emphasis was to be on an audit of actual activities undertaken. More important was the legislative ambiguity over which kinds of projects would be permitted. A broad list of eligible activities was included in the legislation to give recipient jurisdictions considerable flexibility. In addition, three potentially contradictory national goals were announced for the program: to assist poor and moderate income residents; to eliminate slums and blight; and to address emergency situations. Federal authorities would not be able to second-guess the local use of funds unless the use was "plainly inconsistent" with one of these goals.

Such provisions maximized local discretion. Senate liberals had asked that 80 percent of block grant funds be spent in low income areas in each community, but this requirement was deleted in the final bill. In its place was the ambiguous requirement that localities give "maximum feasible priority" to serving low- and moderate-income residents. This compromise paved the way for final passage of the bill as each side read it as a victory for greater or lesser local discretion. However, subsequent regulations and program reauthorizations sparked a battle over the meaning of this vague language and whether recipients had complied with its provisions.

In employment and training this issue was resolved through a different compromise. As discussed earlier, CETA was enacted as a hybrid block grant that retained numerous categorical programs. Although Title I of CETA resembled CDBG in its broad discretion and use of streamlined application, reporting, and auditing requirements, specialized programs in other titles retained federal control over particular activities and target populations that Congress was unwilling to abandon.

3. A final set of policy disputes revolved around program funding. Two questions were at issue here. First, the White House and Congress disagreed about overall funding levels. Second, state and local governments fought bitterly—among themselves and through members of Congress—over funding formulas and the types of jurisdictions that would be eligible for automatic entitlements under them.

Throughout the debates over grant reform proposals, the Nixon administration sought to restrict the levels of funding in both CD and job training. Although in general the president's proposals did not use the presumed economies of block grants as a rationale for reduced funding in the programs at hand, Congress routinely increased authorization levels for such programs during this period. The administration tried to resist, but met with only modest success.

The disputes over the administration's aggressive use of program impoundments during 1973 were more serious. In order to force congressional action on CDRS, the administration requested no new funds for community development in the fiscal 1974 budget. In addition, several controversial housing programs were suspended, including public housing and low-income subsidy programs. Altogether, more than one billion dollars was involved. As the president's budget message explained, the intention was "to accelerate major reforms"; once Congress accepted the administration's proposals for housing vouchers and CD revenue sharing, "new funds [could] begin to flow." [38]

Instead of forcing quick congressional action on the administration's proposals, this impoundment strategy stirred up a storm of opposition from reform supporters and advocates alike and actually delayed and sidetracked progress for many months. Even many Republicans in Congress were angered, complaining that the president's approach "almost smacks of blackmail." [39] As for the mayors, many felt that the tactic gave credence to suspicions that New Federalism was a ruse for spending cuts—a "Trojan horse," filled with "broken promises."

Equally disruptive were disputes among states, municipalities, and counties over which units of government would qualify for automatic grants under a block grant formula. A critical issue in CDBG was how cities that had received large amounts of categorical aid would be treated under the programs slated for consolidation. Many such cities would inevitably lose funds under any kind of formula allocation, even if funds were given only to other equally deserving communities. Although this situation led some cities to oppose any formula for the distribution of block grant funds, most of the losers agreed that some type of formula was needed and were placated by the "hold harmless" provision that temporarily provided larger payments to former grant recipients and eased the pain of transition.

Different levels of government also became embroiled in disputes over formula entitlements in the CD and CETA programs. In general, states argued that all block grant funds should be sent to them and that they should decide which localities were to receive what amounts of funding. Although this position could be backed by legal theory, it found little support in the political arena. The administration favored such an approach in its initial manpower block grant proposal, but abandoned it as politically unrealistic when the states proved politically incapable of supporting this position in Congress. Local governments successfully argued that they had had the most experience in administering the programs slated for consolidation and that their jurisdictions contained the highest concentrations of jobless workers most in need of training programs. They also proved to have the strongest political ties with members of the Democratically controlled Congress.

In contrast, governors were often slow to organize, take a position, and advocate it in Congress. Thus it came as no surprise that, even with the administration's backing, an amendment to increase the role of states in the 1970 manpower training reform bill failed dismally on the Senate floor by a vote of 28 to 46.[40] In future legislation, the administration refused to champion a stronger state role. According to the states' lobbyist on manpower programs, when CETA was finally enacted in 1973, the states were consigned largely to "the jackrabbits and the sage"—controlling funding, planning, and administration only in the least densely populated areas of most states.[41]

In CDBG, the most bitter disputes over funding allocations arose among local governments themselves—especially between cities and counties. For three years, the counties fought, and eventually won, a bitter battle over whether they would be included in the CDBG formula. "The mayors saw us as ripping off the cities," observed the counties' lobbyist.[42] Indeed, the cities' lobbyist considered the outcome "outrageous." The counties did not belong because they "weren't active in urban renewal or model cities," he charged, and they would block federal funds from going to smaller cities within the counties.[43] In fact, some urban lobbyists alleged that including counties in the formula was just part of the Nixon administration's political strategy to "get the money to the suburbs where its political strength was."[44]

The counties countered such objections with a sound case and excellent political tactics. Certain "urban counties," they pointed out, had many of the developmental problems of cities and performed many of the same functions. In certain states, in fact, counties were more significant units of government than cities. Politically, they let the cities carry the ball in enacting the block grant, while the counties focused exclusively on ensuring that qualified members would be included in the formula. This they did brilliantly, by designing their amendment to the formula so that it would appeal to a majority of members on the all-important House Banking Committee. Unlike cities, which became eligible for automatic formula entitlements with a population of 50,000 or above, counties became eligible at the 200,000 level. As the counties' lobbyist explained: "There's nothing magic about the 200,000 eligibility level. We looked at the districts of the members and calculated how high we'd have to go to get a majority. That's how we did it. We needed 21, I think. It was Henry Reuss. 200,000 was just enough to include him."[45]

POWER CONTESTS.   Building a majority in favor of grant reform at each point in the policy process often meant overcoming partisan distrust between Congress and the executive branch, as well as smoothing ruffled feathers, resolving personality disputes, and rising above turf fights in the ego-driven world of congressional politics. The policy manifestations of these disputes have already been discussed in some of the preceding sections. However, their causes merit closer attention. When it came to the distribution of federal aid, state and local governments were almost always at odds because of conflicting territorial interests. Some of the other power contests were dominated by other forms of self-interest.

In 1972, for example, a CD block grant was scuttled because of jealous opposition from the chairman of the House Banking Committee, Wright Patman (Democrat of Texas). Like many other senior committee chairmen, Patman balked at the very idea of a block grant because it infringed on his congressional prerogatives. More important, he used the legislation to carry on a "vendetta" against the chairman and members of the Housing Subcommittee. For years he had resented this subcommittee's unique autonomy, resources, and activism. The CD legislation gave him an opportunity to finally strike back. Using his powers as chairman of the full committee, he delayed considering the housing bill for months, then went through the bill's hundreds of pages line by line. Despite appeals from the administration and other members of the House, the bill was not reported from committee until just before the electoral adjournment, whereupon the leadership refused to bring it to the floor in the crowded, hectic final days of the Ninety-second Congress.

In another case, both CD and CETA were sidetracked for much of 1971, 1972, and 1973 by the bitter battles between Congress and the president over funding, vetoes, and impoundments. Congressional Democrats "badly misjudged the President's mind in 1970" with respect to CETA and provoked a veto by giving the president too much public employment and too little reform. Two years of legislative work were wasted. "After that, tempers had to cool down" on both sides—a process that took almost two years.[46]

Impoundments on CD provoked similar distrust on the congressional side, and personality disputes between leading actors in the White House, HUD, and Capitol Hill aggravated the situation. When the administration suspended or froze more than a billion dollars' worth of urban renewal and housing grants, Congress reacted strongly and negatively. Far from hastening the enactment of a CD block grant, as the administration had hoped, the impoundments encouraged Congress to hold the urban block grant "hostage" in return for resumed funding of the housing programs.[47] Before initiating hearings on new development legislation, the Senate held "oversight" hearings in which members blasted the housing moratorium. By the end of 1973, Senate Democrats were withdrawing from the compromises they had made in the 1972 bill.

This situation finally eased when the growing Watergate crisis forced Nixon to replace White House aides John D. Ehrlichman and H. R. Haldeman with respected former congressman Melvin R. Laird, and prickly HUD Secretary George Romney with James T. Lynn. Because of the housing moratorium, Lynn encountered significant resistance from Senate Democrats at his confirmation hearing. Once approved, however, he overcame congressional distrust by working closely and directly with important members of the House. "Lynn was extremely popular in the House," said one key congressional staffer, "and he spent literally nine-tenths of 1974 on the Hill negotiating in members' offices."[48] His efforts were aided by the constructive and professional attitude of Congressman Thomas L. Ashley (Democrat of Ohio), who led the fight to forge community development and housing legislation in both 1972 and 1974 and who "genuinely believed in the block grant concept."

Block Grants and Political Fragmentation in the 1970s

No specific policy initiatives better illustrate the pervasive fragmentation of the national policymaking process in the 1970s than Richard Nixon's diverse special revenue sharing proposals. The president proposed block grants in six functional areas, yet he obtained them in only two. Both of these enactments were passed only after being significantly modified. In the end, despite presidential backing, each failure or success hinged on the peculiar alignment of interests, actors, and program experiences within each policy arena.

This was not for want of presidential effort and resources. Nixon did all he could to heighten the salience of these proposals—to transform them from matters of interest to a few specialists into visible elements of his domestic agenda. In an era of what was later criticized as the "imperial presidency," he also brought considerable resources to bear on behalf of his objectives. He enjoyed popular support throughout most of his presidency, and he benefited from public dissatisfaction with existing programs. He took unprecedented steps to manipulate the federal budget on behalf of his policy objectives, and he had the backing of the increasingly influential intergovernmental lobby.

Yet in the fields of education, rural development, law enforcement, and transportation, these resources proved inadequate to counteract the forces of fragmentation represented by the subsystem and rational choice models of the policy process. In fact, the legislative events in the areas of education and transportation revenue sharing came very close to what the analysts of subsystem politics would predict. These were close-knit policy communities dominated by program specialists, both in and out of government, who viewed the president's SRS proposals as threats to their policy concerns and interests, and they rallied to defend the categorical programs. Interest groups and agencies that defended categorical programs found a ready audience in Congress in all of these areas, where the electorally motivated "categorical imperative" was alive and well. As the ranking House Republican on the Education Subcommittee observed: "Categorization is inherent in the system, really. Members like to make announcements of programs and projects. With a block grant, someone else makes the announcement." [49]

The politics of the CETA and CDBG programs reveals that these outcomes, too, were surprisingly consistent with sophisticated models of congressional and subsystem behavior. The community development and employment and training communities were not tightly closed subsystems, operating in a policy vacuum impervious to presidential and public influence. On the contrary, both were open to outside influence and novel ideas. At the same time, the supporters of grant consolidation in these fields did not simply follow the advice of outsiders calling for rationality in a wilderness of opposition. Rather it was a case of key policymakers getting cues from professionals in these areas. Furthermore, major groups within the subsystem strongly advocated block grants, especially in community development. One would be hard pressed to find another area in which Congress considered elected state and local officials, as opposed to functional bureaucracies, the key program beneficiaries and where relevant committees considered them the major reference group.

As for the categorical imperative, these successes demonstrate that it is clearly not the sole determinant of policy outcomes. Grant consolidation is not beyond the realm of possibility, and members of Congress respond to public policy concerns as well as electoral incentives. Nevertheless, strong dissatisfaction with the past performance of programs can erode congressional incentives to retain them in their existing form. In the examples just discussed many members seemed more interested in *avoiding blame* for prior failures than in *claiming credit* for often questionable program benefits. Such distancing opened the door for members who sought to reform existing programs in order to promote better performance. Yet categorical incentives were not entirely absent. They were evident at various stages throughout the process. The Senate's manpower reform bill of 1970 was so heavily categorized that President Nixon vetoed it. Even the final CETA bill was only a "hybrid" block grant; only 42 percent of the funds appropriated to CETA in its first full year in operation were allocated to the block grant title of the bill, and this proportion declined steadily thereafter.[50] In community development, even the ranking Banking Committee Republican rebelled at sponsoring the administration's block grant legislation until his favorite program—water and sewer grants—was removed from the bill. Likewise many supporters of the model cities program refused to include it in the block grant until the very end, when the program's authority was scheduled to terminate.

Thus even the successful enactment of block grants had much to do with the distinctive characteristics of these two policy arenas. Some participants claimed that these block grants would have passed even without the president's support. As the League of Cities lobbyist commented with respect to CDBG: "It almost passed without the administration. There was never any concerted opposition to the block grant, if you stripped away the politics of Nixon's New Federalism. Most of the opposition came from the stinko placed on it by Nixon."[51] This was strictly a minority view. Most participants gave the president considerable credit for placing the block grant concept squarely on the agenda and keeping it there despite the obstacles. But there is no question that serious work was under way to develop CD and job training block grants in both Congress and the bureaucracy before the president's initiative was announced. Once the president became involved in the process, the limits of his influence were also made abundantly clear: his inability to obtain legislation on his own terms led to conflict, stalemate, delay, and eventually, substantial compromises.

In short, during the 1970s the policy system was sufficiently fragmented to prevent a president at the height of his powers from obtaining block grants quickly and on his own terms, even within the most favorable of arenas. Additional views of this segmented system are provided in chapters 4 and 5, which trace the political fates of Nixon's proposals for general revenue sharing and welfare reform.

4

The Unique Politics of General Revenue Sharing

IN MANY WAYS, general revenue sharing was the principal legacy of Nixon's federalism agenda. Enacted in 1972, GRS provided more than $6.1 billion a year in no-strings grants to virtually all general-purpose governments in the United States. The idea behind revenue sharing was to combine the advantages of raising revenues at the national level with the advantages of local discretion over spending, by giving state and local governments maximum flexibility in the use of federal funds. Thus revenue sharing carried the principles behind block grants to their logical conclusion.

Despite this similarity of purpose, the politics of revenue sharing were unique. Opposing GRS was a coalition of fiscally conservative Republicans and southern Democrats who believed that revenue should be raised by the level of government that spends it. They were joined by an unusually united group of committee and subcommittee chairmen—some staunchly liberal—who believed that GRS would rob them of their prerogatives as committee leaders. On the other side was an equally odd coalition of liberal northern Democrats and mainstream Republicans. The first group supported GRS in response to strong lobbying by Democratic mayors and governors, the second in response to the president, local politics, and the ideological appeal of decentralization.

These unique coalitions epitomized the segmented political patterns of the 1970s. As the influence of political parties declined and interest groups proliferated, both voters and politicians grew increasingly independent and policymaking became more idiosyncratic. Issues were addressed on a case-by-case basis, and political coalitions were constructed accordingly.

In addition, GRS demonstrated the growing influence of a new form of interest group residing within government itself: the intergovernmental lobby, which comprised associations of mayors, governors, and other state and local officials. The intergovernmental lobby played an even more critical role in the enactment of general revenue sharing than in the politics of block grants, where success depended primarily on whether the interest group was a dominant member of the policy community. Thus block grant legislation was obstructed in fields like education, which were dominated by functional specialists. In contrast, the intergovernmental lobby worked aggressively to pass GRS legislation over the objections of most senior members of Congress. In the process, GRS epitomized an advanced form of rationalizing politics. Members of government not only formulated policies to counter the outcomes of prior programs, but they formed political coalitions both for and against the issue.

Faltering First Steps

As already mentioned, congressional response to Nixon's first revenue sharing proposal of 1969 and 1970 was decidedly cool, especially among Democrats. Wilbur D. Mills (Democrat of Arkansas), the powerful chairman of the House Ways and Means Committee, which had jurisdiction over GRS, refused even to hold hearings on the proposal. Like many fiscal conservatives, he was opposed to revenue sharing because it separated the authority for spending public funds from the responsibility for raising taxes. Another complaint was that revenue sharing threatened to weaken congressional authority to allocate funds and determine their specific uses. Mills was supported in his opposition by John W. Byrnes of Wisconsin, the conservative ranking Republican on the committee, and by most of the Democratic leadership in Congress.

The president's strong support on the one hand and widespread Democratic opposition in Congress on the other added a highly partisan dimension to the revenue sharing debate that program advocates from the state and local level were unable to overcome. Eighty-nine Republicans sponsored the president's first revenue sharing bill in the House, but it had no Democratic cosponsors. In the Senate, thirty-two Republicans supported the president's bill, joined by only two Democrats. Although there was Democratic support for some alternative proposals, few would have denied that revenue sharing had become "an increasingly partisan controversy" during Richard Nixon's first term.[1]

Even Democratic mayors and governors were unable to do much about the situation, in part because their own coalition on behalf of GRS was still shaky. Spending on revenue sharing in the president's first bill was modest (about $1 billion in the first year), and governors and mayors still harbored lingering suspicions and bitterness after their 1968 dispute over state and local roles under the Law Enforcement Assistance Administration (LEAA) block grant.* The administration had helped the major intergovernmental groups reach a compromise over GRS by dividing revenues in each state in rough proportion to each government's share of state and local spending, but the alliance remained fragile. Accordingly, in 1970 the administration's attempts to overcome partisan divisions in Congress through the lobbying of state and local elected officials did not succeed.

The Enactment of GRS

This strategy did succeed in the Ninety-second Congress, with the help of a more active and united intergovernmental lobby. President Nixon made revenue sharing the centerpiece of his domestic agenda, increased initial expenditures under his proposal from $1 billion to $5 billion a year, and raised the local governmental share of funds from approximately 30 to 50 percent.

The increased authorization and formula changes were designed to reward local government officials for their earlier lobbying on behalf of GRS and to generate renewed enthusiasm for the program.[2] As a result, state and especially local governments launched a massive lobbying campaign on behalf of GRS, seeking first to secure hearings on the president's proposal in the Ways and Means Committee and then to secure its passage. The signs of intergovernmental activism were everywhere. The mayors made revenue sharing their highest priority issue in the Ninety-second Congress, and they published articles in municipal publications on how to lobby Congress.[3] The counties promoted revenue sharing in newspaper ads, flew members in to lobby for the program, and began a newsletter focused on GRS. Donald Haider has summarized the impact of these activities:

> The passage of general revenue sharing is the most successful grass roots lobbying effort undertaken thus far. . . . In spring, 1971, delegations of mayors, governors, and county officials swarmed over Capitol Hill demanding congressional passage of this program. . . . The Dem-

* In LEAA, governors, backed by a coalition of conservative southern Democrats and Republicans in Congress, succeeded in replacing President Johnson's proposal for project grants to large cities with a law enforcement block grant exclusively to states.

ocratic leadership and Chairman Mills eventually capitulated to this outpouring of favorable support.[4]

Congressional leaders did capitulate, but slowly. The intense pressure by local Democrats convinced congressional leaders that they must at least grant the issue a hearing. Mills was persuaded to do so, but he announced that his hearing was strictly for the purpose of killing GRS.[5] Democratic mayors and governors pressed for a more positive response, and they made inroads among junior members of Congress. This intraparty split convinced top party leaders—Democratic National Committee Chairman Lawrence O'Brien, House Speaker Carl Albert, Majority Leader Hale Boggs, and Chief Whip Thomas P. (Tip) O'Neill—that the Democrats had to advance an alternative proposal. In O'Neill's words:

> The tide of so much pressure from the mayors more than anybody else was influential. . . . Nixon kept on pressing . . . and we began to feel pressure from the newer members of Congress who were more likely to succumb to pressure than the old hands. Finally Wilbur was called in and the leaders decided that they would have to go along and do something about revenue sharing.[6]

During the first week of hearings on GRS in May 1971, Mills himself met with O'Brien and several mayors and governors and expressed support for a need-based program of revenue sharing directed strictly to urban areas, with no state involvement. This change of heart was widely attributed not only to leadership pressure, but also to Mills's own decision to seek the party's presidential nomination and his corresponding need to build a base of support among local political leaders.

Although opposition to the very idea of revenue sharing remained strong throughout Congress, Mills's reversal greatly improved the prospects for enacting some form of revenue sharing program, with the result that lobbying activity turned to specific provisions of alternative GRS legislation. As Mills developed his own proposal over the summer and fall of 1971, the president and city officials urged that the states be given a role in his program in order to keep the intergovernmental coalition together. Mills agreed but reversed the relative shares of states and cities from the first Nixon bill, giving local governments two-thirds of the funding and states one-third. Moreover this share was tied to incentives for states with income taxes, in order to encourage the broadening of state revenue sources. He also enhanced the program's liberal cast by placing greater emphasis on need and by restricting its use to several priority activities.

The provisions of the GRS program continued to change somewhat through the remaining stages of the legislative process. According to Beer this was a classic case of legislative compromise and adjustment to competing pressures.[7] Yielding to his presidential ambitions, Mills agreed to play down the bill's encouragement of state income taxes, since they aroused highly negative emotions in the key primary state of New Hampshire. The restriction that funds be spent only on priority activities was also negated by eliminating the requirement that recipients maintain their own level of effort on these activities. Despite considerable opposition in the House Rules Committee and on the House floor, the revised bill was passed by the full House on June 22, 1972.

Adjustment also took place in the Senate, where the chief point of controversy was the program's formula. An amendment by senators from rural southern and western states increased allocations to thirty-four principally rural states.

The revenue sharing formula passed by the House was based on five criteria: the total population of the states, the size of the urbanized population, per capita income, general state and local tax effort, and state income tax collections. This formula tended to favor populous, urbanized states with high individual income taxes (such as New York and California), while penalizing the ten states that lacked an income tax. The formula was also extremely complex as it prescribed one allocation system for states and another for local governments. As a result, the relative mix of funds for state and local governments varied greatly from state to state.

Instead the Senate Finance Committee proposed a simple three-part formula based on population, relative income, and combined state-local tax effort. This version aided low-income, mostly southern states and, through its emphasis on overall tax effort, the central cities in many states. To help compensate for this reallocation of funds and to control the exploding costs of federal aid to state supplemental social service programs, the Senate Finance Committee also included a new authorization of federal social service grants that capped federal expenditures but directed more funds toward urbanized states. Under the Senate legislation, only four states lost funding.[8]

The Finance Committee's bill passed the full Senate with relatively few changes. Attempts to increase allocations to more populous states failed. As in the House, stiff but unsuccessful challenges were also registered by leaders of the Appropriations Committee, who viewed the multiyear commitment of funds under the program as an assault on the integrity of the appropriations process—and on the prerogatives of the Appropriations Committee.

The House and Senate conference committee that was organized to iron out the differences between the two bills carried legislative adjustment a step further by designing the grandest compromise of all. Unable to bridge the gap between the two formulas, the conference committee decided to incorporate both into the final program and let each state choose the one most advantageous to it. The committee also decided to keep the Senate program of social service grants but to base the funding allocation on population alone.

Eager to adjourn Congress as the 1972 elections approached, both houses hastened to take up the conference bill and passed it easily. President Nixon signed it on October 20, 1972, and said it marked the start of his "New American Revolution."

The Segmented Politics of Block Grants and Revenue Sharing

As Nixon's rhetoric in signing GRS suggests, revenue sharing was part of his broad agenda for reforming American federalism. Whatever its merits as an integrated policy, Nixon's New Federalism aroused surprisingly little coherent response from those in the political arena. Each element became the focus of a unique political coalition, as illustrated by roll call votes on revenue sharing and block grants in the House of Representatives.

In the House, the crucial test vote on GRS occurred on the rule that allowed revenue sharing to be considered on the floor. Because of its large size, the House establishes a rule for each major bill that sets time limits on the debate and defines permissible amendments. The Ways and Means Committee requested and received a "closed" rule, which prohibited House members from amending the carefully constructed GRS legislation and allowed only a single up or down vote. Because this rule gave an advantage to proponents of the legislation, and because a rules vote often represents a truer test of sentiment by members who may feel compelled to vote for final passage, this constituted the key test of revenue sharing in the House.

In view of the strong partisan divisions between the White House and Congress, the fact that this was a presidential election year, and the president's emphasis on revenue sharing, one might have expected that the fate of GRS would be decided by partisan attachments. Samuel Beer shows that the key rules vote could indeed be considered a "party vote," but only in the technical sense that a majority of Republicans supported GRS, and a small majority of Democrats opposed it.

Much more important in determining the fate of GRS, Beer found, were divisions among the majority Democrats that were based on committee status and seniority. House committee and subcommittee chairmen opposed GRS almost two to one, whereas a majority of rank-and-file Democrats voted for it.[9] In contrast to many other issues on which Democrats are divided, region and ideology were not important factors in this case. Southern and northern Democrats were split in their support and opposition to GRS by similar margins, and ideology was found to correlate only modestly with the vote on GRS. Thus, Beer concluded, the way Democrats voted on revenue sharing was influenced by factors internal to government itself—most notably their attachments to categorical programming and the activities of the intergovernmental lobby. Senior Democratic leaders formed a "categorical phalanx" that opposed GRS because it would erode their prerogatives as committee chairs. In contrast, less electorally secure junior Democrats were not as attached to existing programs. However, they felt more vulnerable to the high-pressure lobbying by mayors and governors.

Block Grants and the Categorical Phalanx

The review of block grant politics in chapter 3 indicates that junior and senior legislators were fairly uniform in their attitudes toward block grants. The bills that passed garnered support from most committee and subcommittee leaders as well as junior members. The opposition of the House Banking Committee chairman Wright Patman to the CDBG block grant was an exception that proves the rule, since all the ranking Democrats on the Housing Subcommittee worked for its adoption. On the other hand, block grant failures were universally opposed by junior and senior Democrats alike.

Thus at the committee level block grants elicited a policy-specific response rather than systematic opposition from committee chairmen. It is possible, however, that the pattern found in the revenue sharing vote emerges only on the floor, not in committee. Especially in the House, the dynamics of the floor are distinctive, and many other actors are engaged. As in the case of GRS, winning the support of Wilbur Mills and the Democratic party leadership did not ensure that other committee chairmen would follow suit.

Although plausible, such a thesis is not easy to confirm, in part be-

cause there were few meaningful floor votes testing block grant sentiment. The failures never made it to the floor, and successful block grants
tended to be passed almost unanimously.

However, two test votes that occurred during this period allow us to
examine this hypothesis. The first was the 1968 test vote on the so-called
Cahill amendment, which proposed to replace a Johnson administration
program of categorical aid for urban crime control efforts with a law
enforcement block grant. The second was the 1971 vote on the Esch
amendment, which sought to substitute a job training block grant for a
categorical employment program.

In both cases, the categorical phalanx not only failed to materialize
among Democratic members of Congress, but the relationship was reversed. The following table shows (in percentages) that committee chairmen were actually more likely to support the Esch amendment than were
rank and file Democrats:

Vote	Chairmen	Rank and file	
Yes	18	8	
No	82	92	(N = 236)

In sharp contrast, committee and subcommittee chairmen were substantially less likely to support GRS than were the Democratic rank and
file (numbers in percentages):[10]

Yes	36	55
No	64	45

The reverse relationship pointed to in the first table, with chairmen
somewhat more supportive of the manpower block grant than the party
rank and file, reflects sectional and ideological influences. Northern
Democratic chairmen (98 percent) and junior Democrats (95 percent)
alike were almost unanimous in opposing the Esch amendment. Only
southern Democratic chairmen proved more supportive of the Esch
amendment than were the rank and file, with 40 percent of them voting
for the block grant. All these chairmen were extremely conservative, having 1971 Americans for Democratic Action (ADA) scores of 25 or less.
In contrast, Beer found that southern Democratic chairmen were the
group most strongly opposed to general revenue sharing.[11]

Similarly, the categorical phalanx was absent from the vote on the
Law Enforcement Assistance Act. The simple correlation between committee status and the vote on LEAA disappears completely when party

and region are controlled. As in the case of manpower, southern Democratic chairmen actually proved somewhat more supportive of the block grant concept than did their rank and file counterparts.

Comparisons with GRS

The absence of a categorical phalanx on two crucial block grant votes suggests that Congress responded differently to block grants and GRS. In fact, House members' votes on the Esch and Cahill amendments hardly correlate at all with their votes on GRS. The gamma correlation between the GRS and Cahill amendment votes was .05 (out of a possible 1.00 if all members voted identically on each), whereas the GRS correlation with the Esch amendment was .17.

Thus GRS and the two block grant proposals tapped different attitudes on Capitol Hill as well as different sources of political support. The votes on the Esch and Cahill amendments tended to follow party lines: almost all Republicans supported the block grant position on these amendments (95 and 98 percent, respectively), whereas the preponderance of Democrats opposed it.

Within the Democratic ranks, ideology proved to be a determining factor in distinguishing supporters and opponents of the two block grant proposals. All but one of the Democratic supporters of the Esch amendment was conservative (defined here as having a 1971 ADA rating of less than 50), although most conservative Democrats opposed the amendment (numbers in percentages):

Vote	Conservatives	Liberals	Total
Yes	28	1	12
No	72	99	88 (N = 235)

A majority of conservative Democrats supported the Cahill amendment, whereas more liberal Democrats overwhelmingly opposed it (numbers in percentages):

Yes	70	7	39
No	30	93	61 (N = 185)

When it comes to ideology, the contrast between block grants and revenue sharing is marked. Conservative Democrats (and Republicans) proved to be most strongly opposed to GRS, rather than in favor of it. And although the vote on GRS was technically a party line vote, this was just barely the case, unlike that for the Esch and Cahill amendments. The gamma correlation between the party and the vote on GRS equaled .40 as against .99 on the Esch amendment and .98 on the Cahill amendment.

These differences have a great deal to do with the influence of public interest groups. The intergovernmental lobby was not a single entity that marched in lockstep on every policy that promised more decentralized control. It was a coalition of different governments with different interests, which achieved unity on some issues and was bitterly divided on others, depending on the specific policy.

The mayors, for example, supported GRS vigorously but were opposed to both the Esch and Cahill amendments. Although they had worked to enact a manpower block grant in 1970, the mayors chose to endorse a public jobs program in 1971 when they were forced to choose between this and the Esch block grant proposal. Mayors and governors were bitterly divided on the Cahill amendment, with the former supporting the president's proposal for direct law enforcement grants to cities and the latter leading the support for block grants to the states.

In the absence of mayoral pressure, northern Democrats gave full rein to their partisan and ideological proclivities and opposed these two block grant proposals. These congressmen were also expressing the views of their urban constituents and, in the case of LEAA, their party's president. In the case of GRS, however, the party and constituency pressures were in competition. Caught between their partisan and institutional suspicion of GRS and mayoral pressure to support it, a majority of rank-and-file northern Democrats eventually yielded to the mayors. Thus the intergovernmental lobby tended to reinforce partisan and ideological differences in the two block grant votes but to dampen them in general revenue sharing.

In summary, block grants and general revenue sharing elicited different types of political behavior even though both were key elements of the New Federalism and thus shared certain programmatic features. This was the case both in Congress and in the debates of public interest groups. Moreover, the case studies of block grant politics suggest that individual block grant proposals met with different responses. Although a partisan-conservative coalition was constructed in support of certain block grant proposals, like the Esch and Cahill amendments, only one block grant—LEAA—was thus enacted. In all the other cases, such coalitions failed to gain a solid majority.

More significant were the policy-specific coalitions that developed around block grant proposals in each functional area. Where consolidation and decentralization already enjoyed substantial support in the policy subsystem, compromise proposals were eventually developed and won almost unanimous support on the floors of both chambers of Congress. Crucial test votes on the block grant concept were anomalies in these fields. In contrast, where little consensus existed in the policy arena, block grants did not even draw Republican or conservative support. Thus what began in the Nixon White House as a broad, coherent initiative on behalf of program decentralization became in Congress a functionally discrete set of policy issues, each immured in its own political problems.

The National Dimensions of Nixon's New Federalism

Nixon's New Federalism cannot be fully understood without some consideration of the centralizing elements of his domestic policy agenda. The best example was the family assistance plan (FAP)—a sweeping proposal to replace the existing state-centered welfare system with a nationally financed program of uniform minimum support payments to needy families. But other, less obvious examples abound as well. During the Nixon presidency the federal government dramatically increased entitlement expenditures, enacted new regulatory statutes, created a federalized program of income assistance payments to the elderly poor, established the first major public employment program since the New Deal, and launched an aggressive program of wage and price controls to regulate the entire national economy.

It would be misleading to portray each of these actions as independent decisions of the president. Richard Nixon was not a liberal Democrat in disguise, bent on expanding the power and functions of the national government. A simple listing of enactments and expenditures in the early 1970s obscures the administration's ambivalence toward many of the programs involved. Much of the apparent activism reflected the president's efforts to accommodate the liberal Democratic Congress, which in the early 1970s was beginning a period of institutional ascendancy as rewards and opportunities for legislative activism proliferated. As the earlier discussion of CETA, CDBG, and housing impoundments makes clear, the president fought significant battles with Congress over spending levels and new programs.

However, many of these disagreements were over questions of degree, not direction—that is to say, over the specific character of new programs or the size of budget increases, not about the need to create programs or enlarge them. President Nixon did not object to increased domestic spending, but he tried to moderate its rate of growth. He did not oppose having public service jobs funded through a training and employment block grant, but he fought a separate jobs program. When his objections were overruled by Congress, he twice signed into law public employment programs unlike any since the 1930s.

Nor was Nixon always the reluctant pragmatist. The family assistance plan was his initiative; he was under no obligation to propose it. Nor was he forced by Congress to propose wage and price controls or stricter environmental and occupational health programs. Beneath his mantle of conservatism, Nixon was a presidential activist in keeping with the temper of his times. Just as he was willing to concentrate power in the White House and launch historic foreign policy initiatives, Richard Nixon was perfectly comfortable with expanding the domestic role of the national government whenever that fit within his broader political and policy agenda.

A National Welfare Policy

In 1969 President Nixon proposed a sweeping change in American welfare policy as an integral component of his federalism reform initiative. Dubbed the family assistance plan, this proposal would have greatly expanded the federal government's financial and administrative role in welfare policy and established for the first time a minimum national income for all poor families. Combined with the decentralizing thrust of general revenue sharing and the president's block grant proposals, FAP would have completed the most significant restructuring of federal, state, and local government responsibilities since the New Deal.

FAP had begun to take shape even before the president's inauguration. A transition task force on welfare policy, chaired by revenue sharing advocate Richard Nathan, recommended a major overhaul of the principal federal-state welfare program, aid to families with dependent children (AFDC). The task force urged that AFDC's system of state-determined benefit levels be replaced with minimum national standards for dependent children in order to raise extremely low welfare payments in the South, and that the federal share of overall welfare costs be increased to aid states in the north with higher welfare payments. When the president endorsed these proposals in principle as a means of redressing the "welfare mess," aides began drafting a specific proposal for consideration in Congress.[1]

At this stage, the plan was converted into a more radical reform of the welfare system by "holdover Democrats" at the Department of Health,

Education, and Welfare (HEW).[2] Departmental analysts objected that truly significant welfare reform could not be accomplished within the constraints of the AFDC program, which offered no benefits to families with a father present or to working parents, no matter how poor. They argued that raising benefits without structural program changes would contribute to the further breakup of poor families and would create economic disincentives for low-wage work. Instead, they sold the new Republican administration on a broader negative income tax proposal that guaranteed every poor family, including the working poor, a minimum national income. To provide an incentive for work, they recommended that benefits be phased out gradually as employment income grew, thus eliminating AFDC's penalty for work.

This concept was embraced enthusiastically by the new Republican appointees at HEW. Ironically, HEW Secretary and long-time Nixon confidant Robert H. Finch accepted a proposal that Great Society architects like Wilbur Cohen had categorically rejected as too radical.[3] The plan found strong support in the White House as well, not only from Nathan but from another holdover Democrat, Daniel Patrick Moynihan, who had become Nixon's urban policy adviser. Moynihan had long advocated adopting a European-style program that would make child allowances available to all families in America, and in the Johnson administration he had emerged as a forceful critic of AFDC's negative impact on black families.

Needless to say, a proposal as important and sweeping as FAP was not accepted uncritically by the Nixon administration or the president himself. Strong objections came from several members of the Nixon cabinet and from Arthur E. Burns, the president's chief economic adviser. Burns argued that the proposal would greatly increase dependency on welfare by bringing millions of new working families into the welfare system. Others complained about the program's cost. Less extreme alternatives were proposed during the next several months while the policy battle was waged in the Nixon White House.

The impasse was broken by the president himself, who became directly involved in the issue and finally decided to proceed with a modified proposal.[4] The administration was under increasing pressure to launch some kind of domestic policy initiative, and in the end Nixon "wanted a major social program, not a 'me too' Great Society" proposal, in the words of one administration official.[5] Nixon had been swayed by Moynihan's arguments that FAP was an "income strategy" that would alleviate poverty by placing greater income directly in the hands of poor people and by letting them choose how to improve their situation. It was viewed as a promising alternative to the "service strategy" used by programs of the Great Society, which relied heavily on middle-class professionals and community organizations to deliver education, training, family assistance, and other social services to the poor. When assured by Moynihan that the plan would be a far more successful assault on poverty and would "get rid of social workers," the president overrode objections and signed on.[6]

In his 1969 television address on the New Federalism, President Nixon launched his drive for revenue sharing, proposed a manpower block grant, and urged "reversal of the trend toward ever more centralization of government in Washington."[7] However, the first half of his message was devoted, not to decentralization, but to a proposal that "the Federal Government build a foundation under the income of every American family . . . that cannot care for itself." He stated, "The present welfare system has to be judged a colossal failure. . . . It is bringing States and cities to the brink of financial disaster. . . . It breaks up homes. . . . Benefit levels are grossly unequal."[8] Specifically, the president said that every family of four should be guaranteed a minimum national payment of $1,600 a year, plus food stamps. With added day care, job training, and higher federal matching rates, the legislation he called for would have raised existing costs of federal welfare spending by $4 billion annually, while expanding coverage to seven million new working poor recipients. It also required states with higher existing benefits to supplement the minimum federal payment, and it provided for federal administration of welfare payments in the remaining states. In answer to critics' charges that the plan would increase dependency on welfare, the final version included stronger work incentives and penalties than were originally proposed, so that the president could claim that he supported "workfare" not welfare.[9]

Thus did Nixon send to Congress what was later termed "the most important piece of domestic legislation proposed in the past 50 years."[10] There it began a frustrating legislative journey during which it twice brushed with success before being defeated. Caught between liberal and conservative notions of how to deal with welfare, the FAP plan fell prey to political contradictions that would doom all subsequent attempts at fundamental welfare reform in the United States.

Nixon assumed that a liberal and Democratic Congress would be forced to accept his proposal, and twice the House of Representatives did so. Although Wilbur Mills had misgivings about the proposal, he agreed to support it, as did John Byrnes, the conservative ranking Republican on the Ways and Means Committee. On the House floor, the bill passed easily with only slight modifications by a vote of 243 to 155. Although it won the support of a majority of both parties, warning signals about the kind of reception it might get in the Senate could be detected in the response of southern Democrats, who opposed the measure 85 to 17.[11] Although southern states were big winners financially under the proposal, many southerners opposed the "high" benefits provided under the plan. Despite the program's benefit structure and workfare requirements, they argued that it would undermine work incentives in the low-wage areas in the South and charged that there would be "no one left to press shirts" if the program passed.[12]

Such arguments found strong support in the Senate. The plan met vigorous opposition in the Finance Committee, which was dominated by conservatives and southerners. Opponents there were led by Senators Russell Long and John Williams, the chairman and the ranking member of the powerful committee. They produced charts showing that in some communities with relatively high welfare benefits, some recipients could suffer slight income losses under the proposal if they went to work, once the loss of in-kind housing, food, and medical benefits was factored in. Although the plan was modified, further opposition came from liberals and the National Welfare Rights Organization, who charged that benefits were set too low and work requirements were too onerous. The full committee finally voted down FAP and agreed instead to a temporary demonstration program. Even that proposal was eliminated on the Senate floor, and the session ended before advocates could attempt to restore it in a House-Senate conference committee.

The president tried again in 1971, calling FAP his "first priority" in the Ninety-second Congress. The plan was introduced as H.R. 1 with several changes; for example, it ended the requirement for state supplemental payments and raised the $1,600 floor to $2,400 but eliminated food stamps. Again the bill passed the House with a majority from both parties, but southerners still opposed it and the margin of victory on the key procedural vote fell by more than half, down to 234 to 187.[13]

Prospects were even bleaker in the Senate. The Senate put aside consideration of FAP in 1971 when the president asked for a delay after announcing his wage and price control program. In 1972 the Senate Finance Committee again refused to report out the program, replacing it with a workfare program advocated by Chairman Long. That, too, was replaced on the Senate floor by a demonstration program. Efforts to replace this modest provision with the House version of FAP or a more liberal Senate proposal were defeated. Because the two chambers could not see eye to eye on these measures, both the test program and the

House version of FAP were deleted from the final bill in conference, and only a relatively noncontroversial program of national income assistance for the elderly and disabled was enacted into law as the supplemental security income (SSI) program.

A Rising Tide of Entitlements

Richard Nixon may not have won an explicit national income floor, but during his tenure the federal government implemented an implicit national welfare policy through a vast and complex web of in-kind entitlement programs. Between 1969 and 1974 expenditures for federal programs providing food, housing assistance, and medical care for the needy increased by more than 250 percent. In addition, as just mentioned, the 1930s system of providing for the elderly poor was nationalized in 1972 through enactment of the SSI program.

This active domestic spending contrasts sharply with the Nixon administration's general reputation for budgetary penury. In many ways this reputation was undeserved. It was based almost entirely on the administration's efforts to slow—not reverse—the growing costs of annually appropriated programs. Elsewhere, Nixon's record for fiscal activism bears surprising similarity to that of his Democratic predecessors. Moreover, as a later section of this chapter demonstrates, this was true with respect not only to spending but also regulation.

There was nothing new about the rising tide of entitlements in the early 1970s. Federal spending on such programs had grown significantly during the Johnson administration with the establishment of new programs like medicaid and medicare and the expansion of existing programs. Direct payments to individuals—including food stamps, federal retirement, and veterans payments, but not social security—increased by 56 percent between 1964 and 1969. Entitlements channeled through state and local governments such as medicaid and AFDC grew by more than one-third.

By most relative measures, however, spending increases during the 1960s were less impressive. Payments to individuals increased substantially in constant dollars, from $20.5 billion in 1964 to $27.4 billion in 1969 (see table 5-1), but such spending remained virtually unchanged as a percentage of GNP or of total federal outlays. Larger increases occurred in programs earmarked specifically for the poor, but these programs were still small even by 1969 (see table 5-2).

By virtually every measure, real and relative, the greatest increases in spending for individuals occurred during the Nixon administration. En-

TABLE 5-1. Federal Spending on Entitlement Programs,
Fiscal Years 1964, 1969, 1974
Billions of dollars unless otherwise specified

Item	1964	1969	1974
Direct payments to individuals (minus social security and medicare)	13.0	20.3	40.7
Grants for individuals	2.8	3.8	13.6
Total	15.7	24.1	54.3
As a percent of federal budget outlays	13.3	13.1	20.2
As a percent of GNP	2.6	2.7	3.9
In constant 1972 dollars	20.5	27.4	48.3

SOURCE: *Budget of the United States Government, Historical Tables, Fiscal Year 1986*, tables 6.1, 6.2, 11.2 Figures are rounded.

TABLE 5-2. Federal Spending on Selected Means-Tested Programs,
Fiscal Years 1964, 1969, 1974
Millions of dollars

Program	1964	1969	1974
Food stamps	30	248	2,845
Child nutrition	181	237	751
Medicaid	196	2,191	5,549
Housing assistance	193	342	1,794
TOTAL	600	3,018	10,939

SOURCE: *Budget of the United States Government, Historical Tables, Fiscal Year 1986*, table 11.3.

titlement spending—including both direct payments to individuals and grants for individuals—more than doubled during this period (table 5-1). Even in constant dollars, spending for such programs rose 76 percent between 1969 and 1974. Still larger increases occurred in programs targeted to the poor. Food stamp outlays multiplied tenfold during this period. Housing assistance to the poor was up five times. The medicaid budget more than doubled. In contrast to the 1960s, entitlement spending relative to other federal outlays and the national economy as a whole also increased sharply.

Two programs in particular, food stamps and SSI, illustrate the depth of these changes. The food stamp program was transformed under Nixon. It began as a commodity distribution program for excess agricultural production. Changes during the Johnson administration allowed localities to choose between operating food distribution centers and offering food coupons that permitted impoverished recipients to purchase approved foods at a substantial discount. Nonetheless, when President Johnson left office, the program still was not offered in six states, only about one-third of all U.S. counties participated, and only about 22 percent of eligible people were enrolled in the program.[14]

TABLE 5-3. Growth of the Food Stamp Program,
Fiscal Years 1964–74

Year	Number of states	Number of program areas	Participants (thousands)	Federal cost (millions of dollars)
1964	22	43	360	28.6
1965	29	110	632	32.5
1966	41	324	1,218	64.8
1967	42	838	1,831	105.5
1968	44	1,027	2,419	173.1
1969	44	1,489	3,222	228.8
1970	46	1,747	6,457	549.7
1971	47	2,027	10,584	1,522.7
1972	47	2,126	10,594	1,797.3
1973	48	2,228	12,106	2,131.4
1974	50	3,062	13,524	2,714.1

SOURCE: U.S. Advisory Commission on Intergovernmental Relations, *Public Assistance: The Growth of Federal Function,* A-79 (GPO, 1980), p. 82.

Six years later, when Richard Nixon left the White House, food stamps represented a form of surrogate welfare reform: all states participated in the program; every county was obliged to distribute stamps instead of surplus commodities; the number of poor recipients had more than quadrupled; and spending had mushroomed (see table 5-3). These changes were the result of amendments that substantially altered the character of the program. Unlike AFDC, food stamps came to have uniform federal standards for eligibility and benefit levels. Food stamp benefits were put on a sliding scale with AFDC to compensate for low welfare payments in the South. Thus by 1974 food stamps constituted a form of minimum national income, albeit at a very low level. Moreover, all counties were required to participate, the program was indexed to inflation, and the federal share of administrative costs was increased.

The SSI program, enacted in 1972, established an explicit national income floor for the aged, blind, and disabled. It was one component of FAP that finally won approval in Congress. As a result, poverty among the elderly has declined sharply in recent years, and SSI stands as the major success story in the federal antipoverty effort.[15]

SSI began as a relatively unnoticed element of the family assistance plan that dealt with the non-AFDC portion of the social security–dependent population. Although these adult groups made up more than one-fourth of the total welfare population, the provisions for them were not as controversial as those for AFDC recipients. In general, the elderly poor, the blind, and the permanently disabled were viewed as the most deserving of the "deserving poor," and questions regarding work disincentives and the morality of AFDC recipients did not pertain to most of these participants.

Nonetheless, SSI was not enacted until 1972 owing to Senate opposition to the rest of the welfare reform proposal. When the AFDC provisions were finally separated in 1972, however, SSI was passed with little fanfare as part of a broader package of social security tax and benefit increases and changes in the medical provisions. As enacted, the program established uniform federal eligibility standards for participation, minimum benefit levels that increased payments in a majority of states, largely federal administration of the program, and incentives for state supplements.[16]

Regulatory Federalism

The Nixon administration also presided over and contributed to the greatest expansion of federal regulation of state and local governments in American history. Equally important, this expansion was not accomplished merely through new accretions of traditional grant-in-aid requirements. It was the result of new forms of federal regulation that were more intrusive, more coercive, and more extensive than any before. These new forms of regulations marked such a departure from prior practice that some authorities believed they were ushering in a new era of federal-state relationships:

> State and local governments . . . have been affected greatly by the massive extension of federal controls and standards over the past two decades. These extensions have altered the terms of long-standing intergovernmental partnership. Where the federal government once encouraged state and local actions with fiscal incentives, it now also wields sanctions—or simply issues commands. The development of new techniques of intergovernmental regulation presents a challenge to the balance of authority in, and the effective operation of, American federalism.[17]

Most people think of regulation as a form of policy that is directed at private industry or individual citizens. Minimum wage and hour requirements, antitrust statutes, and rules governing rates and entry in transportation all fit that common conception. In the 1960s and 1970s, however, there was a dramatic increase in federal regulations aimed at state and local governments. This included both regulations targeted at these jurisdictions as separate entities—affecting everything from their employment practices to the operation of municipal sewage systems—and those that sought to enlist states as agents in regulating the private sector on behalf of federal policies.

New forms of regulation were developed to accomplish these new aims—forms that were very different from anything that state and local governments had experienced before. Traditional intergovernmental regulations—designed to ensure that federal funds were used as intended—were attached to specific federal grant programs. They required state and local governments to prepare audits and reports on the use of federal aid and often to submit detailed plans and applications in advance. Although the requirements were sometimes annoying and burdensome, the principles behind them were almost as old as federal aid itself and the burdens could be avoided by simply refusing to apply for a specific program to begin with.

The newer intergovernmental regulations can be divided into four types, all of which were more intrusive and difficult to avoid than ordinary grant requirements. The most extreme in this respect were direct mandates, which simply instructed state and local governments to comply with a given federal policy. Crossover sanctions were also highly coercive, in that failure to comply with the grant requirements of one program led to the reduction or elimination of funds under other, entirely separate programs. More common were partial preemptions, whereby the federal government preempted a policy area, set minimum national standards, and encouraged states to administer and apply these standards. The most common new regulations were crosscutting requirements, which applied to all or most federal aid programs across the board.[18]

Most of these new forms of regulation were first developed during the 1960s. None were invented by the Nixon administration, but they gained a firm foothold during this period, particularly between 1969 and 1974. Fully half of the thirty-six most intrusive intergovernmental regulations identified by the ACIR were enacted during these years (see table 5-4). Thus it is ironic that an administration committed to greater decentralization contributed to one of the strongest centralizing movements in the history of American federalism. In fact, because block grants and general revenue sharing brought federal aid to many communities for the first time, the new federalism actually became the vehicle for conveying some forms of federal influence more deeply into American society than ever before.[19]

Nixon's attitude toward this regulatory buildup ranged from reluctant

TABLE 5-4. Original Enactment of Major Intergovernmental Regulations, by Date and Administration

Item	Pre-Johnson (1931–63)	Johnson (1963–68)	Nixon-Ford (1969–76)	Carter (1977–80)
Number enacted	2	8	21	5
Percent of all intergovernmental regulations enacted	6	22	58	14
Predominant regulatory objectives	Labor rights	Civil rights; consumer	Environment; health and safety; civil rights	Energy conservation; environment

SOURCE: Calculated from ACIR, *Regulatory Federalism; Policy, Process, Impact, and Reform*, A-95 (GPO, 1984), pp. 19–21.

to forcefully enthusiastic. Some of the major regulations enacted in this period, like the Safe Drinking Water Act of 1974, were opposed by the Nixon administration as unwarranted intrusions on state prerogatives; and some, like the landmark provisions outlawing discrimination against women and the handicapped, were tucked away in large omnibus bills, their effect on federalism unrecognized for the time being.[20] However, most of the major regulations of this period enjoyed the full or partial backing of the president, as can be seen in the following examples.

Environmental Protection

The Nixon administration's regulatory activism is best seen in its environmental policy. Although the president eventually let Congress take the lead in this area, at first he seemed to be vying with it over who could appear tougher on environmental issues. In the process, he not only responded to the mood of the early 1970s, but he also helped elevate environmental issues to a prominent position on the policy agenda. The landmark environmental statutes enacted in consequence extended the reach of federal regulations to unprecedented lengths. More important, this centralized rulemaking stemmed not only from an analytical conclusion that effective pollution control required more national standards, but also from the political needs of those competing for the presidency in 1972.

Beginning on New Year's Day in 1970, Nixon attempted to seize the initiative on environmental issues through a series of highly publicized actions. Calling it his "first official act of the new decade," he signed the National Environmental Policy Act, which established a Council on Environmental Quality in the Executive Office of the President and required that federal agencies and federal grant recipients file detailed environmental impact statements before undertaking construction or other projects with environmental ramifications.

Three weeks later, the president devoted one-third of his State of the Union address to environmental concerns. He subsequently sent Congress a thirty-seven-point program for "total mobilization" on environmental issues.[21] Finally, in late 1970, he implemented a plan establishing the Environmental Protection Agency and consolidating most of the federal government's growing environmental responsibilities there.

The most significant environmental action of that year, however, was the enactment of the Clean Air Act Amendments of 1970. This legislation established national air quality standards for various pollutants, required states to develop implementation plans for achieving these standards, and regulated automobile emissions. Because states were given little choice in assuming primary responsibility for administering the act, some analysts have argued that the act is a form of "legal conscription" and thus is inconsistent with the principle of federalism:

> Of all the intergovernmental mechanisms used to nationalize regulatory policy, none is more revolutionary than the approach first applied in the Clean Air Act Amendments of 1970. . . . It is a mechanism that challenges the very essence of federalism as a noncentralized system of separate legal jurisdictions. . . . It is an approach allowing national policymakers and policy implementors to mobilize state and local resources on behalf of a national policy program.[22]

In a seeming reversal of roles, it was the Nixon administration that first proposed establishing federal emissions standards for air pollution. Senator Edmund Muskie (Democrat of Maine), the leader on most environmental issues in Congress, initially favored giving state and local governments a larger role in making and administering air pollution policy. But Muskie's leadership in this area was challenged by other members of Congress, and he was embarrassed by a blistering attack on his air pollution record in a major report sponsored by Ralph Nader.[23] When the House responded quickly to the president's proposal for national standards by passing an even more forceful bill, Senate activists felt compelled to join the House in a game of environmental escalation, passing a stronger bill still. The toughest bill of all emerged from the House-Senate conference, as the strongest provisions of both proposals were merged into one.[24] Although the administration at this point made a modest attempt to restore somewhat greater administrative discretion to the legislation, there was never any doubt that the president would sign it.

At first, President Nixon appeared to take the lead on water pollution as well. In 1970 he proposed strengthening existing legislation with federally approved effluent standards and increased federal funding for municipal sewage treatment facilities. The administration also attempted to exert leadership in this area unilaterally by resuscitating the Refuse Act of 1899, which required permits for dumping wastes in navigable waterways. As with the clean air amendments, however, Congress outdid the president by proposing even stronger legislation. Its Federal Water Pollution Control Act Amendments of 1972 increased federal jurisdiction over intrastate waterways, established a federal permitting system for all municipal sewage and industrial discharges, set ambitious goals for zero pollution discharges by 1985, required advanced technology regardless of cost, and authorized $18 billion in federal grants for sewage disposal facilities.[25] In short, it was "the most complex and extensive environmental legislation ever passed."[26] Primarily because of its enormous costs, Nixon withdrew his support and vetoed the legislation, but his veto was easily overridden by Congress.

Other Regulations: From Health to Highways

The growth of intergovernmental regulations in the early 1970s extended far beyond environmental policy, and the Nixon administration's support for an expanded federal role was often greater in these areas. Among the devices developed in this period were crossover sanctions, which stipulated that federal funds for several programs would be jeopardized should recipients fail to comply with regulations in a separate single program. Despite their unprecedented coercive character, the Nixon administration endorsed such regulations in both health care and transportation.

Congress and the Nixon administration were at odds in almost every area of health care in the early 1970s, including spending levels, health care block grants, and national health insurance. However, the administration's efforts to control rising health care costs enjoyed strong support from Congress, which passed the National Health Planning and Resources Act in 1974. This act directed states to pass legislation establishing complicated certificate-of-need programs to evaluate all proposed construction and development projects undertaken by health care facilities. Failure to comply with the program's intricate national standards and detailed administrative procedures would threaten not only federal planning funds but also public health, alcoholism, and mental health grants. According to one analyst, this legislation "intrudes upon state and local operations to a greater degree than almost any other grant program." [27]

National health planning legislation was bitterly opposed by both medical interests and state and local elected officials. Ironically, states had pioneered the concept of hospital cost control, and a majority of them already had laws on the books when this bill was passed. But both the administration and key members of Congress insisted on having a more uniform national system and argued that it should be placed in the hands of nonprofit organizations.

Few federal regulations have done more to annoy sparsely populated western states than the national speed limit, set at 55 miles per hour, which is widely viewed as inappropriate and unenforceable. Yet the Nixon administration exerted continuous leadership with a series of ever stronger proposals for a national speed limit in response to the Arab oil embargo in 1973. Early that year the administration requested that states voluntarily lower their speed limits to save lives and conserve energy. The president made a personal plea in midsummer, and by year's end a majority of states had complied. [28]

Soon more direct pressure was applied. With the president's strong backing, a national maximum speed limit was enacted on a temporary basis in January 1974; it was enforced by a provision requiring that all federal highway aid be withdrawn from any state refusing to comply. By March all fifty states had reduced their speed limits. [29] Later that year the president signed legislation making permanent what had begun as a temporary measure.

In summary, by the time Richard Nixon left office the federal government had firmly institutionalized new patterns of interaction with state and local governments. If the expanded federal role seemed somewhat vulnerable immediately after the Great Society, it was now permanently established. New regulatory techniques had become widely accepted, and they supplemented enormous increases in federal domestic spending. Together, these developments left no room for doubt over which level of government was now the senior partner in virtually all areas of intergovernmental collaboration.

The Politics of Nixon's New Federalism

Richard Nixon's federalist legacy was a complex one. In attempting to rationalize the intergovernmental system, Nixon devised a strategy that combined both centralizing and decentralizing elements. From a personal standpoint, the president clearly emphasized decentralization in this equation. He sought a net increase in state and local power and responsibility in the intergovernmental system. Ironically, the final outcome was quite the opposite. Despite the failure of FAP and the notable achievements of revenue sharing, CDBG, and CETA, Nixon left behind what was probably a more centralized federal system than the one he inherited. Federal expenditures for many domestic functions had increased dramatically, and an unprecedented federal intergovernmental regulatory presence had been institutionalized.

This paradoxical state of affairs is related to the political changes of the 1970s, particularly institutional fragmentation, increasing professional influence, and declining partisanship. Each of these factors influenced the fate of Nixon's block grants. Despite the president's best efforts to elevate this issue on the public agenda, the only block grants to succeed in Congress were those that already had consensual support within individual subsystems. Those that did not failed.

The legislative outcome of welfare reform, revenue sharing, and environmental regulation, which were far more salient issues in the Nixon presidency, also varied, depending in part on the degree of policy consensus. Where that was absent, the administration had to mobilize political allies and find other available forms of political support, which it did successfully in the case of revenue sharing but not in the case of FAP.

Although partisanship did not play a determining role in shaping coalitions or deciding the fate of any of Nixon's major New Federalism policies, it was by no means an irrelevant factor. Party loyalties did influence some of the initial reactions to Nixon's block grant proposals, for example, and partisan coalitions did develop on other issues from time to time. In the end, however, the successful block grants had bipartisan support, and those that failed were rejected on a bipartisan basis.

In fact party coalitions had little to do with the final legislative responses to Nixon's other initiatives. Most regulatory initiatives enjoyed bipartisan support, and some even generated competition over which party was most committed to the goal. Where sharp conflicts existed, as in the case of both welfare reform and revenue sharing, the cleavages cut deeply across party lines. In each case, both the supporting and opposing coalitions were bipartisan.

The parties' inability to frame issues and shape coalitions during the Nixon presidency was not confined to New Federalism initiatives. Many measures of party unity and cohesion reached modern low points under Richard Nixon. Among the most extreme was the decline in party votes in the House, defined as the percentage of all roll-call votes in which a majority of Republicans opposed a majority of Democrats. Party votes in the House fell to 32 percent during Nixon's six years in office, which was down from 48 percent under Eisenhower and 46 percent under Kennedy and Johnson.[30] Such data, reinforced by the evidence of subsystem influence on issues of lesser salience, merely underscore the fragmented character of the policymaking environment confronting Richard Nixon's federalism agenda in the early 1970s.

Part 2
Reagan

Part 2
Reagan

6

The Context of Reagan Federalism

D ESPITE many setbacks, federalism reform appeared to be building
political momentum by the time Richard Nixon left office.
Many observers believed that Nixon had launched a powerful
movement and predicted that it would continue throughout the remainder of the 1970s. As one prominent intergovernmental analyst wrote in
1974, "We should expect the federal government over the next half decade or so to get out of the categorical grant-in-aid business and to continue to shift toward revenue sharing and other broad-purpose fiscal
transfers."[1] The ACIR concurred: "The trend is toward the consolidation of previously fragmented, though functionally related, categorical
grants."[2]

In successive administrations, however, comprehensive efforts at federalism reform gradually diminished, although the Ford administration
did try to consolidate some intergovernmental programs during its brief
tenure. It resurrected the proposed education block grant of the Nixon
era and formulated plans for consolidating health and child nutrition
grants, but all were stalled in Congress. Only one additional block
grant—for social services—was created in early 1975, but it was intended to cap a single runaway federal program rather than consolidate
a mix of overlapping federal grants.

In the remainder of the 1970s no additional block grants were established, and few were proposed. On the contrary, Congress proceeded to
recategorize and recentralize existing ones. Between 1975 and 1977 the
block grant portion of the CETA program was cut from 42 percent of
appropriations to 23 percent.[3] New categorical programs appended to
CETA included countercyclical public employment, a series of youth employment and training demonstration programs, and a new private sector job training program. Less recategorization took place in CDBG, except for enactment of the urban development action grant program
(UDAG). However, the Carter administration sustained efforts to in-

95

crease federal control over CDBG, with the result that local discretion over how and where to spend block grant funds was substantially reduced. As Donald Kettl explained, "Regulation gradually emerged as the key strategy for implementing the new generation of urban aid programs. . . . The creeping growth of new rules . . . gradually shifted power back to the Federal Government."[4] Ironically, revenue sharing and the new block grants in some ways extended federal influence farther than ever before, sending federal funds (and regulations) for the first time to virtually all local governments, regardless of size, and allowing many hard-pressed urban centers to rely more and more on federal aid.

Renewed program fragmentation and regulation were not confined to block grants, however. Between 1975 and 1980, 92 new categorical programs were created, bringing the total to a record 534.[5] And although the pace of intrusive regulatory enactments had slowed from the peak of 1965–75, Congress enacted five major new intergovernmental regulations during the Carter administration, including the Clean Air Act Amendments of 1977, the Surface Mining Control and Reclamation Act of 1977, and the Public Utilities Regulatory Policies Act of 1978.

As these developments suggest, federalism reform was not a priority of the Carter administration, despite the president's anti-Washington rhetoric. Carter's major management reform efforts were directed toward federal agency reorganization, not intergovernmental grants. In fact, the president had come into office promising to reduce the number of federal agencies, boards, and commissions from over 1,200 to just 200. Although this goal was eventually dropped as hopelessly naive, Carter used a tremendous number of staff and considerable political capital to prepare and advance more than 100 different reorganization plans.[6]

Carter's principal proposal for intergovernmental reform was the ill-fated national urban policy initiative of 1978. Far from being a coherent strategy of the kind proposed by Nixon, Carter's plan was an $8.3 billion amalgam of disparate agency initiatives, most of which had already been rejected many times in the past. A disappointed David Broder called it "a smorgasbord . . . 10 strategies supported by 38 recommendations, plus 160 suggestions for improving old programs left scattered in five agencies."[7] Even White House staff viewed it as a "laundry list" of Cabinet requests.[8]

A more lasting Carter initiative may have been his enhancement of the White House staff responsible for intergovernmental affairs. Carter institutionalized and enlarged the intergovernmental affairs office, and he appointed one of his trusted aides from Georgia, Jack Watson, to head it.

Although this office had some policy responsibilities, it concentrated on ombudsman-like activities on behalf of mayors and governors—relaying their complaints to federal officials and interceding for them in their dealings with federal agencies. In this role, however, the office was simply one of many—such as those operating on behalf of women, blacks, Jews, Hispanics, the elderly, consumers, and the business community—established under the broad expansion of political liaison activities in the Carter White House.[9]

Consequently, the Advisory Commission on Intergovernmental Relations concluded in 1980 that the federal system had not been reformed during the 1970s but had become even more unbalanced and was in greater need of comprehensive restructuring than ever before. In summarizing its extensive study of intergovernmental trends in seven functional areas, the bipartisan commission concluded that "contemporary intergovernmental relations . . . have become more pervasive, more intrusive, more unmanageable, more ineffective, more costly, and above all, more unaccountable."[10] Some scholars went even further, arguing that the United States no longer had a true federal system but had become a decentralized unitary state.[11]

The Politics of Federalism: From Nixon to Reagan

In the 1980s federalism reform found a new champion in Ronald Reagan. In his first inaugural address, the new president placed the blame for intergovernmental imbalance squarely on the federal government:

It is time to check and reverse the growth of government which shows signs of having grown beyond the consent of the governed. It is my intention to curb the size and influence of the Federal establishment and to demand recognition of the distinction between the powers granted to the Federal government and those reserved to the states or to the people.[12]

To accomplish these goals, the president set forth a sweeping agenda of budget reductions, tax cuts, personnel freezes, block grants, and deregulation initiatives—all intended to give the federal government a dramatically lower fiscal and administrative profile.

Although Reagan pursued more extreme objectives than Nixon did, he enjoyed relatively more success in achieving them. This was especially true in 1981, when the Reagan administration achieved its most impressive legislative victories. Although the administration's record since 1981 has been far more mixed, those early victories structured and constrained the subsequent policy agenda.

In fact, it is at this level of agenda setting that the contrast between Nixon and Reagan has been the sharpest. Nixon's ultimate objective, it has been argued, was to improve the manageability of government by rationalizing its functions and modestly decentralizing the distribution of power. By that definition he achieved at best a mixed success: revenue sharing was adopted, as were two block grants in modified form, whereas the family assistance plan was twice rejected by Congress, and most of the special revenue sharing initiatives failed altogether. As already mentioned, Nixon's most significant domestic legacy may well have been to increase federal entitlement spending and expand federal intergovernmental regulations to an unprecedented degree. These policies reflected Nixon's pragmatic acceptance of governmental activism but hardly constituted the core of a balanced New Federalism.

Indeed, by the late 1970s these outcomes were part of a pattern that led analysts across the political spectrum to ask whether the government in the United States was spiraling out of control. It was not just the rapid growth of the public sector that was alarming them, but also the extreme pluralism of the policy process, which generated "growth without purpose."[13] This environment made it extremely difficult for Nixon to advance his goals despite committed attempts to do so.

In contrast, Reagan's policies have dominated the political agenda, primarily as a result of his victories in 1981. In that year alone federal income tax rates were cut by 25 percent and business taxes were reduced an additional $50 billion; federal spending for domestic programs was reduced by $35.2 billion (with savings over subsequent years totaling over $130 billion); nine new block grants were established, consolidating seventy-seven programs; and sixty-two additional programs were terminated. In addition, new regulatory review procedures were instituted and various pending regulations were halted or amended, leading the administration to claim that it had reduced the regulatory burden on states and localities by millions of manhours and billions of dollars.[14]

As a result, political commentary today tends to focus not on government out of control, but on the need for further spending cuts to reduce the federal deficit, on the diminished role of the federal government in domestic affairs, and on the resurgence of states as centers of policy initiative. To be sure, Reagan's accomplishments are often exaggerated. He certainly has not achieved all of his goals. The sweeping federalism reform that he sought in 1982 was a total failure, and many of the block grants and program cuts proposed since 1981 have been ignored by Congress. After eight years in office, President Reagan has not turned the clock back to the 1920s, as some analysts claimed he would.[15]

But real change is evident, especially in intergovernmental relationships. Governmental growth is no longer out of control. If anything, the federal role in some domestic affairs has been frozen or partly reversed. Significant structural reforms have been instituted in a variety of grant and regulation programs—although by no means all. Although the evolving mix of programs and policy instruments makes meaningful comparisons difficult, by most relative measures federal intergovernmental spending today is roughly comparable to that of the early 1970s.

These differences in outcomes and perceptions underscore important changes in the structure of politics from the 1970s to the 1980s—changes that extend beyond the realm of intergovernmental policy. Between 1974, when Richard Nixon left office in disgrace, and 1981, when a new Republican president was inaugurated, the political environment and operating premises of American government had changed in fundamental ways, from the "rationalizing" politics of the 1970s to the "reactive" politics of the 1980s.

Unlike Nixon, who hoped to rationalize active government, Reagan has tried on the whole to restrain domestic government. Although not always consistent or successful, Reagan's efforts represent a reaction against fundamental elements of the welfare state itself.[16] In so doing, intergovernmental policies have been only one instrument. State and local government may have been preferred to federal involvement in many circumstances, but often only as a fallback to no governmental involvement whatsoever. In those cases where federal policy appeared to give more free rein to private markets than state and local policies, the Reagan administration consistently endorsed preserving or enhancing the federal role—states rights rhetoric notwithstanding.

Such distinctions are more than a historical curiosity. They point to important transformations in the character and structure of American politics, public attitudes, and the roles of political institutions. The premises underlying public policy have changed considerably since the early 1970s, as have the influence and role of the president, Congress, interest groups, and political parties. Before the effect of these changes on specific public policies can be analyzed, however, it is necessary to examine the economic, institutional, and political context in which this transformation took place.

Economic Disarray

The magnitude of the changes that occurred between 1970 and 1980 can be seen most clearly in the area of economic policy. Flushed with the success of the 1964 tax cut and armed with more and more sophisticated economic models, economists spent the remainder of the 1960s convincing themselves and government officials that they so thoroughly understood the operation of the economy that they could fine-tune economic performance. Recessions had become a thing of the past. "We are all Keynesians," declared Richard Nixon in announcing his comprehensive program of wage and price controls in 1971.[17]

Ten years later, this economic hubris lay buried in stagflation, the seemingly inexplicable and insurmountable combination of economic stagnation and high inflation. Buried with it, in the view of political observer Theodore White, were the electoral hopes of the Democratic party in 1980 and its post-New Deal reputation as an effective manager of the economy. During the 1970s, the inflation rate more than doubled, averaging more than 12.5 percent in 1980.[18] Largely as a result, interest rates temporarily reached a high of 21 percent in late 1980. This trend, in White's view, ate away at the very fabric of American society and destroyed public confidence in the political and economic system. "Inflation is the cancer of modern civilization, the leukemia of planning and hope. . . . [It] comes when a government has made too many promises. . . . Ultimately . . . faith is lost."[19]

To make matters worse, the negative effects of rising inflation were not compensated for by commensurate economic growth. The economy suffered a severe recession in 1974, and employment never fully recovered. By 1980, despite multibillion dollar public jobs programs, unemployment rates were 48 percent higher than the average of the 1960s.[20]

In part, these economic dislocations were attributable to the oil price shocks resulting from the Arab oil embargo in 1973 and the growing power of the OPEC cartel. Oil prices in real dollars rose sharply between 1974 and 1980, and gas lines and shortages imposed additional burdens on the economy. Yet these factors do not fully account for the growth of inflation in the 1970s. Estimates vary, but it appears that only about one-third of the rise in inflation stemmed from higher oil prices.[21]

In their search for other causes of chronic economic distress, increasing numbers of observers pointed to the federal government itself. Conservative Republicans in particular attributed a growing list of social and economic ills to big government as more and more of them came under the sway of refurbished theories of free-market economics.[22] Their message was translated and disseminated by growing numbers of well-funded conservative think tanks that sprouted up in Washington and around the country during the late 1970s. It fell on sympathetic ears in the business community as well, which looked at tax rates and the government's regulation of business as the chief cause of falling productivity and the erosion of American competitiveness worldwide.[23] Thus by 1980 the conventional economic wisdom of the 1970s was not only failing to produce the expected results, it was under increasing intellectual attack by articulate critics throughout society.

Institutional Erosion

Those who concluded that the source of economic ills was federal policy complained not only about "excessive" federal spending and large federal budget deficits, but also about the apparent inability of political institutions to limit spending and deficits. It was this frustration that led some to move for a constitutional amendment to balance the federal budget. Although extreme, such indictments reflected broader concerns about the capacity of American political institutions to govern effectively. A succession of weakened presidents in the 1970s had convinced many that strong executive leadership was no longer possible. Serious consideration was given to the idea of reforming the Constitution in order to strengthen the presidency, and even to the suggestion that American governing structures be replaced with some elements of a parliamentary system.[24]

These views received powerful symbolic affirmation when the government seemed unable to resolve the agonizing hostage situation in Iran, but their origins extended far beyond any single incident or any single president. Although the numerous political and legislative problems that plagued Jimmy Carter were taken to be a sign of a weakened presidency, he was merely the last of several presidents who had found themselves in the same predicament, beginning with Richard Nixon in the final, Watergate-dominated years of his second term. As table 6-1 shows, Nixon's support in Congress on roll-call votes dropped sharply after 1972, and Ford's congressional support remained at historically low levels throughout his tenure. Although Carter enjoyed greater support in Congress than his Republican predecessors, his average was well below that of other modern Democrats.

In part, the decline in presidential influence was the product of the decentralization of Congress, which reached its apogee during the late 1970s as changes in rules, resources, and political incentives all worked

TABLE 6-1. Presidential Victories on Votes in Congress, 1953–83
Percent

President and term	House and Senate votes supporting president
Eisenhower	
First	79.1
Second	65.3
Kennedy	84.6
Johnson	82.6
Nixon	
First	73.2
Second (1973–74)	55.1
Ford	57.6
Carter	76.4
Reagan	
First	72.6

SOURCE: Calculated from table 8-1 in Norman J. Ornstein and others, *Vital Statistics on Congress, 1984–85 Edition* (Washington, D.C.: American Enterprise Institute, 1984), pp. 177–78.

to increase congressional independence. "Subcommittee government" became the order of the day as power, staffing, and independent funds were diffused among 139 subcommittees in the House and 140 in the Senate.[25] Never before had individual members of Congress been as influential and as independent. As James Sundquist observed,

> The [early 1970s] saw the greatest spurt of congressional reform since the Revolution of 1910 tranformed the House. It is not too much to say that in the 1970s the Congress was transformed again.... The dominant element of the new political order is individualism.... Junior members will accept leadership only on their own terms, and subject to their continuous control. They insist on the right to decide day by day and case by case, without coercion, when they will be followers and when they will assert their right of independence.[26]

As a result, effective leadership in Congress demanded herculean efforts. When Tip O'Neill became speaker, his influence was expected to rival that of Sam Rayburn. His long years of experience and substantial personal skills were fortified by a series of compensatory reforms intended to strengthen the power of party leaders in the House and provide some measure of central coordination to overcome the centrifugal effects of decentralized resources. These tightened the speaker's control over the critical House Rules Committee, gave the party caucus in the House new powers, and through the Budget and Impoundment Act established powerful new mechanisms for creating an integrated congressional budget process. Yet by 1980 the general consensus was that "this optimism . . . proved premature. . . . Defeats during the Carter years . . . indicated that even with strong personal leaders, increased substantive leadership powers, a president of the same party, and a two-to-one majority, the leadership could not overcome the independence of House members."[27]

Such legislative fragmentation was both mirrored in and reinforced by the political process outside Congress. The proliferation of interest groups during the Nixon years (see chapter 5) continued unabated during the remainder of the 1970s. Indeed, owing largely to changes in electoral laws, interest group participation in the electoral process expanded dramatically in this period. Between 1974 and 1980 the number of political action committees (PACs) virtually exploded, going from 608 to 2,551, and PAC contributions to congressional campaigns increased from $1.6 million in 1974 to $83.1 million in 1982.[28]

As in the 1960s, many groups continued to form or relocate in Washington in response to the enormous growth in federal programs.[29] Higher education was a case in point. Before the Higher Education Act of 1965 was passed, only two higher education groups were permanently active in Washington, although many more were involved at the state level. Six years later, four additional groups had moved to Washington, and three had been newly created. By the 1980s close to twenty-two such groups were active in the nation's capital, about half of which were founded after the federal government had implemented its new initiatives.[30] Similar examples abound in many other policy areas, from the environment to the handicapped.

Almost the only group that was not experiencing fragmentation was the Republican party. Shaken by the deep losses caused by Watergate and frustrated by the party's decades-long inability to change its minority status among the electorate, national leaders made an unprecedented effort to strengthen the party's organizational structure and financial resources. Between 1967 and 1978 the Republican National Committee increased its permanent staff by 60 percent and its resources by over 500 percent, to almost $10 million.[31] By 1980 the party had a direct mail donor base of well over one million individuals, who contributed more than $6 million that year to Republican congressional and gubernatorial candidates.[32] These "party-building" efforts helped the Republicans capture the Senate in 1980 and provided a foundation for Reagan's subsequent legislative victories. In contrast, centrifugal forces in the Democratic party caused a sitting president to face a major primary challenge that year.

In combination, then, a weakened presidency, a decentralized Congress, and an explosion of interest groups created a difficult environment in which to carry out concerted political action. Seeking a metaphor to compare the political atomization and volatility of the 1970s with the 1960s, Joseph Califano settled on the term "molecular politics."[33] As mentioned earlier, one British analyst despaired that American policymaking had been reduced to "building coalitions in the sand."[34] Since each issue was taken up separately and required a coalition all its own, policy outcomes were often unpredictable and the burdens on leaders almost unbearable. It is little wonder that the fragmentation of the Nixon era gave rise to serious doubts about the "governability" of the American polity itself.[35]

Attitudinal Change

The economic stagnation and perceived institutional weaknesses of the 1970s, reinforced by foreign policy conflicts and Watergate, had important consequences for public attitudes toward the federal government. Compared with the early 1960s, popular support for federal activism had markedly declined by 1980, confidence in American political institutions had fallen, and the public's willingness to entertain conservative alternatives to established federal policies had increased.

It would be a mistake to interpret Ronald Reagan's election as a popular referendum indicating support for the conservative policy agenda he espoused. Most citizens hold mixed and even somewhat contradictory values and attitudes. This allows skillful politicians (and pollsters) to elicit support for quite different policy platforms. Moreover, American elections tend to be retrospective judgments of past performance rather than prospective promises. Still, the electorate wooed by Ronald Reagan in 1980 was looking at a dismal record, which led many people to believe that the government in Washington combined the worst of two worlds: it had become excessively intrusive and overbearing, and at the same time unmanageable and inept.

Survey data demonstrate clearly that public dissatisfaction with the size, scope, and performance of the federal government increased steadily throughout the late 1960s and 1970s. These attitudes toward the federal government were a leading indicator of a much broader decline in public confidence in American institutions of all kinds. Indeed, some analysts argue that the overall decline was the direct result of the decline in government confidence.[36]

These trends are reflected in the responses to three survey questions asked first in 1964—at the inauguration of the Great Society—and then at various points during subsequent years. When people were asked in 1964, "Can you trust the government in Washington to do what's right?" 74 percent replied they could "always" or "most of the time," and only 22 percent replied "only some of the time" (see table 6-2). By 1980 these percentages had almost been reversed. Only 25 percent believed they could trust Washington most of the time; 69 percent now said "only some of the time."

Similarly, 47 percent of Americans surveyed in 1964 agreed that government wastes "a lot of the money we pay in taxes." Fourteen years later that number had climbed 30 points to 78 percent. Finally, the percentage of citizens agreeing that "the federal government has too much power" increased by half between 1964 and 1978. In the year that Barry Goldwater lost his presidential bid, a plurality of citizens thought the federal government's powers were "just about right." Fourteen years later the public had become far more polarized on this question, with a narrow plurality now taking an anti-Washington stance. By 1982 this plurality had been solidified by two years of Reagan rhetoric.

These negative evaluations did not extend to all levels of government. By the time Reagan reached office, larger majorities than ever favored local responsibility for government services; the income tax had become less popular than other state and local taxes; people believed 4 to 1 that states had a better understanding of "peoples' real needs," and that the federal government wastes 50 percent more of every tax dollar.

In short, public opinion was receptive to Ronald Reagan's anti-Washington message in 1980 because the general perception of the government had changed drastically since Nixon's tenure. Although these negative views masked considerable public support for many specific federal programs and functions, they became solidified during Reagan's first two years. By 1981 almost 60 percent of the public had come to agree with the old Jeffersonian maxim, "The best government is that which governs least." The following year, almost two-thirds of the populace indicated that they agreed with the President that the federal government causes more problems than it solves.[37] The White House, the Congress, and the press undoubtedly exaggerated this conservative shift in the electorate—popular support for the broad outlines of the welfare state remained solid—but in politics perceptions can outweigh reality. Seeing the measurably weakened support for federal activism, the administration seized the opportunity to advance its domestic policy initiatives.

TABLE 6-2. Public Attitudes toward the Federal Government, Selected Years, 1964–82

	Percent of responses unless otherwise specified				
Question	1964	1972–73	1978	1980	1981–82
"Can you trust the government in Washington to do what's right?"					
Always/most of the time	76	61	...	25	...
Only some of the time	22	42	...	69	...
"People in government waste a lot of the money we pay in taxes."					
Agree	47	66	77	78	...
"The federal government"					
Has too much power	26	...	38	...	38
Has just about the right amount of power	36	...	18	...	18
Should use its powers more vigorously	31	...	36	...	30
"Local government is closer to the people, so as many services as possible should be local."					
Agree	...	72	...	...	82
"Which do you think is the worst tax—that is, the least fair?"					
Federal income tax	...	19	30	36	36
"How many cents of each tax dollar do you think are wasted?"					
By states	...	...	...	...	0.29
By federal government	...	...	...	...	0.42
"The best government is the government that governs least."					
Agree	...	32	38	...	59
Disagree	...	56	48	...	35
"The federal government creates more problems than it solves."					
Agree	...	...	...	...	63

SOURCES: David R. Gergen, "Following the Leaders," *Public Opinion*, June–July 1985, p. 56; Arthur Miller, "Is Confidence Rebounding," *Public Opinion*, June–July 1985, p. 17; ACIR, *Changing Public Attitudes on Governments and Taxes*, S-12 (GPO, 1983), pp. 1, 16, 52; Lloyd A. Free and Hadley Cantril, *The Political Beliefs of Americans* (Simon and Schuster, 1968), p. 218; National Research Corp.–National Journal, "Opinion Outlook Briefing Paper—The New Federalism Outlook," February 12, 1982, pp. 4, 5; "Opinion Roundup—A Qualified 'Yes' to New Federalism," *Public Opinion*, December–January 1982, p. 36; and R. W. Apple, Jr., "President Highly Popular in Poll; No Ideological Shift Is Discerned," *New York Times*, January 28, 1986.

Reactive Politics and Reagan Federalism

In many ways the major changes in economic performance, institutional processes, and public attitudes that had taken place by the time Ronald Reagan assumed office were the product of earlier governmental policies and performance. Collectively, they laid the groundwork for a new type of government-inspired "reactive politics" that emerged during Reagan's administration. Public policies normally are thought to be shaped by forces and demands external to government. Such forces can include the pressures created by particular crises and events and by interest groups, parties, and public opinion. Because this view of policymaking is closely tied to the normative assumptions of democratic theory, it has often been accepted almost without question. Yet since the 1960s, when the government's share of the gross national product first exceeded 30 percent, it has become increasingly clear that this simple demand model of the policy process is not only incomplete, but also misleading. Three decades of intergovernmental policymaking and reform have shown that the public sector itself is now inspiring many public policies. It does so in three principal ways.

First, actors and institutions within the government may initiate and shape policies independently of the external actors and forces—the general public, interest groups, economic conditions, and so on—normally associated with policy formation. The war on poverty and other aspects of Lyndon Johnson's "creative federalism" are excellent examples of such an internally driven policy process. Johnson's decision to make the war on poverty the centerpiece of his domestic policy agenda was not inevitable or imposed by external actors. As James Sundquist notes, "The war on poverty did not arise, as have many great national programs, from the pressure of overwhelming public demand—the poor had no lobby." [38] Indeed, before deciding to proceed with a broad antipoverty initiative, the Johnson White House seriously considered promoting revenue sharing or a broader agenda aimed at America's booming suburbs. [39]

It would be naive, of course, to think that the war on poverty was an entirely autonomous enterprise of government insiders, although the community action program probably came close to this model. Government decisionmakers were influenced by a variety of outside factors, ranging from intellectual works to John F. Kennedy's campaign experiences in 1960. Moreover, enactment of the program depended on a favorable, or at least nonhostile, response from the outside world. Yet the decision to pursue an antipoverty agenda was in keeping with the tendency of policymaking in the 1960s to rely heavily on the knowledge of specialists, particularly social scientists, to find solutions to social problems. In Samuel Beer's words,

> The intellectual history of federal domestic programs since the days of the Great Society is deeply marked by the influence of . . . complexes of professional expertise. . . . How rarely additions to the public sector have been *initiated* by the demands of voters or the advocacy of pressure groups or the platforms of political parties. On the contrary, in the fields of health, housing, urban renewal, transportation, welfare, education, poverty, and energy, it has been . . . people in government service, or closely associated with it, acting on the basis of their specialized and technical knowledge, who first perceived the problem, conceived the program, initially urged it on president and Congress, went on to help lobby it through to enactment, and then saw to its administration.[40]

Although developed internally, such policies affect the government's political environment in a multiple of complex ways. Federal programs created in the 1960s and early 1970s spawned new interest groups and lobbies, which were developed to represent their clients and service providers. Indeed, in the case of community action and several other Great Society initiatives, the government explicitly set out to organize certain groups of citizens and to alter the existing political landscape. Once formed, such groups often pushed aggressively for still more and larger programs. At the same time, new expectations were created among citizens who now saw their own problems as appropriate targets of governmental attention. Legislators learned to convert these expectations into political opportunities by adopting an entrepreneurial role in policy initiation, focused on inventing new programs and conferring new benefits.

Such a system creates problems as well as solutions. As pointed out in earlier chapters, Nixon's New Federalism represented a second form of governmentally inspired policymaking, which has been labeled "rationalizing politics" by Lawrence Brown.[41] In this instance, policies are shaped in response to earlier program failures and previous governmental action. Nixon's management reforms and block grant proposals were an explicit response to the problems of previous intergovernmental programs, as were many regulatory programs like the National Health Planning Act. The politics of revenue sharing, which was dominated by the intergovernmental lobby, raised the process of intragovernmental politics to a new level.

This political dimension of the New Federalism had important implications for the formulation of public policy. Nixon's initiatives were aimed in part at disrupting the professional and institutional arrangements that legislators had depended on earlier in creating many of the programs targeted for reform. This was clearly evident in Nixon's efforts to replace the "service strategy" of the 1960s with an income strategy and entitlements in public assistance. It was evident, too, in block grants and revenue sharing, which sought to disrupt the "iron triangles" and to consolidate governmental activism within the domain of generalists at the state and local levels. Indeed, the Nixon administration even launched a campaign to build an intergovernmental lobby of state and local elected officials as a political counterweight to bureaucratic professionals at all levels of government. As the Labor Department official quoted in chapter 3 remarked in the case of CETA:

> Probably the strongest interest groups have been the public interest groups [PIGs], and that was sort of creating our own Frankenstein. . . . We'd give them funds to hire planning staffs, and this built up a strong infrastructure. We also had policy assistance contracts . . . to provide a mechanism for educating and sensitizing officials on the new initiative. But yes, we were creating a constituency and an adversary group prior to CETA.[42]

In the end, this effort to disrupt the dynamics of professional policy generation was largely unsuccessful, in part because important elements of Nixon's agenda were not adopted and in part because government technocrats were often found to be important and necessary allies in the effort to rationalize prior policies. As a result, rationalizing politics was layered over the creative federalist model, and new initiatives continued to emanate from Washington, largely as a result of the efforts of policy entrepreneurs in Congress.

The politics of Reagan's New Federalism represents a third form of governmentally inspired policymaking, which can be termed "reactive" politics. In this phase the concern with governmental dysfunctions has spread well beyond government officials and shapes the broader political climate, including public opinion, reform agendas in party platforms, and mass media attention. As a result, reactive politics at times resembles the demand model of the policy process. It is also somewhat similar to the "breakthrough politics" that typified the federal government's initial, often difficult incursions into many new fields of policy.[43] The distinction is that the new public agenda has been formed around issues of past and present governmental performance and can be considered an outgrowth of those policies.

Reagan's Instrumental Federalism

Thus when Ronald Reagan charged that "the most important cause of our . . . problems has been the government itself," his diagnosis may have been simplistic, but it suggested an important truth.[44] The president sounded a new chord in American politics, and it drew a strong response. That is to say, he was given an opportunity if not a mandate for change. From an intergovernmental perspective, it was an opening Reagan filled with "instrumental federalism."

Some have argued that federalism rests at the very center of Reagan's philosophy of governance, that it organizes his stand on a vast range of specific policies. According to Richard S. Williamson, Reagan's former assistant for intergovernmental affairs,

> President Ronald Reagan has a dream. His dream is not to cut the bloated federal budget. . . . His dream is not about tax cuts. . . . His dream is not about regulatory relief. . . . Rather, the President's dream is to change how America is governed. . . . He is seeking a "quiet revolution," a new federalism which is a meaningful American partnership.[45]

The president's own words lend credence to this interpretation. "My administration is committed—heart and soul—to the broad principles of American federalism," he told a gathering of state legislators in 1981.[46]

In contrast, others have argued that, rhetoric aside, federalism reform was merely a Trojan horse for Reagan's plan to slash the federal budget and dismantle social programs—and was not the organizing principle of the president's philosophy. As one of Jimmy Carter's intergovernmental aides put it,

> The driving force behind the Administration's decisions about federalism is primarily a concern with the federal deficit. . . . At the bottom of the New Federalism is, I believe, the Administration's belief that the best way to cut spending is to eliminate the substantial support that the federal government currently provides for a variety of programs administered by state and local governments.[47]

This has been the view of many state and local officials, including Democratic governors who complained that Reagan's 1982 Federalism initiative was "a diversionary tactic" to "solve the federal deficit."[48]

In truth, both views are partly right, and they reveal the instrumental character of Reagan's views toward federalism reform. Altering the balance of power between the federal government and the states has been an important goal of the president and his administration. Far from being the hidden goal of a secret and contradictory agenda, cuts in federal aid have been considered an important tool of intergovernmental reform because they lower the fiscal profile of the federal government. In sharp contrast to Nixon, Reagan has consistently defined federalism reform as a one-sided equation that reduces the federal role but does little to encourage states and localities.[49]

But it is also true that federalism reform per se was not among the President's ultimate policy objectives. Rather, his commitment has been to the sometimes contradictory goals of reducing the influence of the public sector at all levels of government (except for national defense), increasing society's reliance on private markets, and advancing traditional social values. Because decentralization is often consistent with such aims, Reagan has often employed it to implement his objectives. But where the president's federalism goals (which are almost always defined in terms of aggressive decentralization) conflict with these larger ends, federalism concerns have been consistently sacrificed on their behalf. As succeeding chapters demonstrate, this has been true in budgetary, tax, and regulatory policy alike and underscores the president's conviction that "government [at any level] is not the solution. Government is the problem."

7

The Implicit Federalism of Reagan's Fiscal Policies

I N DECEMBER 1980, David Stockman mailed a job application to the
newly elected president. Entitled "Avoiding an Economic Dunkirk,"
this lengthy résumé raised the specter of an economic crisis on the
nation's horizon and spelled out a detailed program for avoiding it.

The fundamental problem, Stockman wrote, was the modern welfare
state itself. Nurtured by unholy alliances of bureaucrats, legislators, subsidized industries, and other client groups, the American welfare state
was growing at an uncontrollable rate and strangling the economy. The
result, he concluded, would be economic collapse: high federal taxes and
high levels of federal borrowing would combine with proliferating regulations to stifle business incentives, hamper productivity, undermine private investment, and drain economic vitality, growth, and competitiveness.

To deal with this complex set of problems, Stockman prescribed a
comprehensive set of reforms. Large, immediate reductions in federal income tax rates were required to restore incentives for private investment
and risk taking. To accommodate tax cuts and to reduce federal interference in the marketplace, federal domestic spending had to be drastically
reduced and large numbers of intrusive and ineffective programs eliminated. Finally, specific federal regulations, and the entire regulatory process, had to be reformed and restructured to reduce excessive interference
in social and economic decisionmaking and to ensure that social benefits
outweighed economic costs.

Stockman's job application was successful, earning him the post of
director of the Office of Management and Budget. From this position, he
was strategically placed to fashion the president's program in domestic
policy, and the product hewed closely to his initial recommendations.

Nowhere in Stockman's agenda were issues of federalism mentioned outright. But, implicitly, intergovernmental issues were inescapable. Terminating "ineffective" or "inefficient" programs meant, in many cases, terminating federal grant programs to state and local governments. Reforming and reducing the costs of federal entitlements affected federalism directly, by modifying intergovernmental programs like AFDC and medicaid, and indirectly, by scaling down the fiscal profile of the federal government. Tax cuts would make this lower profile permanent by putting a fiscal straitjacket around federal activists in Congress. Relieving regulatory costs and burdens altered joint administrative arrangements in some regulatory programs and reduced state and local costs and burdens in others. In short, the comprehensive economic plans recommended to the president constituted a complex strategy for implementing federalism reform as well as economic reform, and the president and his advisers seized on and embellished this dual character.

Such embellishments included an explicit package of federalism initiatives—consisting of seven sweeping block grant proposals—which was added to the 1981 budget proposals. This was followed in 1982 by a huge plan for restructuring federal, state, and local responsibilities. (These initiatives, along with budgetary decisions affecting intergovernmental aid levels and priorities, are reviewed in the following chapters.) However, it was Reagan's implicit agenda—in the form of federal tax and domestic budget cuts—that had greater long-term philosophical and operational implications for the federal system as a whole. As was argued in chapter 6, Reagan's New Federalism policies were one expression of a broader philosophical attack on the modern welfare state. This was not simply a question of giving a greater role to the states vis-à-vis the federal government; Reagan opposed public sector activism at every level of government. His explicit intergovernmental agenda is best appreciated within this wider context.

From a historical standpoint, the preeminence of Reagan's implicit federalism agenda is not unique. Despite all their specific programmatic accomplishments, Roosevelt and Johnson did most to reshape the federal system by nationalizing policy innovation, by expanding public expectations of the federal government, and by altering the political incentives of politicians. Reagan has done much the same in reverse. Federal tax cuts and defense increases have produced unprecedented deficits that have come to dominate the national agenda, reducing federal activism and altering its forms. It is this change in the policy agenda and the resulting shift in the locus of policy activism that promise to be the greatest intergovernmental legacies of the Reagan era.

The political effect of Reagan's implicit federalism agenda has been just as significant. Although ambitious in scope, the president's initial proposals mustered surprising political support in Congress. As a result, anticipated federal spending for domestic programs was reduced by more than $35 billion in fiscal 1982, and grants to state and local governments were cut sharply. Federal income tax rates were reduced 25 percent over a three-year period, and sixty pending regulations were delayed or revised by administrative action.[1] These striking outcomes were produced by a very different style of politics than was evident during the 1970s. These factors in turn redefined the subsequent policy agenda.

Politically, the Reagan administration shunned the tedious process of building a bipartisan consensus for reform in individual policy areas. It succeeded instead in constructing a partisan-conservative phalanx that rolled major portions of the president's program through Congress in one bold sweep. For the single critical year of 1981 the narrow interest subsystem politics and congressional fragmentation that characterized the Nixon and Carter years gave way to a highly visible, majoritarian style of presidential policy leadership.

This pattern of successful party government did not last, but neither did the federal government return to the incrementally expansionist, highly fragmented system of policymaking that dominated the 1970s. With respect to budgetary policy, for example, the legislative changes enacted in 1981 restructured the policymaking environment, and a new politics of budgetary stalemate emerged on most domestic spending issues. Continuing efforts to reduce or eliminate the federal deficit, whether through an amended Gramm-Rudman-Hollings process or some other means, promise to maintain the pressure for additional domestic budget cuts in the years ahead.

In the area of tax policy, Congress waged an incremental effort over four years to restore some of the revenues lost to the federal treasury by the 1981 income tax reductions. This was done without taking on the president's supply-side tax cuts directly, through excise tax increases and loophole closing. Although these patterns of fiscal stalemate and incremental tax increases were temporarily broken with the passage of sweeping tax reform legislation in 1986, the "revenue-neutral" character of that legislation did nothing to resolve the fiscal tourniquet squeezing the federal agenda.

Budgetary Blitzkrieg in 1981

On February 18, 1981, Ronald Reagan sent Congress an "economic recovery program" containing 83 proposals to reduce federal budget

TABLE 7-1. Comparison of Reagan Budget Requests for
Fiscal Year 1982 with Actual Fiscal Year 1981 Expenditures
on Comparable Programs
Billions of dollars unless otherwise specified

Program category	Fiscal 1981 expenditures	Fiscal 1982 request	Percent difference
Total block grants	18.7	14.8	−21
New block grants[a]	12.8	9.7	−24
Existing block grants[b]	5.9	5.1	−14
Total federal aid	105.8	86.2	−19
Major entitlements[c]	311.4	335.3	8
Total domestic spending[d]	511.2	546.1	7
National defense	182.4	226.3	24
Total federal spending	718.4	772.4	8

SOURCE: *Budget Appendix, Special Analyses, Budget of the United States Government,* various years.
   a. The fiscal 1981 figure is the combined expenditures for the programs consolidated into the fiscal 1982 block grants.
   b. Does not include public service employment programs.
   c. Includes social security.
   d. Total federal spending minus defense and international affairs.

outlays by $34.8 billion in 1982. Three weeks later he sent Congress another package of 200 recommendations for an additional $13.8 billion in savings.[2] From an intergovernmental standpoint, the most noteworthy items in these packages were the proposals to (1) establish seven new block grants, with estimated savings in fiscal 1982 of $3.1 billion; (2) cut $5 billion out of income security programs by tightening eligibility requirements and by changing matching ratios in medicaid, food stamps, AFDC, and child nutrition programs; and (3) terminate the remainder of the CETA public employment program, thereby saving approximately $2 billion. Overall, the president proposed reducing federal aid expenditures by $19.6 billion, or 19 percent, below fiscal 1981 levels. By one estimate, two-thirds of the administration's proposed cuts came out of intergovernmental programs, even though federal aid constituted only about 17 percent of the federal budget.[3] In contrast, total domestic spending—including social security—was slated to rise 7 percent, and defense spending was to increase 24 percent over 1981 levels (see table 7-1).

   Although the president did not obtain everything he asked for, he was surprisingly successful, as already mentioned. The final budget to emerge from Congress in 1981 reduced anticipated federal outlays for domestic programs by $35 billion in fiscal 1982 and $131 billion by 1984. This amounted to a reduction of approximately 6 percent below expected 1982 spending levels.[4] Grants to state and local governments were cut even more sharply, falling $6 billion below actual spending in fiscal 1981 and 13 percent below anticipated or baseline expenditures for fiscal

1982. Especially hard hit were grants supporting the delivery of state and local services in education, job training, and social welfare, as well as nongrant programs like housing assistance, Amtrak, government employee benefits, and postal subsidies. Sixty-two programs were terminated altogether, including CETA public employment, and another seventy-seven programs were consolidated into nine new or restructured block grants.[5] Finally, medicaid spending was slowed, and the AFDC and food stamps budgets were reduced by about $2 billion below baseline expenditures.[6]

Evaluations of the effect of these budgetary changes vary. Although most administration officials were jubilant at what they had achieved, David Stockman argued publicly that the cuts agreed upon constituted only half of the domestic cuts needed to complete the president's agenda. Indeed, some observers questioned whether Reagan's victories even amounted to a change in direction. They argued that—far from ushering in a "Reagan revolution"—they merely accelerated budgetary trends that had begun in the Carter administration.[7]

Press accounts at the time were more generous, calling the reconciliation act a "triumph for conservatism rivaling the liberal triumphs of . . . Roosevelt and . . . Johnson."[8] Many policy analysts agreed. Richard Nathan called the Omnibus Budget Reconciliation Act (OBRA) "the single most important piece of social legislation enacted in the United States since the Social Security Act of 1935."[9] Most important from a political standpoint, most members of Congress viewed both the budget and tax initiatives as striking departures from "business as usual." Republicans hailed the "two whopping pieces of legislation." "Part of the Great Society program has been repealed," observed House Republican leader Robert H. Michel of Illinois, and "can't be reinstated."[10] Disheartened Democrats called it "the most monumental and historic turnaround in fiscal policy that has ever occurred."[11]

How Reagan achieved this budgetary victory can be traced to three sets of political factors. Philosophically, the president was aided by a widely perceived crisis in New Deal liberalism and the seeming inability of Democrats to defend convincingly the merits of existing programs or to generate viable policy alternatives. Structurally, the president was assisted by Republican control of the Senate, by the revival of the conservative coalition in the House, and by the relative coherence and technical sophistication of the Republican party. Finally, enactment of the new block grants and budget reductions was achieved through brilliant parliamentary tactics that substantially altered the traditional ground rules of budgetary politics. The budget reconciliation process made it possible to subsume a series of discrete policy decisions under the president's economic program, where the particularistic concerns of individual program advocates were overshadowed by high-visibility budgetary politics.

Reconciliation and the Tactical Transformation of Budgetary Politics

A simple chronology of budget politics in 1981 reveals the role of tactical considerations in the Reagan victory. Early in the year, as the president's proposals were being considered individually by congressional committees, the prospects for enactment were anything but promising. Committees in the Republican-controlled Senate made substantial alterations in sections of the president's proposals, and some committees in the Democratic House threatened to block certain cuts altogether. This pattern was reversed, however, when the reconciliation process was used to shift decisionmaking from committees to the floor and to reframe issues on the president's terms.

The seeds of reconciliation were sown long before Ronald Reagan was elected and Republicans gained control of the Senate. Ironically, they lay in Congress's negative reaction to the budget tactics associated with the New Federalism of Richard Nixon. In 1974 Congress passed the Budget and Impoundment Act in response to the Nixon administration's abuses of its power to impound appropriated funds. Moreover, there was a growing sense within Congress that, in order to effectively challenge any president's budget, the legislative branch required an independent mechanism that would enable it to produce a coherent set of alternative spending priorities.

The Budget and Impoundment Act required Congress to adopt two comprehensive budget resolutions each year: a preliminary one in the spring setting forth general spending targets to guide individual committees' spending decisions, and a binding one in the fall adjusted for actual appropriation and authorization bills adopted by Congress and for any modifications in revenue and expenditure estimates caused by changing economic conditions. In order to ensure that automatic entitlements would not exceed the binding budget ceilings, the act included a "reconciliation" provision permitting statutory provisions of existing legislation to be amended by the budget resolution, in order to "reconcile" them to overall spending limits. This provision was not used until 1980, however, when serious problems with President Carter's fiscal 1981 budget proposal produced a crash effort by White House and congressional leaders to cut federal spending. They used the reconciliation device to reduce the 1980 and 1981 budgets by approximately $5 billion.[12]

This laid the groundwork for the Republicans' use of reconciliation in 1981. The new administration and Republican leaders in Congress seized on the device as a vehicle for making rapid budget cuts before the president's popularity began to slip away. For obvious reasons, administration strategists did not expect congressional committees to willingly make substantial cuts in federal programs or to sacrifice their own influence over policy through program consolidation. A comprehensive budget reconciliation bill, combining spending reductions with consolidations, could be used to bypass committee specialists and to divert political attention from the fate of separately targeted programs and draw it to the president's economic program.

This proved to be a brilliant political move. At a time when individual committees in both chambers of Congress were resisting the president's budget and block grant proposals, the reconciliation vehicle allowed the administration to construct conservative budget coalitions on the floor of each chamber that adopted overall spending ceilings consistent with the president's economic program. The Republican-controlled Senate passed its initial budget resolution on April 2, 1981, by a vote of 88 to 10.[13] The House, in a major victory for the president, rejected the Democratic leadership's proposed budget resolution and on May 7 adopted a lower, administration-backed budget resolution amendment—the so-called Gramm-Latta I amendment—by a vote of 253 to 176.

These initial resolutions instructed recalcitrant committees to develop specific legislative proposals designed to meet the new spending targets and to report these changes to their respective budget committees by June 12, 1981. These budget targets were not binding, however, and so the reconciliation process was implemented in order to establish fixed spending ceilings and make permanent changes in specific legislation. Once again, the Senate led the way, passing its version of the Omnibus Budget Reconciliation Act on June 25, 1981, by a vote of 80 to 15. The House passed its final reconciliation bill, as amended by "Gramm-Latta II," in a dramatic showdown vote of 217 to 211 the following day. A conference version of the reconciliation act was signed into law on August 13, 1981.

As Robert Fulton, former chief counsel for the Senate Budget Committee, observed, the tactical key to the success of the reconciliation act was that it combined a wide variety of program changes and spending cuts in one highly visible package:

Reconciliation made possible a "critical mass" of spending reductions which members could not afford to oppose, and it enabled the media—and the public—to keep a clear view of the progress Congress was making on the President's proposals. It also provided a few highly visible votes upon which maximum leverage could be mobilized by the President and his supporters.[14]

Recognizing the political implications of the reconciliation device, House Democratic leaders made one last-ditch attempt to disrupt the administration's strategy before the act was adopted. They proposed a rule requiring the administration-backed Gramm-Latta II substitute to be considered in five different components, so that House members would go on record for specific cuts in student aid, social security, medicaid, and so forth. However, the president's budget coalition in the house defeated this rule in a critical vote on June 25, 1981, and the stage was set for a single yes/no vote on the Gramm-Latta II reconciliation amendment.

Accordingly, the budget for fiscal 1982 was developed not through the traditional painstaking and incremental work of the appropriations subcommittees, but by and large in a single, massive ad hoc amendment pasted together in a frenzied scramble of last-minute negotiations among Republicans and conservative Democrats. In fact House members had almost no information concerning the contents of the far-reaching Gramm-Latta amendment.[15] As Congressman Norman Mineta (Democrat of California) complained after the budget was adopted:

The haste with which the Administration substitute was thrown together . . . made it impossible for Members to know what they were voting on. Copies of the proposal which was hundreds of pages long were only available to Members just hours before the final vote and after debate had begun on the bill. The legislative document contained handwritten notes scribbled in the margin, dollar amounts of entries pencilled in, others scratched out. In this . . . manner, Congress was asked to consider the largest single bill ever brought before it, affecting virtually every activity of government.[16]

In the end, then, reconciliation allowed the issue to be framed in the president's terms. "The Reagan administration cast it this way," said one newspaper report. "You were either for the president and economic recovery, or you were against it. Cool deliberation took a back seat. . . . Substance gave way to symbolism." [17]

Philosophical and Institutional Dimensions of the Reconciliation Act

The reconciliation act may have provided a vehicle for the president's victory, but it was not the ultimate cause. The legislation mustered support largely because of two political factors: the philosophical and structural disarray of the Democratic party, which hampered attempts to challenge the administration's program; and the surprising strength of the Republican party in Congress.

THE EROSION OF NEW DEAL LIBERALISM. Conventional wisdom attributes much of the credit for the Reagan administration's legislative successes to the president's landslide victory at the polls, which was seen as a "mandate" for change. Politicians and the public alike were impressed by the president's sizable margin of victory. Moreover, the appearance of a conservative tide was reinforced by the defeat of several prominent liberal senators and the surprising election of a Republican majority to the Senate for the first time in a quarter century.

Equally important was the contrast between the new administration's ideological vigor and the philosophical malaise of the Democrats. The administration exuded confidence, believing that it had found in "supply-side economics" an answer to the seemingly intractable problems of stagflation, lagging investment and productivity, and soaring interest rates. Moreover, as chapter 6 explained, public opinion polls seemed to indicate growing popular support for the president's proposal to cut back the government in Washington.

At the same time, according to press accounts in early 1981, the Democratic party was beset by organizational floundering and intellectual anomie. Because much of the policy agenda stemming from the New Deal had been adopted—with the notable exception of national health insurance—there was an understandable policy vacuum in the party. Capturing the tenor of the times, columnist Russell Baker described the New Deal as "an idea whose time had passed." He wrote poignantly:

Only a sentimentalist could weep. A 50-year-old political idea is like a 30-year-old dog or 150-year-old man. . . . So it was with the New Deal: old, stricken in years, and, despite the accretions of Truman's Fair Deal and Lyndon Johnson's Great Society, finally it gat no heat. It certainly gat none in the new generation of Democrats. For years now they have formed a party only in the sense that a party is a conspiracy to get elected and enjoy the pleasures of the feeding trough.[18]

Notwithstanding the "tenor of the times," there are sound reasons for questioning the extent to which Reagan's budget victories were rooted in popular opinion. To connect any shift in the specific details of public policy with the broad contours of public opinion is hazardous at best, and grossly simplistic at worst. Moreover, there is ample basis for doubting that Reagan's 1980 election victory reflected an ideological "mandate."[19] American presidential elections generally are based on retrospective evaluations of past political performance, and many factors suggest that public dissatisfaction with Jimmy Carter was the principal issue in the election. Accordingly, Mann and Ornstein conclude that the election of 1980 was misperceived:

> The consensus interpretation of the 1980 election . . . worked greatly to the [legislative] benefit of Republicans. . . . The Republican win in 1980 was not nearly so sweeping as it appeared to be. . . . But the [narrow] margins of victory [in Senate races] were overshadowed by the [unexpected] victories themselves. . . . The result was an overinterpretation of the meaning of 1980.[20]

For political purposes, however, the actual existence of a mandate for change in 1981 was less important than the widely held perception that one existed. The political events of 1981 clearly demonstrated the power of perceptions and ideas in shaping the course of public policy. The new administration seemed almost uncontested in the realm of new (or very old) ideas, and the president's popularity was growing in early 1981, bolstered by reactions against his attempted assassination and by his reputation as a "great communicator." These factors formed a crucial backdrop for coalition building in Congress.

STRUCTURAL CHANGES IN AMERICAN POLITICS. Reinforcing the apparent popular support for Reagan administration policies were political factors stemming from structural changes in American political institutions. These boosted the president's standing in Congress enormously during the crucial year of 1981. Particularly important were the organizational fragmentation of the Democratic party in Congress and the surprising unity of the Republican party.

DEMOCRATIC FRAGMENTATION IN CONGRESS. The Democratic party's seeming loss of philosophical identity in 1981 was exacerbated by the effects of organizational fragmentation in Congress. As had occurred in the highly individualistic Senate, power in the House of Representatives was greatly decentralized through a series of procedural reforms in 1970, 1971, and 1973 that stripped committee chairmen of power, greatly expanded the number and influence of subcommittee chairs, and strengthened the position of individual members of Congress. The most significant of these reforms originated in a partisan forum. They were developed in the House Democratic caucus and then imposed by the majority on the operations of the House. In effect they produced what some observers have called "subcommittee government," which contributed to the "extreme individualism" in congressional behavior during the 1970s.[21]

This general fragmentation contributed to growing Democratic disunity in the late 1970s, especially among newly elected Democrats whose support of the party seemed to be waning rapidly. Senior Democrats in Congress began complaining that newer members were becoming unpredictable and seemed to lack a stable footing in the party's ideological mainstream.[22] To make matters worse, there was a powerful revival of the conservative coalition in Congress. Indeed, one renegade Democrat, Congressman Phil Gramm of Texas, negotiated directly with the White House and Republican congressional leaders on bipartisan budget legislation and had his name prominently affixed to the key budget amendments that shaped the reconciliation act. Partly because of such efforts, 1981 witnessed the highest success rate ever scored by a conservative coalition during a single session of Congress since the *Congressional Quarterly* began compiling this index in 1957. The conservative coalition won victories in a whopping 92 percent of the cases in which a majority of southern Democrats and Republicans opposed a majority of northern Democrats. This success rate was 20 percentage points higher than in 1980 and 28 points above the average score of the previous decade. It is no wonder that President Reagan achieved the highest presidential support in congressional voting since Lyndon Johnson's triumphs in the Eighty-ninth Congress.[23]

Among southern Democrats, support for the conservative coalition stemmed largely from the president's popularity in the South in 1981 and from increasing Republican competition for congressional seats in the no longer "solid South." Republicans gained nine House seats in that region in the 1980 election and were up thirteen seats from 1976. Not one

House delegation from a southern state was solidly Democratic by 1981, and only two southern states retained two Democratic senators. As a result, White House budget strategists were determined from the start to focus their lobbying efforts on these potentially vulnerable members of Congress.[24]

REPUBLICAN SOLIDARITY. An even more important reason for the president's success in 1981 lay in Republican behavior in Congress. In contrast to the Democrats' disorganization, Republican voting in Congress was marked by a "striking gain in solidarity." This was especially true in the Senate, where GOP control for the first time in twenty-five years raised party unity scores among Republicans 16 percentage points above 1980 levels. On a series of critical votes in the House, the president's economic program evoked similar unity from members of his party. On the first budget resolution, House Republicans voted 190 to 0 in support of Gramm-Latta I, thereby reducing fiscal 1982 spending by $36.6 billion. Six weeks later, they voted 188 to 2 in favor of specific budget cuts and block grants in Gramm-Latta II. Finally, they voted 190 to 1 in favor of the president's tax cut bill, reducing federal income taxes 25 percent over three years.[25]

This striking unity does not mean that the so-called gypsy moths—moderate northern Republicans who threatened to abandon the president's position—had no influence in 1981. Before the key vote on Gramm-Latta II, for instance, they were able to exact certain concessions on spending for medicaid, Amtrak, and mass transit grants. But such amendments are part of the normal give and take of legislative politics. In 1981 the most important factor was the lack of moderate Republican defections on key votes. "We always had 25 or 30 of the Gypsy Moths . . . who voted with us [in prior years]," complained Tip O'Neill. "But as you look at the discipline of the party, last year the Republicans voted in lockstep. . . . The President never lost a vote."[26]

This unity, in turn, reflected the influence of both short- and long-term factors on the Republican party. In the short term, it represented an initial response by a party long out of power, buoyed by the president's popularity and ideological vigor and by the Democrats' disorganization. The Reagan administration's subsequent difficulties in furthering its legislative program and advancing its New Federalism proposals indicate the transient character of the many factors responsible for the president's 1981 victories. For example, Republicans in Congress departed sharply in 1981 from their historic levels of support for federal aid spending. In 1982, however, they quickly returned to earlier patterns of support and, measured by one index, the average federal aid support among eastern Republicans in the Senate actually exceeded their levels in the late 1970s.[27]

At the same time more lasting changes in the structure and composition of the Republican party also contributed to party strength and unity. Students of Congress had observed a trend toward increasing ideological consensus among congressional Republicans in the years prior to 1981, and found that surviving members of the Watergate era and their newly elected colleagues in both chambers were becoming more conservative.[28] For example, the average score of Republican congressmen on the roll call vote index compiled by Americans for Democratic Action—a common measurement of ideology—fell 20 percent during the 1970s, from an average score of 20 in 1971 to just 16 in 1981.

Also contributing to Republican unity were structural developments in national party organization. In the wake of the Watergate debacle, the Republican party grew increasingly active in grooming and assisting new candidates for Congress—a process that, in 1981 at least, helped counteract the longer-term trend toward congressional atomization. Specifically, the party recruited promising candidates for congressional office, staged national training seminars in campaign techniques, provided candidates with polling and consultant services, and distributed substantial campaign contributions.[29] Indeed, the party's success in direct mail fundraising enabled the National Republican Congressional and Senatorial Committees to raise $78.8 million for the 1980 campaign (as of September 1981), which was ten times more than the $7.8 million raised by their Democratic counterparts.[30] Along with the coattails of Ronald Reagan, these party-building efforts in the 1980 campaign helped Republicans elect twelve new members to the Senate and thirty-three to the House.

The Republican party's organizational sophistication was evident in legislative coalition building also. White House and congressional leaders skillfully bound the elements of their electoral coalition together by using sympathetic lobbies to campaign for block grants and budget cuts and to mobilize public pressure on Congress to support the president. The White House employed a special presidential assistant to coordinate and organize business support for the Reagan economic program, and a massive grass-roots lobbying effort was orchestrated to supplement the president's skill as a "great communicator." According to the *Congressional Quarterly*, "The Reagan administration was quick to recognize and exploit the potential of an organized business community. In winning passage of its tax and budget legislation . . . the administration took existing business bands and built them into an orchestra for the Reagan side." [31] The White House helped mobilize such groups into an organized blitzkrieg of fifty-one key congressional districts, generating phone calls, mail, and demands for presidential support from the general public, the local media, and campaign contributors. [32] Apparently spurred by this presidential symphony, Capitol Hill was flooded with letters and calls supporting the president in the battle over reconciliation. Although on close examination some of the president's grass-roots support appeared to be artificially inspired "astroturf"—manufactured by business allies who encouraged or cajoled employees to send letters to Congress favoring tax and budget cuts—the impact on congressional voting, in this case at least, was much the same. [33]

Budget Politics since 1981

Whatever their ultimate significance historically, the budget actions of 1981 stand out as a unique phenomenon in contemporary budgetmaking. Before 1981 the normal pattern in budgetary politics was incremental growth. [34] Although this pattern of overall growth often obscured major differences and shifts in growth rates among individual programs and budget functions, incremental growth remained the norm until 1980, when the budget reconciliation process was first utilized on a small scale under the Carter administration. The large cuts implemented in 1981 were followed by more modest annual reductions in subsequent years.

The unique character of the 1981 reconciliation act is reflected in the outcomes of congressional budgetary actions from 1980 to 1984 (see table 7-2). Congress continued to make incremental budgetary reductions in subsequent years, but they paled in comparison with the 1981 cuts. Measured as outlays, the total annual cuts enacted for the three years between 1982 and 1984 equaled less than one-third of the reductions enacted in 1981 alone, and their magnitude was even less significant when measured in terms of budget authority.

This change in budgetary momentum was not for want of trying on the president's part. The administration continued to propose substantial new domestic spending cuts and structural program changes but met with limited success. As table 7-3 shows, for each fiscal year from 1982 to 1987, the administration consistently proposed lower levels of spending on federal domestic programs than were actually adopted into law, but instead of achieving additional large reductions in domestic expenditures, the administration ushered in a period of relative stability. Federal domestic spending actually increased 10 percent in constant dollars during Reagan's administration, owing mainly to large increases in social

TABLE 7-2. Congressional Budget Actions, 1980–84
Billions of dollars

Budget action	First-year effect	Three-year effect
Omnibus Reconciliation Act of 1980		
Budget authority	−2.8	...
Outlays	−4.6	...
Omnibus Reconciliation Act of 1981		
Budget authority	−53.2	−172.3
Outlays	−35.2	−130.9
Omnibus Reconciliation Act of 1982		
Budget authority	−3.4	−14.9
Outlays	−6.9	−29.9
Omnibus Reconciliation Act of 1983[a]		
Budget authority	2.0	2.3
Outlays	−0.4	−1.8
Deficit Reduction Act of 1984		
Budget authority	−0.9	−7.2
Outlays	−3.9	−12.2

SOURCE: John Ellwood, "The Great Exception: The Congressional Budget Process in an Age of Decentralization," in Lawrence C. Dodd and Bruce I. Oppenheimer, eds., Congress Reconsidered, 3d ed. (Washington, D.C.: CQ Press, 1985), p. 332.
a. Enacted on April 18, 1984.

TABLE 7-3. President's Budget Proposals and Actual Outcomes, Nondefense Outlays, Fiscal Years 1982–87
Billions of dollars; percent change from current services

Year	Current services	Administration proposal	Actual
1982			
Amount	558.7	506.5	560.4
Percent change	...	−9	*
1983			
Amount	577.0	536.6	598.4
Percent change	...	−7	4
1984			
Amount	626.6	603.2	624.4
Percent change	...	−4	*
1985			
Amount	660.7	653.5	693.6
Percent change	...	−1	5
1986			
Amount	729.9	688.1	716.4
Percent change	...	−6	−2
1987			
Amount	734.6	711.7	722.6
Percent change	...	−3	−2

SOURCES: Budget of the United States Government, Special Analyses, section A, various years.
*Less than 0.5 percent.

TABLE 7-4. Percentage Change in Real Domestic Outlays,
Fiscal Years 1981–87

Budget category	1981–1982	1982–1983	1983–1984	1984–1985	1985–1986	1986–1987	Total, 1981–1987
Total nondefense	0.9	2.7	0.4	7.1	0.6	-2.1	9.8
Payments to individuals[a]	3.6	6.2	-2.8	2.8	2.8	1.2	14.7
Grants in aid	-12.3	0.6	1.4	3.9	2.9	-6.3	-10.1
All other	-10.8	0.5	-6.7	17.0	-9.3	-7.5	-20.1
Net interest	15.3	1.3	18.6	12.7	2.2	-0.7	59.4

SOURCE: Calculated from *Budget of the United States Government, Historical Tables, Fiscal Year 1989,* table 6-1.
a. Including grants to state and local governments for individuals.

security, medicare, and interest on the debt, although this was far short of the 47 percent real increase in domestic spending that occurred in the 1970s (see table 7-4). Real spending for federal grants to states and localities actually fell 10 percent from fiscal 1981 to fiscal 1987, but this reflected primarily the steep cuts made in OBRA in 1981 and the elimination of revenue sharing in 1986. Although some components of federal aid continued to decline, notably for government services, grants-in-aid for individuals grew modestly after fiscal 1982. When measured in relative terms as a percentage of GNP or of total federal outlays, total domestic spending and most of its individual components (except for interest on the debt) remained relatively constant after 1981.

This stability in domestic budget outputs was the result of the political stalemate between the president and Congress over fiscal issues. The president's congressional success rating—the percentage of congressional roll call votes on which the president took a position and was successful in Congress—dropped sharply in the House after his initial victories in 1981. It dropped 16 points, or nearly 23 percent, in 1982 alone and continued falling in subsequent years.[35] In terms of presidential support in the House, 1981 was clearly an anomaly.

The Politics of Fiscal Constraint

Although the momentum for additional large domestic program cuts did not continue past 1981, the president's first-year victories had lasting effects. At least for the duration of his tenure in office, the fiscal policies of 1981 permanently restructured the federal government's domestic agenda. In sharp contrast to the policies of the 1970s, Reagan's agenda has remained fixed on issues of retrenchment rather than growth, and few important spending initiatives have been seriously proposed, much less implemented, in the 1980s. As table 7-2 suggests, since 1981 the

TABLE 7-5. Indicators of Congressional Activity, 1975–86

Congress	Bills introduced	Bills passed	Recorded votes
Senate			
94th (1975–76)	4,114	1,038	1,290
95th (1977–78)	3,800	1,070	1,151
96th (1979–80)	3,480	977	1,028
6-year average	3,798	1,028	1,156
97th (1981–82)	3,396	803	952
98th (1983–84)	3,456	936	673
99th (1985–86)	3,386	940	740
6-year average	3,413	893	788
House			
94th (1975–76)	16,982	968	1,273
95th (1977–78)	15,587	1,027	1,540
96th (1979–80)	9,103	929	1,276
6-year average	13,890	975	1,363
97th (1981–82)	8,094	704	812
98th (1983–84)	7,105	978	906
99th (1985–86)	6,499	973	890
6-year average	7,233	885	869

SOURCES: Norman J. Ornstein and others, *Vital Statistics on Congress, 1984–85* (Washington, D.C.: American Enterprise Institute, 1985), pp. 144, 146; *Congressional Record,* daily edition, "Resume of Congressional Activity of the 98th Congress," November 14, 1984, p. D1347; and *Congressional Record,* daily edition, "Resume of Congressional Activity of the 99th Congress," January 6, 1987, p. D2.

large structurally embedded federal deficit has focused congressional attention each year on deficit reduction rather than program enhancements.

The restricted nature of the post-1981 policy agenda is evident in both the substantive mix and overall scope of Congress's work load during the 1980s. Virtually all measures of congressional productivity have declined under Ronald Reagan, in both the House and Senate. The number of bills introduced in the House averaged 13,890 per session in the three Congresses from 1975 to 1980 (see table 7-5), but between 1981 and 1986 the number of bills introduced averaged only 7,233 per session of Congress—which represents a drop of 48 percent. The number of bills passed in the House declined 9 percent during this time period, from an average of 975 per session in the late 1970s to 885 in the 1980s. Recorded votes in the House declined an average of 36 percent during the same period.

Similar trends occurred in the Senate, where, on average, 10 percent fewer bills were introduced in the Ninety-seventh through Ninety-ninth Congresses in comparison with the Ninety-fourth through the Ninety-sixth Congresses. The bills passed dropped by 13 percent, and 32 percent fewer votes were recorded in the Senate during this latter period.

To be sure, such data give only a rough idea of actual congressional outputs and activities during these respective periods. They say nothing about the magnitude or content of the legislation passed.* Moreover, averaging the data over six-year periods obscures variations and trends within these time periods. As measured by these indicators, congressional activism actually began declining in the late 1970s, while the number of bills passed increased during the Ninety-ninth Congress, in both the House and Senate, suggesting that the nadir of declining productivity was reached during Ronald Reagan's first term. Barring a substantial upward trend in these indicators in the years ahead, however, there is no question that important forms of congressional activity reached new and lower thresholds, and possibly new equilibriums, in the 1980s.

This new and more constrained congressional agenda has had other manifestations as well, altering both the mix of congressional activities and members' subjective evaluations of the process. Most important has been the growing prominence of budgetary issues. The percentage of budget-related roll call votes in Congress increased sharply in the 1980s in comparison with those of the late 1970s (see table 7-6). This was especially true in the Senate, where the average percentage of budget-related votes increased from 38 percent in the late 1970s to 56 percent in the 1980s.[36] In the more carefully regulated House, the percentage of budget-related votes increased from an average of 48 percent in the 1975–78 period to an average of 55 percent in the 1980s.

That a more restrictive and fiscally constrained policymaking environment was emerging in Congress is borne out by the perceptions of members of Congress. Especially during Reagan's first term, normally active congressmen encountered new limits to their capacity to legislate. "The deficit holds everything hostage," became the new conventional wisdom on Capitol Hill.[37] As one astonished member of the House Energy and Commerce Committee observed in 1983,

> If you had told me . . . that John Dingell wouldn't get out as many bills as [his low-key predecessor] Harley Staggers did, I would have been astounded. But Reagan put all the issues in the Budget Act and

---

* For example, the average page length of bills has been increasing, partly because of the growing number of reauthorizations. On the other hand, the amount of noncontroversial commemorative legislation has increased sharply, while the percentage of substantive legislation has declined.

TABLE 7-6. Selected Budget-Related Roll Call Votes in Congress, by Type, Selected Years, 1975–86

Type of vote	1975	1978	1981	1984	1986
Senate					
Authorizations	121	83	64	38	34
Appropriations	88	80	131	76	78
Budget resolutions	8	18	26	1	14
Reconciliation	...	...	62	47	12
Debt ceiling	3	1	5	3	3
Miscellaneous	4	10	6	2	23
TOTAL	224	192	294	167	164
Percent of all votes that are budget related	38	37	60	61	46
House					
Authorizations	167	216	97	123	120
Appropriations	93	132	86	75	88
Budget resolutions	12	30	13	10	7
Reconciliation	...	...	12	8	9
Debt limit	10	10	2	6	2
Miscellaneous	10	4	1	1	10
TOTAL	292	392	211	223	236
Percent of all votes that are budget related	48	47	60	54	52

SOURCE: Congressional Research Service, derived from all roll call votes listed in *Congressional Quarterly*. Miscellaneous votes include proposed changes in budget process and proposed rescissions. Each category includes votes on passage, amendments, and relevant procedures.

used that as a vehicle for everything he wanted. Virtually everything stopped as we fought those battles. There wasn't much room for authorizing legislation to come down the pipe.[38]

Lobbyists, too, noted the change and adjusted their strategies accordingly. With fewer bills moving through Congress, budget-related vehicles became prime targets for legislating extraneous matters. Moreover, the increased importance of the centralized budget process forced many groups to band together to protect their interests. One comprehensive study of interest group behavior in the 1980s found that coalition building among interest groups was the fastest growing form of lobbying strategy.[39] On the other hand, decremental budgeting and annual reconciliation bills introduced a new form of zero-sum—or often negative-sum—politics into the legislative process, as the revenues to finance one initiative had to be sought from the appropriation for some other program. "What's happening is that we're trying to put a size 9 foot into a size 7 boot," observed one farm lobbyist. "The budget rules simply prevent anything from moving. The budget process is more important to lobbying now than getting things through the authorizing process." [40]

As the data in table 7-5 suggest, all initiatives have not been foreclosed by this new zero-sum legislative environment. Indeed, the pace of new enactments may be quickening in Reagan's second term as members learn how to adjust to their new constraints. But the size and structure of new initiatives is evolving as new legislation is adapted to the new political, budgetary, and procedural environment. "The pressure of the deficit is forcing Congress to think about alternatives in a far more serious way than we would have done otherwise," observed House Majority Leader Thomas Foley. "America does not have to spend more to do more," has become the new watchword of activists like Senator Ted Kennedy. [41]

However, new initiatives have generally been forced to adopt one of three new strategies designed to minimize their impact on the federal deficit. The most difficult but effective technique is to levy a new tax for the specific problem to be addressed, as was done in the case of the superfund program for cleaning up toxic waste sites and the 1982 highway reauthorization bill, which contained a five cent increase in the federal gasoline tax. The second technique is to reassign funds from existing programs to pay for a new initiative, as was done with the omnibus drug initiative of 1986. Third, Congress can attempt to pass new regulations and unfunded mandates to deflect program costs from the federal budget to third parties, as was done with the urban nonpoint pollution monitoring standards adopted in the Clean Water Act reauthorization in 1986. Some new initiatives, like those being developed in catastrophic health care, combine both the regulatory and the "pay-as-you-go" budgetary approaches.

Nothing illustrates both the post-1981 shift to zero-sum budgetary politics and Congress's relentless efforts to test the limits of budgetary constraints more clearly than the Balanced Budget and Emergency Deficit Control Act of 1985, popularly known as Gramm-Rudman-Hollings. This legislation established a fixed, statutory schedule for eliminating the deficit over a five-year period, in annual increments of $36 billion. The full implications of this legislation for domestic spending remain unclear. They depend in part on overall economic performance, on the political vulnerability of defense spending, and above all on the strength of Congress's commitment to faithfully implement the process. If the "sequestration" procedures contained in the act are followed, pressure for additional domestic budget cuts is likely to increase rather than diminish in the years ahead. Half of the cuts required by the process will be siphoned from domestic programs, leading to further attenuation of the federal domestic role. Moreover, grants-in-aid to state and local governments are particularly vulnerable to sequestration since few grant programs are protected from across-the-board cuts under the process. If sequestration should be put into effect, additional reductions in intergovernmental aid are expected to be in excess of $12 billion in just the first three years.[42] Yet such drastic cuts may never be implemented through the process, which has been weakened by the courts and discredited in Congress. As members of Congress attempt to balance the fiscal imperatives of deficit reduction with the political imperatives of congressional activism, the conventional wisdom regarding Gramm-Rudman by early 1987 was that "no one is taking the process seriously anymore."[43] Whether the Gramm-Rudman "fix" or the budget "summit" agreement negotiated at the end of that year can effectively restore the process remains unclear. The agenda of rationalizing fiscal policy continues, but fittingly, it is neither the president's agenda nor Congress's.

Reagan's Budget Legacy

Whatever the ultimate fate of the Gramm-Rudman-Hollings process, the tax and budgetary policies enacted in 1981 have had important, long-term intergovernmental consequences. In particular, the activist, entrepreneurial Congress of the 1970s was constrained by the new budgetary politics of the 1980s. Although additional domestic spending reductions were modest after 1981, a new and lower equilibrium was achieved in new spending initiatives. Given the importance of congressional entrepreneurship for shaping the intergovernmental system of the 1960s and 1970s, this in itself was an important consequence of Ronald Reagan's implicit federalism.

Equally important, the newly constrained agenda has shaped the kinds of new policies emerging from the Congress as well as their total volume. Federal budget politics have evolved from being distributive to redistributive in nature, meaning that the resources available for domestic programs are now reallocated within a stable or shrinking funding base rather than being funded from a budgetary base that expands incrementally over time.[44] In the process, the character of congressional initiatives has shifted to "low cost social justice"[45]—often ad hoc forms of spending, tax, and regulatory policies in which the means of financing may acquire greater priority in program design than the substantive goals of the program itself.

Undermining the Welfare State through Tax Policy

Although budget policy has had the most obvious indirect impact on intergovernmental relations under the Reagan administration, Reagan tax policy may prove to be more important in the long run, particularly with the enactment of comprehensive tax reform legislation in 1986. There is no question that federal income tax policy has undergone a virtual revolution under Ronald Reagan. Individual income tax rates were reduced 25 percent over a three-year period under the Economic Recovery Tax Act of 1981. The top marginal tax rate was reduced by three-fifths, from 70 percent to 50 percent in 1981 and then down to 28 percent in the Tax Reform Act of 1986. On the revenue side, the combined effects of the individual tax rate reductions and incentives for personal savings and corporate investment enacted in 1981 reduced federal revenues $282 billion below what they would have been during the period between 1982 and 1984.[46] Although some of these lost revenues were restored through increased excise taxes and "loophole closing" in the Tax Equity and Fiscal Responsibility Act of 1982 and the Deficit Reduction Act of 1984, the comprehensive tax reform legislation passed in 1986 shifted an additional $120 billion from individuals to corporations over five years.

The significance of these changes for federal revenue collections and the structure of the federal tax code has been widely recognized. Indeed, the tax reform act has been called "one of the most important pieces of tax legislation ever passed."[47] It is less widely recognized that, taken collectively, these changes constitute a frontal assault on the revenue base of the modern welfare state, not only in Washington but also at the state and local levels. This assault has three dimensions.

First, the massive tax reductions adopted in 1981 dwarfed the budget cuts adopted that year and weakened the fiscal underpinnings of future federal spending. Citing David Stockman's published admission that the tax cuts would "pin the craven politicians to the wall," some have charged that this was part of a deliberate strategy to force additional domestic budget cuts. As Congressman Ted Weiss (Democrat of New York) put it, "There is substantial evidence that the huge deficits we are now experiencing are not the result of administration bungling, but have been purposefully created . . . to convince the American people that we can no longer afford programs that serve human needs."[48] Stockman himself denies that the administration's tax and budget policies were so elegantly coordinated in 1981, but he admits that the tax cuts and budget cuts were conceptually consistent and mutually supportive. He certainly makes no secret that his personal policy goal was "a radical anti-welfare state premise [that] . . . implied dismantling vast segments of the Second Republic's budget, slashing all the expenditures that reflected its statist enterprises." Having achieved substantial reductions in tax rates and revenues, Stockman admits that after 1981, "my aim had always been to force down the size of the domestic welfare state to the point where it could be adequately funded with the revenues available after the tax cut."[49]

Although both the president and Congress demonstrated a willingness to live with far higher federal deficits than had been anticipated, the preceding section of this chapter makes clear that the dramatic tax reductions had important policy consequences. When combined with sizable defense increases, the resulting deficits had a dampening effect on subsequent domestic policy initiatives and the growth and maintenance of the welfare state. Large deficits also induced members of Congress from both parties to try to reverse some of the 1981 tax cuts and raise additional revenues. Although these attempts were partly successful in 1982 and 1984, the president managed to limit them and also to prevent the Democrats from using the tax reform act as a vehicle for raising taxes.

The second important point is that Reagan's tax policies eroded support for the welfare state through their attacks on progressive taxation. The progressive federal income tax was one of the primary factors contributing to the enormous growth of federal activity and spending in the twentieth century.[50] Yet close observers of President Reagan note that reducing federal income tax rates, and especially reducing the top marginal rates for the highest taxpayers, was the single issue closest to Ronald Reagan's heart. It generated the most enthusiasm from him among all the 1981 initiatives.[51] The results of the president's early efforts went beyond his wildest dreams: Congress virtually abandoned the principle of progressivity and adopted a modified flat tax in the 1986 Tax Reform Act.

This move has important implications for the future of the welfare state. Progressivity has allowed higher levels of taxation (and thus spending) at key points in American history, such as the World War II years, when both the number of Americans subject to the income tax and the federal tax burden were enormously expanded.[52] After 1988, however, federal tax rates will bear less relationship to individuals' ability to pay. Thus raising additional federal revenues through tax increases is likely to become more difficult because the tax resistance level of the average voter will be reached at a lower overall level of collections.

Third, Reagan administration tax policies have included unprecedented challenges to provisions of the internal revenue code that support state and local governments' capacity to raise their own revenues and provide services. Both key intergovernmental components of the tax code—the exemption for interest earned on municipal bonds and the federal income tax deduction for state and local sales, income, and property taxes—were targeted for elimination or substantial reduction by the Reagan administration, and both were significantly restricted by the Tax Reform Act of 1986. In this sense, Ronald Reagan has used tax policy to attack the welfare state at every level of government, not just in Washington, and so has clearly set his policies apart from those of activist decentralizers like Richard Nixon.

The 1981 Tax Cuts

On August 13, 1981, Ronald Reagan signed the Economic Recovery Tax Act (ERTA) of 1981, calling it "a turnaround of almost a half a century of . . . excessive growth in government bureaucracy, government spending, government taxing." [53] While tax policy was turned around, the tax process was turned upside down by the frenzied process by which the legislation was enacted. The administration's initial tax reform proposal was unveiled on February 18, 1981, as part of the president's omnibus economic recovery package. It proposed $54 billion in tax reductions in 1982, which was to be achieved in two basic ways. Most of the expense was to come from the first of three years of 10 percent across-the-board rate reductions for individual taxpayers, with much of the remainder from liberalized provisions for depreciating capital assets. Both were intended to stimulate long-term economic growth and investment, the first by promoting individual savings and the second by allowing faster write-offs of capital investments.

The individual tax rate reductions were the political core of the tax reform plan, as well as its most costly component. Although they enjoyed the weakest support on Capitol Hill, they quickly became the chief priority of the president. He translated his own experience with the economic disincentives of high marginal tax rates during World War II into a belief that large tax cuts were the key to stimulating economic recovery and shrinking big government.[54]

Patterned after the Kemp-Roth "Tax Relief Act of 1977," massive tax reductions were considered a "fringe idea" in Congress until they were incorporated into the 1980 Republican platform.[55] They were initially included in the president's bill because of their potential political appeal to working- and middle-class taxpayers. Indeed, Stockman argues that the broad, across-the-board cuts were just a "Trojan horse" for lowering the top tax rates. Those were the key to stimulating investment and entrepreneurial risk taking, in his view, but they lacked sufficient appeal on their own. "It's kind of hard to sell 'trickle down'"[56] he observed. In contrast, flat rate reductions ensured that there was something for everyone in the package. The president and many other supply-side theorists appeared to be less cynical about across-the-board tax cuts, however. They viewed the cuts as a direct means of broadening the appeal of conservative policies to blue-collar and other nontraditional constituencies.

Whatever their appeal to conservatives, these tax cuts lacked sufficient support in Congress to be viable on their own. This was particularly true among liberal Democrats, who opposed the nonprogressive nature of across-the-board cuts and who were skeptical of further tax breaks for business. Yet support was also soft among Senate Republicans and conservative southern Democrats, who were the president's allies on budgetary policy. Both groups viewed the large cuts as fiscally irresponsible and preferred to concentrate on altering depreciation rules and other provisions advocated by business to increase investment.

White House strategists were determined to avoid Jimmy Carter's stigma of weakness and were convinced that early success on budget and tax issues would breed further success on other items on the Reagan agenda. Thus, in its bid to attract additional support, the administration revised its package twice in early June, adopting a strategy of "25 percent plus ornaments."[57] It reduced its proposed reduction in individual rates from 30 percent to 25 percent over three years, modified its proposals to promote business investment, and endorsed additional "sweeteners" like ending the marriage penalty, which appealed to individuals or voting blocs in Congress. When business "remained cool" to the new plan, the White House endorsed a business-backed, $40 billion proposal for accelerated depreciation sponsored in the House by Congressman Barber Conable of New York, the ranking Republican on the Ways and Means Committee, and Congressman Kent Hance of Texas, a leader of the conservative southern Democratic "boll weevils." This approach was sufficient to pass in the still reluctant Senate, but only after the addition of costly amendments to index federal income tax rates for inflation, to promote employee stock ownership plans, and to encourage further savings through tax-preferred "all savers certificates."

After their defeat on the reconciliation act in late June, the Democratic leadership in the House went all out to lure back conservative Democrats and retain a working majority on the House floor. A partisan bidding war emerged as House Democrats joined the administration "in a blatant move to attract votes."[58] In order to pay for a competitive array of special tax preferences, Democrats scaled back the individual tax rate cuts and targeted them more heavily to middle- and low-income voters. To this they added provisions already adopted by the Senate, like all savers certificates and a marriage penalty provision, plus additional tax preferences for "almost everyone."[59] This included new tax credits for child care, research and development, and royalty income; exemptions for overseas income, inheritance taxes, and Keogh plans; and provisions benefiting farmers, truckers, utilities, and mass transit operators.[60]

Despite the temptation to wash its hands of legislation that was spiraling out of control, the White House responded to the Ways and Means proposal by opening a new round of vote bidding. In Stockman's memorable phrase, "the hogs were really feeding," as tax subsidy provisions were matched nearly one for one.[61] In the search for votes, both sides had expanded their packages far beyond what anyone had anticipated in the beginning. The Chamber of Commerce spokesman was "astounded" at the Democrats' costly proposal for "expensing" business investment spending. For its part, the administration filled its final offer with arcane complexities and revenue losses that made its original plan look "moderate."[62] The revenue implications of the final package were so severe, Stockman reports, that he and key White House aide Richard Darman contemplated killing the proposal at the last minute.[63] Nevertheless, because of the political stakes involved, both sides were determined to win a victory on the House floor. Thus the open bidding process rendered many of the differences between the two proposals largely "symbolic," and only the duration of individual tax cuts (two years versus three) and their application to taxpayers earning over $50,000 remained in serious dispute.

The final vote in the House was expected to be extremely close until the president went on nationwide television on July 27. In what was called a "masterpiece of propaganda," he rallied public opinion behind his program and stimulated an unparalleled "telephone blitz" by constituents to members of Congress.[64] Although the authenticity of this popular response has been questioned (there are many reports that businesses seeking tax breaks organized workers to call their congressmen on company phones on company time), the result had a "devastating effect" on the Democrats' efforts to hold their supporters, and the key vote was not even close at 238 to 195.[65] Despite the last-minute Democratic defections, the final vote divided the parties more sharply than any other tax vote in the House since 1921.[66]

TABLE 7-7. Revenue Effects of the Economic Recovery Tax Act of 1981, Fiscal Years 1981–87[a]

Billions of dollars

Item	Actual, 1981	Projections					
		1982	1983	1984	1985	1986	1987
Total federal receipts under							
Prior Law	605	670	747	849	982	1,062	1,176
ERTA	603	631	652	701	763	818	882
Difference	−2	−39	−95	−148	−189	−244	−294
Revenue loss as percent of GNP	...	1.3	2.8	3.9	4.5	5.4	5.9

SOURCE: Charles Hulten and June O'Neill, "Tax Policy," in John L. Palmer and Isabel V. Sawhill, eds., *The Reagan Experiment* (Washington, D.C.: Urban Institute Press, 1982), p. 113.

a. CBO estimates.

The Long-Term Effects: Rationalizing Tax Policy

Thus the president won a "victory" on tax policy that exceeded even that on the budget. As with the administration's actions on defense spending, however, the unparalleled costs associated with the victory dictated the policy agenda for years to come. The implications were truly staggering. According to the Congressional Budget Office, the cumulative revenue loss to the federal government by 1987 totaled more than $1 trillion, or almost 6 percent of GNP (see table 7-7). These revenue losses "dwarf[ed] other post-war tax reductions."[67] For example, the revenues forgone in just the first two years of ERTA totaled $128 billion, or $110 billion more than the famous Kennedy-Johnson tax cut of 1964.

Revenue losses of this magnitude dominated the federal government's fiscal agenda until 1985, when comprehensive tax reform became the president's top domestic priority for the Ninety-ninth Congress. On the spending side, if the intention of the deep Kemp-Roth tax cuts had been to "starve the budget beast," as David Stockman put it, this strategy proved to be only partly effective. As previous sections of this chapter have indicated, mounting deficits placed continual pressure on the domestic budget and ultimately produced the Gramm-Rudman deficit reduction targets. Yet the stalemate between the president and Congress over severe budget reductions permitted deficits to remain at historic levels. Thus tax increases that would partly restore some of the reductions made in 1981 were driven to the top of the congressional revenue agenda. By enacting ERTA, the tax-writing committees of Congress had put themselves "in the tax raising business for years."[68]

This became immediately evident in 1982 with the enactment of the

Tax Expenditure and Fiscal Responsibility Act of 1982 (TEFRA). Just one year after the enormous tax cuts of 1981, TEFRA raised $98 billion in new revenues over three years with a combination of excise tax increases, restrictions on tax preferences, and compliance reforms. For consumers, the cigarette tax was doubled, the telephone tax was tripled, and airport taxes were increased; for business, the investment tax credit, industrial development bonds, and accelerated depreciation were restricted and the minimum tax on corporations was raised; and for individuals, the medical deduction was restricted and withholding on interest and dividends was instituted.

These provisions—and the strong motivation to restore revenues—were principally the work of Congress, and particularly the Senate. Yet, faced with ballooning deficits, even the president acknowledged the need to raise additional revenues in his 1982 State of the Union address. However, he objected to any increase in excise taxes and remained adamantly opposed to any delay or reduction in the individual tax rate reductions enacted in 1981.

Even the president's modest proposals received a mixed response on Capitol Hill, where supply siders resisted any increase in taxes, liberals questioned a tax increase during a recession, and others seemed reluctant to raise taxes in an election year. But the deficits projected from the tax cuts and defense spending increases were now magnified by economic conditions: lower revenues and increased outlays driven by the 1982 recession and by continued high interest rates. This forced most members to acknowledge the need for further revenues, and the fiscal 1983 budget resolution anticipated increases of $98 billion in additional revenues over three years.[69]

The irony of Congress's taking the lead on raising taxes in an election year was heightened by other unusual aspects of TEFRA's enactment. House Democrats "completely abdicated the House's traditional lead in tax matters" in order to avoid all blame for raising taxes. When the House balked, and the administration refused to offer an alternative plan, the Senate departed from its constitutionally prescribed reactive role in revenue matters and put together a compromise proposal. Making "effective use of a closed Republican conference," Finance Committee chairman Robert Dole of Kansas put together a package that avoided tampering with the major 1981 tax cuts but did combine substantial excise tax increases with stricter compliance and provisions for closing loopholes. Dole then succeeded in making skillful use of his slim Republican majority on the Senate floor, maintaining nearly "complete control of the process" in passing the legislation on a party line vote.[70]

Because TEFRA was attached to the budget reconciliation bill already passed by the House, the legislation went directly to a House-Senate conference. There it received reluctant presidential support and was accepted with few major changes. The resulting compromise passed the House with both parties badly split.

Despite passing TEFRA, Congress had only begun the task of rationalizing tax policy to the revenue needs generated by ERTA, by continuing service demands, and by defense and domestic spending policies. Driven by an "overwhelming concern with the deficit,"[71] Congress launched a series of tax bills and revenue measures over the next two years, beginning with a five cent increase in the federal gas tax later in 1982. Donald Susswein, former tax counsel for the Senate Finance Committee, has aptly summarized this frantic congressional search for additional revenues:

> Soon after the '81 give-away, when I came on board [the Finance Committee staff], we began trying to put together revenue enhancing options which ultimately became the '82 tax bill. After we enacted the '82 tax bill, there was the '82 gas tax bill. 1983 saw the reform of Social Security, which had some tax consequences to it. Then, right after the summer of '83, we started working on what became the '84 bill.[72]

To comply with its fiscal 1984 budget resolution, Congress was supposed to enact legislation to collect $73 billion in additional revenues in 1983. On a sharply partisan vote in July, the House passed legislation placing a $720 cap on benefits from the third and final round of 10 percent tax cuts, but this was immediately rejected by the Senate. When an $8 billion revenue raising bill was defeated on a procedural motion in October, the Senate halted work on its own bill and further action was delayed until 1984.

As Susswein suggested, this legislation became the basis for the Deficit Reduction Act of 1984 (DEFRA). Once again, Senate Republicans provided leadership on the issue. After both tax-writing committees reported $50 billion multiyear revenue packages in March, Senate leaders arranged a "Rose Garden" agreement on a compromise package with the House leadership and the White House.[73] Again the package placed restrictions on tax preferences (for industrial development bonds, income averaging, and retirement benefits) along with increased excise taxes on liquor and telephones. Again the president agreed to support modest excise tax increases in exchange for insulating the heart of his economic program from change. This ensured that the entire 25 percent cut in individual tax rates would finally be implemented and protected from erosion by the indexation of tax rates to inflation. Having won a consensus by the major parties in each branch of government, the compromise passed both houses of Congress by large margins.

Institutionalizing the Reagan Tax Revolution

Despite the long-term implications of ERTA's reductions in federal revenues, the Tax Reform Act of 1986 (TRA) will most likely be remembered as the most important tax legacy of the Reagan administration. The substance and complex politics of tax reform are clearly beyond the scope of this study. However, the TRA has had both obvious and hidden consequences for intergovernmental relations that will undoubtedly be of lasting significance.

Fundamentally, the TRA built upon and institutionalized Reagan's 1981 revolution in tax policy. For two years it diverted efforts away from raising additional federal revenues and so maintained the deficit's pressure on domestic spending. Moreover, it enabled the president to lower top marginal tax rates, as he had set out to do. By curtailing statutory progressivity in federal tax rates and establishing a modified flat tax structure, the TRA erected new roadblocks to the future expansion of federal income tax revenues.

Equally important, the tax reform act constituted a direct assault on the revenue base of state and local governments. As proposed by President Reagan, tax reform would have eliminated the two largest tax "subsidies" for states and localities. The fiscal implications of this policy dwarfed the intergovernmental aid cuts proposed or implemented by the Reagan administration. Although only parts of this intergovernmental strategy were adopted by Congress, the president's proposals on tax reform illustrate with unusual clarity that federalism policy in the Reagan administration was actually the means to other political ends.

The Origins of Reagan Tax Reform

How Reagan's tax reform evolved and why it was placed at the top of his agenda are complex questions. Support for tax reform was widely shared by professional economists, who saw it as a means of improving equity and long-term economic growth by evening out tax-induced distortions in investment.[74] These views carried considerable weight in the Treasury Department. However, the president's endorsement of the concept was also influenced by political considerations and the opportunities it provided for furthering his policy agenda.

Politically, Reagan's order to the Treasury Department to prepare a study of comprehensive tax reform was largely an electoral maneuver, designed to beat the competition to the issue in the event that Walter Mondale made this a key component of his presidential bid.[75] When Mondale failed to do so, Republican political strategists urged the president to seize what they perceived to be a "realigning" issue that could lay the basis for a permanent Republican majority. As one presidential political adviser put it,

> Passage of tax reform, with strong Republican support, will erase the cartoon of our party as defender of the rich and privileged. . . . The dramatic relief for the working poor and the provisions assuring that every corporation and every individual bears a fair share of our national tax burden, would reflect very well on . . . all Republican candidates for the next generation.[76]

Tax reform had appeal on policy grounds, as well, since it provided a means of furthering the policy agenda first outlined in the 1981 tax cuts. Stockman maintains that the concept of tax reform was first sold to the president during a golf game with Secretary of State (and former economics professor) George Shultz. After hearing Shultz argue that less government interference in investment decisions could promote long-term growth, Reagan was said to have concluded that tax reform "was a way to reduce the deficit without increasing taxes" by reaping the revenue benefits of a stronger economy.[77]

Dubbed by some within the White House as the "second installment on Kemp-Roth," tax reform developed ideological appeal for the president and others in the administration, even though it threatened the substantial tax benefits enjoyed by important Republican constituencies. The presidential message transmitting the tax reform proposal to Congress attacked the existing revenue code as an instrument of excessive government intrusion into the marketplace, which "slows economic growth . . . by interfering with free markets and diverting productive investment into tax shelters and tax avoidance schemes."[78] The president was particularly excited about the prospects for further lowering the top tax rate. According to Treasury Secretary Baker, when administration officials proposed providing additional tax relief to the middle class and raising the top rate in the president's plan from 35 percent to 40 percent, the president responded: "Absolutely not. I want real tax reform, I don't want to just diddle around with the margins . . . a top rate of 40 percent means it's antigrowth." Were it politically possible, Baker explained, the administration would have preferred "a flat 10 percent rate across-the-board—figure out what our income is, send 10% in and go on about our business, but unfortunately the political system is not such that we can do that." [79]

A final virtue of tax reform, in the administration's eyes, was that it challenged the fiscal underpinnings of active government at the subnational level as well as in Washington. The income tax deduction for state and local taxes was as old as the federal income tax itself, as was the exclusion of interest earned on tax-exempt municipal bonds. Despite their relevance to a balanced system of fiscal federalism and their relationship to funding the administration's own initiatives for devolution, both provisions were curtailed or eliminated under the president's tax reform plan.

The motivation for this was partly fiscal, since the elimination of deductibility alone provided an additional $33 billion in federal revenues to help fund lower tax rates. Yet the president made clear from the beginning that the elimination of deductibility also was intended to undermine the revenue base of fiscally active states and localities. In his first speech to rally citizens' groups around his tax plan, he denounced the deduction for state and local taxes as "one of the major pressures pushing up the tax rates of the American people" and an unfair tool to "subsidize the big-spending policies of a few high tax states." [80]

The Politics of Tax Reform

The underlying consistency between tax reform and the president's commitment to limited government is only one important aspect of the Tax Reform Act of 1986. Equally important, from a political perspective, is how this sweeping legislation survived countless obituaries and achieved enactment at all. Although this chapter cannot accommodate a detailed analysis of the factors responsible for its enactment, the significant point is that, relative to the legislation that preceded it, the politics of H.R. 3838 were unique. In contrast to both TEFRA and DEFRA, the president took the initiative while Senate Republicans voiced reluctance and initial opposition. In contrast to the tax cut of 1981, key Democrats in the House embraced tax reform and kept the legislation—and the political momentum—moving.

In the process, the focus of tax politics shifted abruptly from narrowing the deficit to broadening the tax base. Like congressional tax reformers before him, from Senator Bill Bradley (Democrat of New Jersey) to Congressman Jack Kemp (Republican of New York), the president insisted on "revenue neutrality" in his proposal in order to focus attention on reform rather than raising revenues.

Coming in the wake of Mondale's overwhelming electoral defeat in 1984 on a platform of raising taxes, and given congressional exhaustion with the treadmill of modest annual revenue enhancements, many members of Congress were only too happy to comply. Some demurred along the way, hoping to keep the focus on deficit reduction. Early in 1985, Senate majority leader Bob Dole wrote that "the first priority for the 99th Congress should not be tax changes, but deficit reduction." [81] Similarly, Congressman Thomas Downey of New York, a prominent Democrat on the Ways and Means Committee, observed that "we are literally fiddling while the nation burns. We're trying to reform taxes and the fact is that we need to raise taxes, not reform them." [82] But the politics of tax reform, driven above all by partisan jockeying and institutional blame avoidance, left little room for maneuvering on this point.

The confluence of interests between the president and congressional reformers like Senator Bradley emerged most clearly after tax reform passed the House and arrived in the Senate. After one of reform's nearest brushes with political demise, Senator Robert Packwood, the Republican chairman of the Senate Finance Committee, jettisoned his own beleaguered proposal and advocated a new and radically different approach modeled after the Bradley-Gephardt "fair tax act."

This had both substantive and political implications. Substantively, it had the effect of strengthening many of the president's original policy goals. Bradley-Gephardt was a relatively pure piece of legislation, designed by economists to portray an ideally reformed system. Because economists' prescriptions for reform had much in common with the president's objectives, though often for very different reasons, [83] using Bradley-Gephardt as a model strengthened the administration's hand. It not only accepted the condition of revenue neutrality, it also reduced tax preferences dramatically and thus reduced federal interference in the marketplace. And because the political appeal of lower tax rates provided the incentive for eliminating special preferences, Bradley-Gephardt foreswore a progressive rate structure and offered dramatically lower tax rates. In the end, this combination of bipartisan support, powerful presidential backing, and the imprimatur of "good government" economics proved sufficient to hold a coalition together in the anarchic Senate and produce a bill surprisingly to the president's liking.

Intergovernmental Dimensions of Tax Reform

The shift to a relatively pure tax reform approach, combined with the high-profile politics of a major presidential initiative, had important implications for provisions of the tax code that bear most directly on state and local governments. This was particularly true of tax-exempt municipal bonds, which were significantly restricted by the Tax Reform Act.

The legal basis for exempting interest on state and local bonds from federal taxation originated in the nineteenth century, and this practice has been part of the federal income tax code since it came into being in 1913. Since then tax-exempt bonds have been the principal device used by localities for financing long-term capital projects like schools, roads, and government facilities. Since 1970 such traditional borrowing has been supplemented by an explosion of nontraditional bonds for housing, economic development, pollution control, and hospitals (see table 7-8). In many jurisdictions, such subsidized borrowing established the financial basis for an explosion of "public-private partnerships."

Despite their long heritage and importance to state and local governments, tax-exempt bonds were under constant attack throughout the 1980s as an inefficient subsidy and unacceptably large drain on federal revenues. The revenue loss totaled $20.4 billion in 1983. This was more than triple the revenue forgone just five years earlier, and it made the interest exclusion on bonds by far the fastest growing federal "subsidy" to state and local governments.[84] Although Congress played a key role in restricting bonds in 1982 and 1984, a far more sweeping assault was proposed by the president's tax reform plan. The initial tax reform plan developed by the Treasury Department in 1984 advocated the complete elimination of interest exemption for all bonds, including traditional governmental issues. Although this proposal was modified in the final proposal sent to Congress five months later, the restrictions on bonds remained so severe that they were estimated to reduce total bond issuances 62 to 80 percent.[85] Despite further modification of these proposals in Congress, the final tax reform bill may reduce tax-exempt issuances by as much as 60 percent, and cut federal revenue losses by approximately $4 billion over five years. Ironically, given the president's rhetorical commitment to federalism, nontraditional bonds issued by state and local governments fared far less well than similar bonds issued by colleges, nonprofit hospitals, and other nongovernmental entities.

The president's attack on the deductibility of state and local taxes was even more extreme and, given the scope of revenues involved, potentially

TABLE 7-8. Trends in the Volume of New Long-Term Tax-Exempt Bonds, by Traditional and Nontraditional Purposes, 1970–82

Billions of dollars

Item	1970	1971	1972	1973	1974	1975	1976	1977	1978	1979	1980	1981	1982
Traditional purposes													
Education	5.0	5.7	5.0	4.8	4.7	4.4	4.9	5.0	4.7	4.6	4.1	3.4	4.7
Transportation	3.2	4.3	3.0	1.6	1.7	2.2	3.0	3.0	3.5	2.4	2.6	3.5	6.2
Water and sewer	2.2	3.2	2.4	2.3	2.0	2.5	3.0	3.3	3.3	3.1	2.9	2.9	5.0
Public power	1.1	1.3	1.2	1.6	1.5	2.2	2.7	3.4	4.5	3.5	3.4	6.3	7.1
Other and unidentified	5.7	7.3	6.8	3.6	7.6	11.6	10.5	11.4	11.4	8.3	9.5	10.1	16.8
Subtotal	17.2	21.8	18.4	13.9	17.5	22.9	24.1	26.1	27.4	21.9	22.5	26.2	39.8
Nontraditional purposes													
Housing	0.7	2.1	2.2	3.2	1.9	1.6	3.4	3.7	6.1	12.4	15.8	6.2	14.3
Industrial development	0.1	0.1	0.3	2.7	0.5	1.3	1.5	2.2	3.4	7.1	9.2	12.6	12.7
Pollution control	n.a.	n.a.	0.6	1.7	2.2	2.5	1.9	2.6	2.7	2.1	2.3	4.3	5.3
Hospitals	n.a.	0.4	0.5	0.7	0.8	2.0	2.3	3.3	2.1	3.4	3.6	5.4	9.5
Student loans	n.a.	n.a.	n.a.	n.a.	n.a.	n.a.	0.1	0.1	0.3	0.6	0.5	1.0	1.6
Subtotal	0.8	2.6	3.6	8.3	5.4	7.4	9.2	11.9	14.6	25.6	31.4	29.5	43.4
Refundings	0.1	0.5	1.7	1.6	0.7	1.1	3.2	8.8	8.7	1.2	2.0	1.3	4.3
TOTAL	18.1	24.9	23.7	23.8	23.6	31.4	36.5	46.8	50.7	48.7	55.9	57.0	87.5

SOURCE: U.S. Advisory Commission on Intergovernmental Relations, Strengthening the Federal Revenue System: Implications for State and Local Taxing and Borrowing, A-97 (GPO, 1984), p. 117.
n.a. Not available.

even more significant. Again the president followed the advice of Treasury Department economists. They believed that deductibility was an economically inefficient subsidy and sought to use the revenues captured by its elimination to lower overall tax rates. Thus the president proposed the total elimination of deductibility for state and local sales and income taxes, which produced a five-year revenue gain of $149 billion to the federal treasury.[86]

Some have charged that, in making this proposal, the president sought more than increased federal revenues and greater tax equity. They regard the elimination of deductibility as a vehicle for exporting the "Reagan revolution" to the states, eroding their capacity to finance responsibilities devolved by the federal government.[87] Assistant Treasury Secretary Ronald Pearlman seemed to support this view when he stated, "We agree there will be more pressure [against raising state and local taxes] from those who no longer benefit from the deduction. That's as it should be."[88] Even the president contributed to this interpretation when, in a 1986 fund-raising letter, he attacked Democratic governors who "turned right around and increased state sales and income taxes, wiping out the tax cut given to you by our Administration."[89] By thus seeking to reduce taxes and government revenues at all levels of government, Reagan made clear his philosophical differences with Nixon with respect to New Federalism.

Whatever the aims, these proposals were serious and partly successful. The final tax reform bill passed by Congress and signed by the president contained the first significant limitations on deductibility since the tax code was created, eliminating the deduction for state and local sales and personal property taxes for a five-year savings of $17 billion. Because the discriminatory effect of this partial repeal of deductibility may weaken support for preserving the remaining taxes, especially at a time of continuing need for further federal revenues, some believe this was only the first step toward the president's original request: the total elimination of deductibility.

Conclusion

In a speech to the National Association of State Legislatures in 1981, Ronald Reagan declared that "with our economic proposals, we're staging a quiet federalist revolution."[90] Taken collectively, the tax and budgetary policies propounded by the new administration did indeed constitute a broad but implicit strategy for intergovernmental reform. The dramatic tax and budget reductions developed by the White House were designed to reduce substantially the federal government's profile in domestic affairs, to alter those budgetary priorities that remained, and to stem the tide of new domestic initiatives. The president's tax policies were intended both to ensure the implementation of these budgetary aims and to eliminate federal subsidies for governmental activism at the state and local levels. Thus these fiscal policies leave no doubt that Nixon's philosophy of decentralized activism was far different from Reagan's view that traditional forms of governmental activism were inappropriate throughout the public sector.

These distinctive views were expressed in quite different political environments. In contrast to the political fragmentation that overwhelmed many of Nixon's initiatives, Reagan's fiscal policies were swept through Congress in 1981 on a wave of unparalleled Republican unity and a reenergized conservative coalition. This highly visible, majoritarian pattern was the institutional manifestation of the reactive politics that candidate Reagan exploited in seeking office.

This pattern of policymaking did not survive intact beyond 1981—although elements of it, most notably the heightened levels of party unity and partisan-based agenda setting and coalition building, did persist on important pieces of legislation. Even so, the initial policies adopted were sufficient to restructure the subsequent policymaking environment, institutionalizing a fiscally interdependent policy agenda that precluded a return to the politics of the fragmented, incremental expansionism that had prevailed in the 1970s. The fiscal policies of 1981 ushered in a new era of rationalizing politics, forcing policymakers to cope with the effects of policies previously adopted. And, as the president intended, this new pattern of politics had important implications for intergovernmental relations.

At the broadest level, the new rationalizing politics struck at the heart of the congressional activism that had driven the intergovernmental system for two decades. In the new era of zero-sum budgetary politics, the opportunities for successful policy entrepreneurship were substantially reduced. Fewer bills were introduced in Congress. Fewer bills were passed. Fewer amendments were introduced and voted on. The business of Congress was focused more narrowly on budgetary issues. Although some signs of entrepreneurial adaptation were emerging by the Ninety-ninth and One Hundredth Congresses, the redistributive budgetary politics of the 1980s had become institutionalized. Thus new forms of policy activism are now defined by the limits they impose.

Reagan's policies have had a more direct effect on intergovernmental relations as well. Federal aid as a whole has been significantly affected by the politics of budgetary constraint. Overall levels of aid have been reduced in competition with other budget sectors, and priorities among federal aid programs have been altered. These and other explicit dimensions of Reagan's intergovernmental policies are reviewed in the next two chapters.

8

Federal Aid Budgets and Block Grants in the 1980s

REAGAN ADMINISTRATION budget and tax policies constituted a far-reaching though implicit strategy for restructuring the federal government's role in the federal system and its relations with state and local governments. But Ronald Reagan had an explicit federalism agenda as well. Especially during the first two years of his administration, "federalism reform" was given a prominence on the nation's policy agenda unparalleled since the days of Richard Nixon.

Both before and after becoming president, Reagan left little doubt that federalism reform would be a major priority of his administration. The need for a comprehensive restructuring of intergovernmental roles and responsibilities had been a central theme of his 1976 campaign for president, and he saw to it that federalism reform was a plank in the 1980 Republican platform. Upon election, he devoted time to discussing this issue in his first inaugural and State of the Union addresses. A complex proposal for sorting out intergovernmental functions and "returning" to states billions of dollars of federal programs and tax sources was made the centerpiece of his 1982 domestic program. These federalism initiatives were "even closer to the heart of Ronald Reagan than the budget cuts," reported presidential assistant Robert B. Carleson. "The budget cuts became the first priority because of the economic situation we inherited, but the president has been calling for these changes in the federal system throughout his entire political career."[1]

Reagan's explicit reform strategy consisted of four parts. First Reagan proposed to reduce, and alter the priorities among, federal grants-in-aid. Whereas the macro budget policies were designed to alter the broad financial profile of the national government within the federal system (see chapter 7), specific changes in grants-in-aid to state and local governments had more immediate and obvious effects on the intergovernmental system by reducing national involvement in traditional state and local responsibilities. Thus the president recommended, and obtained, the first absolute decline in federal aid expenditures since the 1940s and a 25 percent reduction in the number of federal assistance programs. The administration's budgets also altered the priorities among remaining programs. Particularly significant was the termination of the general revenue sharing program—the crown jewel of the Nixon administration's New Federalism strategy. Also terminated was the public jobs component of the CETA program, which was enacted under Nixon and expanded under Ford and Carter.

Block grants were the second component of Ronald Reagan's federalism reform strategy. Ironically, his administration placed even greater emphasis on this reform device than had the Nixon administration, yet it was less committed to the concept. In his first six years in office Reagan submitted thirty-one proposals for new or substantially revised block grants. Although he was initially far more successful than Nixon had been in securing block grants—nine were enacted in 1981 and one in 1982—he made little progress in this area after 1982. Unlike Nixon, however, Reagan did not advance the block grant as a managerial device or as a useful end in itself. Rather, this was intended to help the federal government disengage itself from what were considered to be traditional state and local functional responsibilities.

The third element in the president's federalism reform strategy was a sweeping "sorting out" initiative—a grand design for permanently restructuring intergovernmental roles and responsibilities (see chapter 9). Under this 1982 proposal, the federal government was to assume total financial responsibility for the $19 billion state share of the medicaid program, while turning back to the states more than forty other federal aid programs—including AFDC and, initially, food stamps—along with a number of excise tax sources that were to pay for them. Despite its bold outlines and high political profile, Reagan's proposal was never formally sent to Congress. Efforts to mobilize the nation's governors and reach an agreement on a compromise bill broke down because of differing objectives, logical and fiscal inconsistencies in the proposal, divisions within the administration, and strong opposition from Congress and the affected interest groups.

The fourth component of Reagan's federalism strategy was regulatory relief (see chapter 10). Here, as in the block grants, Reagan sought both continuity and change. His was the first administration to recognize intergovernmental regulation explicitly as a unique and significant form of federal regulation, and it undertook a series of initiatives designed to redress federal regulatory burdens on state and local governments. Yet, apart from regulatory changes adopted in the context of the 1981 block grants, most of the Reagan administration's deregulatory efforts were achieved through unilateral administrative action and are vulnerable to rapid reversals in the future. But deregulation is only part of the story. More telling, and far more in keeping with past federal practices, has been the Reagan administration's consistent willingness to support and promote new federal regulatory initiatives—from uniform trucking standards to changes in local affirmative action policies—when they serve the larger social and economic objectives of the president.

Owing to the widely divergent outcomes of Reagan's efforts, from unprecedented success in the early block grant proposals to the premature failure of the swap proposal, as well as the inconsistency between the president's rhetorical goals and his actions, evaluations of his New Federalism program have been mixed. Some see it as the central accomplishment of his first administration, dwarfing his achievements on the federal budget.[2] Others question whether it will have any long-term significance. They note that the sorting out plan was never even introduced and that, apart from 1981, no new block grants have been enacted and few significant cuts have been made in intergovernmental funding.[3]

Both interpretations appear to contain an element of truth. The Reagan administration's achievements fell far short of the president's goals, but they were certainly significant when measured by historical standards. Reagan's policies altered and accelerated downward trends in federal aid spending, realigned national priorities, and placed intergovernmental issues and federalism reform prominently on the policy agenda. Yet far from being divorced from the president's budgetary priorities, many of the administration's most lasting and significant intergovernmental accomplishments were achieved within the context of budgetary policy. This combination had a powerful though often indirect effect. After six years of concerted effort on both the budgetary and federalism fronts, the Reagan administration has significantly altered and in many instances reduced opportunities for national policy entrepreneurship and has introduced new patterns of intergovernmental policymaking.

Intergovernmental Budget Policy: De Facto New Federalism?

Conventional wisdom suggests that Ronald Reagan substantially reduced total domestic spending while rapidly increasing spending on de-

TABLE 8-1. Growth Rates in Federal Aid Spending, Selected Fiscal
Years, 1955–87
Amounts in billions of dollars

	Current dollars		1972 dollars	
Year	Amount	Percent change	Amount	Percent change
1955	3.2	...	5.6	...
1959	6.5	103	10.0	79
1960	7.0	...	10.8	...
1964	10.1	44	14.7	36
1965	10.9	...	15.5	...
1969	20.3	86	24.2	56
1970	24.0	...	27.0	...
1974	43.4	82	37.9	40
1975	49.8	...	39.2	...
1979	82.9	66	48.1	23
1980	91.5	10.4	48.2	0.2
1981	94.8	3.6	46.1	−4.4
1982	88.2	−7.0	40.4	−12.4
1983	92.5	4.9	40.7	0.7
1984	97.6	5.5	41.3	1.5
1980–84	...	6.6	...	−14.2
1985	105.8	8.6	43.1	4.4
1986	112.4	6.1	44.5	3.0
1987	108.4	−3.6	41.7	−6.3
1985–87	...	2.4	...	−3.5

SOURCES: Based on U.S. Advisory Commission on Intergovernmental Relations, *Significant Features of Fiscal Federalism, 1985–86*, M-146 (GPO, 1986), p. 19; and *Budget of the United States Government, Historical Tables, Fiscal Year 1989*, table 12.1.

fense and interest payments. In truth, overall domestic spending measured in both current and constant dollars continued to increase during the Reagan administration, although the rate of growth diminished. But this overall growth masks important changes in domestic spending priorities. Some spending, such as direct payments to individuals and interest on the debt, has increased throughout the 1980s, whereas spending on civilian payrolls and natural resources has declined.

No area has been harder hit by budget reductions than federal grants-in-aid; within grants, payments to governments for the provision of services have been most deeply cut. The growth rate in current spending for grants-in-aid has not only slowed dramatically during the 1980s, but it actually declined in fiscal 1982 and 1987 (see table 8-1). These were the first absolute declines in federal aid levels since the 1940s. Real spending on federal grants also declined from 1980 to 1987, in sharp contrast to

TABLE 8-2. Index of Change in Constant Dollar Outlays for
Selected Expenditure Categories, Fiscal Years 1980–87

Category	1980	1981	1982	1983	1984	1985	1986	1987
Total U.S. budget outlays	100	104	107	113	115	123	124	123
National defense	100	107	118	128	133	142	148	152
Direct payments to individuals	100	106	110	117	114	117	120	122
Net interest	100	119	137	140	166	187	191	189
Total grants to state and local governments	100	94	82	82	84	92	91	85
Payments to individuals	100	105	101	106	109	120	123	127
Other grants	100	88	72	70	70	76	74	67

SOURCES: Lillian Rymarowicz and Dennis Zimmerman, *The Effect of Tax and Budget Policies in the 1980s on the State-Local Sector*, Rpt. 86-2E, (Washington, D.C.: Congressional Research Service, 1986), p. 51; and *Budget of the United States Government, Historical Tables, Fiscal Year 1989*, table 6.1.

the preceding thirty years of rapid growth. All this was part of a deliberate administration strategy to reorder federal spending priorities and to eliminate or reduce "ineffective" and nontraditional federal programs.[4]

There have been wide variations in the budgetary treatment of different grant programs as well. In some cases, such as grants to states for the support of individuals, spending has continued to grow during the Reagan years, although again at a slower rate. Indeed, grants for payments to individuals have grown more rapidly during this period than has overall spending for direct entitlements such as veterans' assistance, social security, and medicare (see table 8-2). More than 60 percent of this increase has been due to higher outlays for the medicaid program. Real AFDC spending actually fell slightly during Reagan's first term, despite an increase in poverty.

By far the largest reductions have been in the category of federal grants to governments. Real outlays expended on grants to state and local governments fell by 33 percent between 1980 and 1987, and the decline would have been even greater if additional highway aid stemming from the 1982 increase in the federal gas tax had been excluded. The largest reductions occurred in general-purpose assistance, economic development, employment and training, and social services (see table 8-3). With one major exception, the most severe cuts occurred early in Reagan's first term, in fiscal 1982 and 1983. Real spending for many of these programs actually increased modestly in fiscal 1985, in anticipation of the 1984 election. The exception was general revenue sharing, which was repeatedly slated for termination in the president's budgets and allowed to expire at the end of fiscal 1986. This single step reduced federal grant outlays to local governments by approximately $5 billion in fiscal 1987.

TABLE 8-3. Selected Grant Outlays to State and Local Governments,
by Function and Program, Fiscal Years 1980, 1985
Millions of 1980 dollars unless otherwise specified

Grants	1980	1985	Percent change, 1980–85
Total for all functions[a]	59,524	45,513	−23.5
Transportation	13,087	13,027	−0.5
Highways	8,676	9,548	10.0
Mass transit	3,129	2,547	−18.6
Airports and other	1,282	932	−27.2
Community and regional development	6,486	3,905	−39.8
Economic development	452	275	−39.2
Local public works	860	6	−99.3
CDBG	3,902	2,896	−25.8
Urban renewal grants	1,047	351	−66.6
Education, training, and social services	21,783	14,405	−33.4
Compensatory education	3,370	3,192	−5.4
Social services	2,763	2,081	−24.7
Human development	1,548	1,449	−6.4
Community services	547	285	−47.8
Temporary employment assistance	1,797	0	0
Training and employment	6,924	3,729	−68.8
Other	4,834	3,767	−22.1
General purpose assistance	8,478	4,658	−45.1
General revenue sharing	6,829	3,478	−49.1
Other	1,649	1,170	−29.0
All other grants to governments	9,690	9,420	−2.8

SOURCE: Rymarowicz and Zimmerman, *Effect of Federal Tax and Budget Policies*, p. 11.
a. Excludes grants that provide payments to individuals.

Three important points should be noted about these trends in federal aid spending under Ronald Reagan. First, federal aid reductions did not constitute a complete reversal of earlier patterns of intergovernmental fiscal relations. Rather, they accelerated trends that had already begun in the waning years of the Carter administration. Second, those programs targeted for the deepest cuts by the Reagan administration were the professionally administered services at the core of the Great Society. Reagan shared Nixon's dislike of the "service strategy" of the 1960s and chose to attack it head on rather than obliquely by promoting direct aid to individuals. Third, block grants and general revenue sharing, which were central to Nixon's New Federalism, were targeted for deep cuts and eventual elimination by the Reagan administration.

TABLE 8-4. Federal Grants as a Percentage of Total State-Local Outlays, Total Federal Outlays, and Gross National Product, Selected Fiscal Years, 1955–87

	Federal grants as a percentage of		
Year	Total state-local outlays	Total federal outlays	Gross national product
1955	10.2	4.7	0.8
1960	14.5	7.6	1.4
1965	15.1	9.2	1.6
1970	19.0	12.3	2.4
1975	22.6	15.0	3.3
1976	24.1	15.9	3.5
1977	25.5	16.7	3.5
1978	26.5	17.0	3.6
1979	25.8	16.5	3.4
1980	25.8	15.5	3.4
1981	24.7	14.0	3.2
1982	21.6	11.8	2.8
1983	21.3	11.4	2.8
1984	20.9	11.5	2.6
1985	20.9	11.2	2.7
1986	20.5	11.3	2.7
1987	18.2	10.8	2.5

SOURCE: ACIR, *Significant Features of Fiscal Federalism, 1988* (GPO, 1988), vol. 2, p. 15.

Trends in Intergovernmental Spending

By most relative measures, federal grants to state and local governments reached their zenith in fiscal 1978, the second year of the Carter administration: federal aid accounted for 26.5 percent of total state and local outlays, 17.0 percent of the federal budget, and 3.6 percent of the total economy (see table 8-4). Although federal aid in current dollars continued to rise until fiscal 1982, by each of these relative measures it had begun to subside in the later years of the Carter administration.

This was particularly evident in fiscal 1981, when the final budget policies achieved by the outgoing Carter administration were combined with additional midyear reductions implemented by Reagan. Before Carter left office, Congress eliminated the state share of general revenue sharing and substantially reduced CETA public employment grants. Both Carter and Reagan also made the first significant use of the budget reconciliation process. However, federal grant outlays as a percentage of all federal spending had already declined 9 percent between fiscal 1978 and 1980, and federal aid as a percentage of GNP had declined 5 percent. Indeed, some advocates of greater federal social spending were aware by the early 1980s that a reversal of prior growth trends was inevitable. As one put it, "Changes in the economy [would] have foretold an end to the earlier rate of growth in social welfare spending, regardless of who ha[d] been in office." [5]

Assault on the Service Strategy

If the direction of budgetary change was not a surprise to many informed observers, the magnitude of cuts in certain areas was. By far the largest cuts recommended and adopted by the Reagan administration were concentrated in the areas of community and economic development, education, social services, and employment and training (table 8-3). While total aid declined 8 percent and all aid to governments fell 24 percent between 1980 and 1985, real outlays for community and regional development were reduced by nearly 40 percent; real outlays for education, employment and training, and social services were cut by one-third. Particularly hard hit were many of the hallmark programs of the Great Society: community services, the descendant of the community action program, was cut nearly in half; local public works and regional development grants were practically eliminated; urban renewal and training and employment services were cut by two-thirds. Within education, the largest cuts occurred in the 1960s programs of bilingual education, compensatory education, and the small stimulative grants consolidated into the chapter two education block grant. [6]

The proponents of the Great Society devised these programs to break the cycle of poverty, to raise educational standards, and to promote regional economic development—not by giving the poor and unemployed cash or a government-sponsored job, but by delivering carefully planned and coordinated professional services prescribed by professional norms and the latest social science research. As Samuel Beer observed:

> The Great Society acquired a special character by its emphasis upon spending for services provided largely by state and local governments. . . . To a pronounced degree there was a "professionalization of reform." In the fields of health, housing, urban renewal, highways, welfare, education, and poverty, the new programs drew heavily upon specialized and technical knowledge in and around the federal bureaucracy [and] . . . enhanced [the] importance of scientifically and professionally trained civil servants at all levels of government. [7]

It was precisely such programs that were most objectionable to Ronald Reagan and the right wing of the Republican party. Both viewed them as forms of government-sponsored "social engineering" that undermined traditional values and social relationships. During his 1976 drive for the presidency, Reagan complained that "thousands of towns and neighborhoods have seen their peace disturbed by bureaucrats and social planners."[8] Earlier, while he was governor, Reagan denounced the war on poverty as "a matchless boondoggle," which "abandon[ed] tried and true principles" and replaced them with the judgments of "a self-appointed group of experts operating out of either Washington or Sacramento [who] cannot have all the answers to the problems that beset us." He pointed, as an example, to an antipoverty project he had vetoed because it employed seven administrators to provide employment services to seventeen unemployed individuals. Such programs, Reagan declared, amounted to little more than "the arrogant misuse of poverty funds for political nest-building."[9]

This last objection has prompted some observers to interpret Reagan's attack on the service strategy as more than a disagreement over methods and as part of a conscious strategy to "defund the left." As one reporter observed during the budget cuts of 1981, "One of the fondest conservative dreams is that the federal budget cuts will 'defund the left'—bankrupt the social action, civil rights, and other liberal groups that depend so heavily on federal funds."[10]

That dream flowed partly out of the president's conviction that liberal activists were dependent on a Washington power base for support. "It is far easier for people to come to Washington to get their social programs," he observed in early 1981. "All their friends and connections are in Washington."[11] But some of the president's conservative supporters went further in their political diagnosis. They argued that federal programs directly subsidized the administration's liberal opponents, and that the key to conservative success lay in "eliminating the power of the federal bureaucracy . . . to subsidize activist organizations which are working . . . to render irrelevant the election returns."[12]

The conservatives' perception was not entirely fanciful. A few interest groups representing public service clients and providers were forced to make drastic personnel and operational reductions when the administration severed federal contracts with them.[13] Most were not dependent on direct subsidies, however, and were targeted in other ways.

Ironically, it was state and especially local government associations, as a group, that were most dependent on federal subsidies and were most seriously affected by the Reagan cutbacks. These were the very organizations that the Nixon administration had consciously sponsored and assisted in order to provide lobbying assistance and technical support on behalf of common interests in the first New Federalism, but they were viewed as "wily stalkers of federal aid" or "merely [another] leg of that 'iron triangle'" by conservatives in the Reagan administration.[14] Thus between 1981 and 1983 the National League of Cities lost $3.6 million in federal contracts and training grants (one-half of its total budget) and was forced to fire 58 percent of its staff. The U.S. Conference of Mayors lost over $1.5 million in federal contracts in this period and made similar staff reductions. Owing to the combined effects of federal contract reductions and mismanagement, the National Association of Counties was driven to the brink of bankruptcy and underwent massive personnel and organizational changes. The National Conference of State Legislatures lost one-third of its budget and a similar share of its staff. Only the National Governors' Association escaped relatively unscathed, in part because of the administration's intergovernmental biases.[15]

In addition to eliminating direct grants and contracts to Washington-based interest groups, the administration attempted to undercut indirect subsidies and programmatic support for federally oriented "liberal" organizations. Reagan repeatedly sought to defund or eliminate the legal services corporation and the community services program. Both were peculiar legacies of the Great Society's attempts to represent and organize the poor, and both had earned reputations for challenging established institutions and practices, both governmental and private.[16]

The administration also attempted to alter regulations governing federal contract audit procedures in ways that would have severely restricted contract recipients from publicly promoting policy positions, particularly through congressional testimony. These proposed regulations were significantly modified, however, in response to strenuous congressional objections and opposition from defense contractors and other unintended targets of these rules changes. The White House was more successful in removing policy-oriented advocacy groups from participating in the federal government's version of the United Way, thus channeling the charitable giving of federal employees toward more traditional service-oriented organizations.

Third, and most important, the administration used block grants to disrupt, if not "defund," the left. Block grants were intended to force interest groups to focus their activities away from Washington and thus move the center of policy decisionmaking to new and presumably unfamiliar terrain at the state and local levels.

This was expected to have two results. First, it would alter the kinds of interests that would be involved in policy decisions, thus affecting the shape of specific policies. As Robert Carleson, a conservative White

House architect of the president's federalism strategy, observed: "We have consciously set out to force political decisions and the struggles that accompany them down to the state and local level. The so-called iron triangles in Washington for too long have had a virtual monopoly on political influence in Congress and in the agencies." [17] Second, the structural changes imposed by block grants were expected to reduce the overall magnitude of public sector activity. Administration strategists assumed that if the "iron triangles" were disrupted, the supporters of domestic social programs would be less able to maintain spending and programmatic activities at existing levels. "The block grant is the ideal vehicle for permanently reducing the growth of spending," argued Carleson.[18] As the president himself observed, "It would be a hell of a lot tougher [for social programs] if we diffuse them and send them out to the states." [19]

Budgetary Implications of the Reagan Block Grants

Reagan's use of block grants to reduce the scope of the public sector and advance conservative social policy objectives was very different from Nixon's. Although not unaware of or indifferent to the potential merits of block grants as a political device for restructuring policymaking arenas and altering program priorities, most Nixon administration officials viewed block grants as a worthwhile end in themselves. They favored block grants as an efficient administrative mechanism for combining the federal government's revenue-raising capacity with state and local familiarity with local needs and expertise in service delivery. In contrast, the Reagan administration has seen block grants as an effective transitional device for weakening the "Washington establishment" by providing a "halfway house" on the road to total federal withdrawal from affected policy areas.[20] As the president himself observed in a speech to the National Conference of State Legislatures, "The ultimate objective . . . is to use block grants . . . as only a bridge, leading to the day when you'll have not only . . . the programs that properly belong at the state level, but . . . the tax sources now usurped by Washington . . . ending the round trip of the peoples' money to Washington, where a carrying charge is deducted, and then back to you." [21]

Reagan's budgetary treatment of block grants also differed from Nixon's. As earlier chapters have shown, the Nixon administration demonstrated a consistent willingness to accept higher spending levels for block grants in order to ease the administrative transition to these grants and enhance political support for them in Congress. In contrast, Reagan's major block grant proposals embodied large reductions in spending as well as changes in program structures. Such cuts were not entirely without justification, given the economic conditions at the time and potential administrative savings for states resulting from reductions in application, compliance, and paperwork requirements. For these reasons, the nation's governors had offered to accept a 10 percent reduction in budget authority for programs consolidated into block grants. Yet they were hardly prepared for the budget request that accompanied the president's initial block grant proposals in 1981. In his fiscal 1982 budget, Reagan proposed creating seven sweeping new block grants and reducing their budget authority almost 25 percent below fiscal 1981 spending on the programs proposed for merger. Thus, rather than rewarding block grants with favored budgetary treatment, as Nixon had done, Reagan recommended them for some of the deepest spending cuts in his entire budget. As table 7-1 showed, block grants were recommended for deeper cuts than total federal aid, whereas most other major segments of the budget were to have increases.

This harsh budgetary treatment was not confined to fiscal 1982. Although block grants enjoyed less prominence in later administration budgets and far fewer were enacted, a similar fiscal fate was recommended for most of the president's subsequent block grant proposals. As part of its fiscal 1986 budget, for example, the administration proposed terminating one block grant and cutting the budget of another by 10 percent. Thus the message to state and local governments remained consistent and clear: the president would continue to support the general goal of grant reform, but—in contrast to alternative objectives like national defense, tuition tax credits, and urban enterprise zones—Reagan would not adjust his fiscal priorities to advance this cause.

The president's budgetary treatment of GRS was similar and ultimately had far more devastating consequences. Whereas revenue sharing had been the centerpiece of Nixon's New Federalism and the federal program most dear to state and local governments, Reagan has held a far more hostile view of efforts to harness the federal tax apparatus to provide funds for state and local governments. In fact, the president proposed terminating or severely modifying revenue sharing on several occasions. In 1975 and again in 1982, Reagan advocated folding GRS into a broad package of federal program and revenue turnbacks to the states. In late 1981 he proposed a 12 percent cut in GRS spending as part of a broader across-the-board reduction in federal domestic expenditures.[22]

However, the White House had to back down temporarily in 1983, when strong lobbying by local government officials forced it to agree to reauthorize GRS at its existing funding level for another three years. But the Reagan administration returned to more drastic solutions in its fiscal 1986 budget and proposed terminating GRS in October 1985, one year before it was to expire. Continued large deficits led the administration to argue again that "the Federal government can no longer afford general revenue sharing." [23] In 1985 this argument carried the day in Congress, which, after exploring various options, agreed to let the program expire in October 1986.

Block Grant Politics

In 1981, under unceasing prodding from the administration, Congress consolidated seventy-seven categorical programs into nine block grants, a one-year total that surpassed the combined total of all previous enactments. Reagan's early success stemmed from new tactics—he tied grant reform tightly to new budget procedures—and new political resources. Subsequently, however, only one block grant was enacted as Congress—now reinforced by stronger partisan and ideological suspicions of block grant objectives—reverted to its historic pattern of opposition and held block grants in a budgetary stalemate.

Reagan's Proposals and Early Congressional Reactions

The new parliamentary tactics used to push through the 1981 block grants altered the ground rules of grant consolidation politics. Early in the year, when the president's proposals were being considered individually by congressional committees, the prospects for significant grant reform seemed dim. Committees in the Republican-controlled Senate made substantial alterations in the president's proposals, and committees in the Democratic House threatened to block them altogether. Things changed dramatically, however, when block grants were linked to the president's budget proposals through the reconciliation process. This shifted decisionmaking from committees to the floor and reframed the issues on the president's terms.

Originally, the president proposed consolidating more than eighty programs into seven new block grants in the fields of education, health, social services, and community development. In elementary and secondary education, he proposed consolidating forty-three programs into two: a local education block grant composed of major programs for disadvantaged, handicapped, and special needs students and a state block grant

TABLE 8-5. Number of Categorical Grants Proposed for
Consolidation by Administration and Enacted into
Block Grants by Congress, 1981

Proposed block grant	Programs consolidated	Enacted block grant	Programs consolidated
Local education	10	State education	37
State education	30		
Health services and mental health	17	Preventive health and health services	6
Preventive health	10	Alcohol, drug abuse, and mental health	10
		Maternal and child health	9
		Primary health care	1
Social services	12	Social services	1
Emergency assistance	2	Low-income energy assistance	1
		Community services	7
Community development	1	State community development	3
TOTAL	85	TOTAL	77

SOURCE: David B. Walker, Albert J. Richter, and Cynthia C. Colella, "The First Ten Months: Grant-in-Aid, Regulatory, and Other Changes," *Intergovernmental Perspective*, vol. 8 (Winter 1982), pp. 8–9.

composed of thirty-three mostly small programs for purposes like metric and environmental education and desegregation assistance (see table 8-5). Two block grants also were proposed in public health: a preventive health care block grant that was to replace ten programs ranging from family planning to rat control, and a health services block grant consolidating seventeen categoricals like community health centers and maternal and child health grants. The social services proposal merged twelve programs, including the existing Title XX block grant, most community action programs, and child welfare and adoption services. An emergency assistance block grant combined only two grants—low-income energy assistance and emergency welfare assistance. Finally, the president proposed easing restrictions on the existing community development block grant and turning the federally administered portion of the program for small communities over to the states. He also proposed terminating several categorical programs like planning and weatherization grants and rehabilitation loans and allowing state and local governments to pick them up—if they so desired—with block grant funds.

Structurally, these were very bold block grant proposals as they ignored virtually every feature that had contributed to block grant success in the past. No attempt was made to construct consolidations in areas of professional consensus or to focus on politically vulnerable programs. Nor was any effort made to respect Congress's traditional concern with maintaining fiscal accountability and protecting basic national purposes. Rather, the Reagan proposals resembled and expanded upon Nixon's unsuccessful concept of special revenue sharing. Within the broad range of eligible activities specified in each proposal, most of the Reagan block grants gave virtually unlimited discretion to state recipients—without planning, application, or detailed reporting requirements. As one city lobbyist remarked, they "made general revenue sharing look restrictive" by comparison.[24] Earlier block grant enactments were also very expensive. They consistently had higher appropriations than the programs they replaced, in order to prevent most recipients of existing programs from losing funds in the shift to a new block grant formula. But there was no such attempt to "buy" consolidation under the Reagan proposals. Rather, they generally cut funding levels 25 percent below expected spending levels.

Finally, most of CETA and CDBG funds had gone directly to local governments on a formula basis, in part because these governments had more influence in Washington than states did in the early 1970s. Although some of the Reagan proposals required the states to "pass through" some revenues to local governments, they sent no funds directly to local governments, even in program areas of principally local concern. Instead, they sent all the block grants—and their attendant cuts—to the states, greatly "upping the ante" on the governors' prior offer to accept modest reductions in federal aid in exchange for greater administrative flexibility.

Thus initial congressional and interest group responses to the Reagan block grant proposals were sharply negative. Throughout the spring of 1981 congressional committees in both the House and Senate deleted controversial provisions—and entire programs—from the president's proposals. In the Republican-controlled Senate, for example, defections by key moderate Republicans on the Labor and Human Resources Committee stalled progress on the administration's health and education bills for weeks. When compromise legislation finally was reported from committee, the largest and most sensitive education programs had been saved from consolidation, and the health proposals had been reworked into three less ambitious block grants. The Senate also retained legal services as a separate program, substantially scaled back the social service block grant, and restructured community action grants into a separate block grant. In short, although the Senate eventually acceded to considerable

program consolidation, this occurred only after lengthy and difficult negotiations that concluded with substantial amendments to the president's
proposals.

During this initial period, the president fared even worse in the Democratically controlled House, where most of the proposed block grants
were bottled up or killed entirely in their respective committees. As one
senior aide with the Subcommittee on Health and Environment recalled,
"The block grants were window dressing to disguise budget cuts. And
many health programs historically were not funded by the states. Some,
like family planning, were simply not negotiable. So the president's proposals were rejected out of hand."[25] Similarly, Education and Labor
Committee chairman Carl Perkins (Democrat of Kentucky) charged that
the president sought to "dismantle programs" rather than reform them,[26]
while Congressman William Ford (Democrat of Michigan) likened the
education block grant to sending "bags of money to a State" in a Brinks
truck. "We cannot send a check to Michigan addressed to: 'To whom it
may concern' and hope somebody will cash it and divvy it up properly,"
he said.[27]

As Congressman Ford's statement suggests, the issue of consolidation
was of greater concern to many senior Democrats than the Reagan budget cuts. Operating on the assumption that many of the president's cuts
were popular and unavoidable, Democratic strategists attempted instead, in the words of one observer, to "protect the [categorical] delivery
systems."[28] This would protect Democratic priorities in the long run and
permit rapid program recovery under a later Democratic administration.

The president's block grant proposals also came under scathing attacks from affected clientele and interest groups outside of Congress.
Many saw the block grants merely as a thin disguise for drastic budget
cuts. Others, like the Ad Hoc Coalition on Block Grants (representing
more than 100 separate groups and professional associations) focused
on consolidation as "a radical transformation in the relationship between citizens and their government." In a letter sent to all members of
the House, the coalition charged that the president's proposals would

repeal landmark legislation, eliminate essential programs, undermine
principles of fiscal accountability and lay the groundwork for confusion, neglect, and new bureaucracy at the state level. . . . These proposals will certainly mean . . . less assistance to those in genuine need
. . . and a brutal political struggle at the state level where the most
vulnerable . . . are almost certain losers.[29]

During congressional hearings, witnesses drew ties between the administration's budgetary and block grant strategies. In testimony before the Senate, the executive director of one group concluded that "the problem with block grants . . . is that by removing the targeting [to specific clienteles], you remove the constituency for funding. Pretty soon you can pretend there was no need for funding at all." [30]

Even many state and local government officials—the presumed beneficiaries of grant consolidation—appeared lukewarm or hostile toward the president's proposals. Most state officials reacted tentatively to the block grants, supporting the concept but acting wary of the large budget cuts proposed and the rapid transfer of program responsibility. Local officials were even less in favor of the new grants as they were anxious about both the budget cuts and state control. Mayor Richard Hatcher, of Gary, Indiana, then president of the U.S. Conference of Mayors, spoke for many when he condemned the proposals as "deep budget cuts dressed up to look like block grants and sent to state capitals, where we'll have to go through another layer of bureaucracy to find them." [31] Consequently, much of the hoped-for support for the block grants by the intergovernmental lobby was dissipated in guerrilla warfare between state and cities over block grant funding, eligibility, and design.

Throughout much of early 1981, therefore, prospects for enactment of the Reagan block grant proposals seemed very dim. One respected journalist covering their progress in Congress concluded only one week before House passage of the Omnibus Budget Reconciliation Act that "the political furnace required to melt categorical grants together into large, simple blocks hasn't reached the critical temperature yet, even in this year's overheated congressional atmosphere." [32] This view was shared by many academic experts, as well. "I don't think the block grant proposals will pass Congress," said Professor Frederick Mosher. [33]

Passage of the Omnibus Reconciliation Act

These expectations were dramatically reversed on June 26, 1981, when the House passed its version of the Omnibus Budget Reconciliation Act of 1981. As amended by the so-called Gramm-Latta II amendment, the reconciliation act

—established 9 new or revised block grants for public health, social services, elementary and secondary education, and community development—consolidating or terminating 139 categorical programs in the process;

—reduced funding for the consolidated programs by 25 percent;

—terminated the public service employment titles of the Comprehensive Employment and Training Act; and

—eased federal restrictions on several large existing education and urban programs, including CDBG and title I education grants for educationally disadvantaged students.

In addition to reducing the number of federal aid programs by one-quarter and reducing funds for consolidated programs by a similar amount, the new block grants greatly strengthened the role of states as grant recipients—to the marked detriment of local nonprofit agencies, local school districts, and small municipalities.

The politics of the reconciliation act have already been discussed in chapter 7. In the case of grant consolidation, members of the House were offered a stark choice between two multibillion dollar packages of budget cuts, program changes, and grant reforms. The House Budget Committee package contained an estimated $37.7 billion in reductions from fiscal 1982 outlays for current services. These cuts stemmed from legislative changes devised by each House committee, but the changes did not include any of the president's new block grant proposals. The only additional block grants in the House Democrats' package were four narrowly defined and tightly controlled block grants in public health, one of which consisted of a single program. An alternative budget package was presented in Gramm-Latta II, the substitute amendment devised by the administration and House conservatives that reduced projected fiscal 1982 outlays by $38.2 billion and established eight new block grants. Although there were some differences, these block grants were patterned closely on the president's recommendations.

The normal rules of block grant politics broke down in the confrontation over reconciliation. Key decisions about program structure were removed from the arena of individual committees, often dominated by categorical program sponsors and beneficiaries, and placed before Congress and the country as a whole, where they became part of a litmus test of support of the president's program. In the process, the fundamental legislative issue was transformed from "Does each specific program change make sense to program specialists and supporters?" to "Do you support the economic recovery plan of a highly popular president?"

Under the latter formulation, block grants became a secondary issue for many, obscured in a massive and hurriedly compiled 1,000-page bill and nearly overshadowed by a host of competing budgetary and structural issues in defense, transportation, energy, and entitlements. As one moderate Democrat complained on the House floor: "We are dealing with more than 250 programs with no hearings, no deliberation, no debate."[34] "Normally this package would be one hundred different bills," observed a congressional staff member, "and Congress would spend months on each one."[35] At the end of it all was a simple up or down vote on the total package with no exceptions or deletions.

The House Democratic leadership did not want the issue to be cast in such stark terms, even in the context of reconciliation. The leadership-controlled Rules Committee proposed that reconciliation be brought to the floor under a rule allowing five different votes on major sections of the reconciliation bill. Rather than let the Republicans offer a single omnibus amendment to the Democrats' bill, the rule required that the Gramm-Latta substitute be brought up in separate pieces. The hope was to isolate several politically popular programs in each amendment and force the president's supporters to go on the record voting for specific cuts in college student aid programs, food stamps, social security and medicare, energy and public health programs, and cost-of-living adjustments for federal workers.[36]

Not surprisingly, Republicans bitterly fought this attempt to disrupt their strategy, the success of which depended on a single yes or no on the president's economic package. They charged that the allowable amendments ignored subsequent changes in their package that made it more attractive politically. In fact, the Republican minority leader called them "bastards of the worst order for which we disclaim any parental responsibility."[37]

More surprising than Republican opposition was the outcome. The Republicans won their fight on the rule, and the leadership's attempt to structure debate on the Democrats' terms was defeated. In a show of conservative support and extraordinary Republican unity, 27 Democrats joined all 189 Republicans in supporting a substitute Republican rule that required a single vote on the Gramm-Latta II reconciliation amendment. This procedural vote virtually guaranteed adoption of the Gramm-Latta amendment itself, since the House leadership expected to attract more support on the less visible and arcane procedural issue than on the substantive budget cuts themselves.

THE BROYHILL AMENDMENT. The major exception to this pattern of presidential victories on reconciliation—and a case in which block grants per se became an issue in the debate—was the defeat of the so-called Broyhill amendment. Named for the ranking Republican on the House Energy and Commerce Committee, this amendment covered health care, energy, environmental, and transportation issues in that committee's jurisdiction. Ironically, this was an area in which the president had unusually strong support within the committee itself and his early prospects for success seemed brightest.

By and large, Democratically supported reconciliation plans were reported from each committee, "reconciling" the programs in each jurisdiction with the broad committee spending limits adopted in the first budget resolution. These recommendations were then compiled by the Budget Committee into a single omnibus reconciliation bill. In most cases, the administration attacked the committee plans for being full of "accounting tricks" and gimmickry that would save only a quarter of the promised $118 billion by fiscal 1984. "Committee after Committee played the same havoc," alleged David Stockman, with creative cuts, "preposterous savings claim[s]," and "flagrant ploy[s]." [38] Although this charge was considered excessive even by many Republicans, there was no question that many of the committee bills contained exaggerated claims or easily reversible savings. More important, they contained very little in the way of structural reforms like block grants. Consequently, OMB began to work with the Republican members and staffs of each House committee on an omnibus Republican substitute, which became the Gramm-Latta amendment.

This pattern of Democratic dominance did not emerge in the House Energy and Commerce Committee, which had jurisdiction over the president's block grant proposals for public health programs and low-income energy assistance. When it came time to report its recommended reconciliation cuts, the committee was deadlocked 21 to 21 over two different legislative packages and thus failed to report formally any recommended savings. These two packages differed in many respects, most notably with regard to block grants for health care. The Democrats' proposal, which contained the four narrow health grants described earlier, retained many more strings and consolidated only twelve programs rather than the twenty-five requested by the president. The Republican proposal contained three broader block grants and deeper spending cuts in several areas.

As a result of the committee's deadlock, the Budget Committee incorporated the proposals favored by the Energy Committee's leadership, but it recommended a separate vote on the conservative-supported Broyhill package. The Broyhill provisions were initially folded into the omnibus Gramm-Latta amendment and would have been adopted with the rest of Gramm-Latta II. But these provisions were taken out of the package and prepared as a separate amendment when two "boll weevils" on the Energy Committee informed the administration that that they could support Gramm-Latta only if the Energy and Commerce Committee's provisions were removed. Having received concessions on natural gas regulations, they had promised Energy Committee chairman John Dingell that they would support his part of the bill, and they felt bound by their commitment.[39]

Desperate for every vote, the administration and House Republican leaders agreed to separate the Broyhill amendment from the rest of Gramm-Latta II, and they planned for a separate vote on it. Although many deals were made with northern Republicans to keep them in line on the Broyhill amendment—deals that loosened a proposed cap on medicaid payments to states, took family planning grants out of the proposed health services block grant, and increased spending on Conrail, Amtrak, and the energy conservation block grant—Republican leaders concluded at the last minute that a loss on the Broyhill amendment, which still seemed likely, would jeopardize the entire Gramm-Latta package, so it was never offered. Thus, by default, the Democrats' provisions on health care and other energy and commerce issues went unchallenged and remained in the bill.

THE 1981 RECONCILIATION CONFERENCE. Even with its loss on the Broyhill amendment, the administration had won a historic victory. Gramm-Latta II allowed it to advance its economic agenda in the Democratically controlled House. Because the House and Senate had passed different versions of reconciliation legislation, however, the president's modified budget and block grant proposals were to be sent to a conference committee to iron out the differences. Fearing that its policy goals would be diluted further during this conference or that a way might yet be found to stymie them entirely, the administration requested that the Republican-controlled Senate simply pass the House version of the reconciliation bill and avoid such a conference.[40] Senate Republican leaders angrily refused to engage in such an unprecedented sacrifice of their legislative prerogatives, and the largest House-Senate conference in history was assembled. More than 250 members of Congress representing 59 different House and Senate subcommittees assembled to reconcile differences affecting over 200 federal programs.[41]

As with earlier versions of omnibus reconciliation, many of the most controversial issues in conference, such as the sale of Conrail and the placement of an annual cap on federal medicaid payments to the states, had nothing to do with grant consolidation. Once again, however, health grants were the exception. Because the Broyhill amendment was never offered, the House and Senate took widely divergent positions on block grants. The Senate passed three block grants for health care that consolidated twenty-five different grants—including three extremely controversial programs for family planning, community health centers, and migrant health care. All three sustained deep budget cuts. The House passed four smaller, tightly earmarked, and regulated block grants and retained all three of these programs as separately authorized grants.

These structural differences created obstacles to agreement. As one House committee staffer recalled, "There were two entirely different concepts involved. It took time for the Senate to realize they couldn't get a big block grant for health. Once they realized that, then there were logical ways that programs broke down into pieces." [42] In the end, the conference reported the four health care block grants that the House had passed, but with modifications in their budgets and with nine additional programs folded in. For example, the preventive health and health services block grant was enlarged, its budget was reduced, and the reporting and structural features of the four block grants were standardized. But the House refused to consolidate several controversial programs, with the result that the primary care "block grant" consisted of one program and was made so restrictive that only a single state chose to participate. As in the House, family planning grants were particularly controversial in conference. Senate conferees were heavily pressured by right-wing conservatives to terminate the program, but the House insisted it was "not negotiable." The logjam was finally broken when the chief Senate negotiator, Senator Orrin Hatch (Republican of Utah) obtained a letter from the White House publicly acknowledging the political need for its continuation.[43]

In health care, the conference followed the usual pattern of blending provisions from the House and Senate bills, leaving a group of block grants broader than the House's version and narrower than the Senate's. In other areas, a more obvious effort was made to weaken the block grants, much as Stockman had feared when he sought to avoid a conference committee. In social services, for example, the House had folded the community services program into the larger social services block grant (SSBG), while the Senate retained it as a separate program. The conference agreed on the Senate version and removed the program from the SSBG. Other programs that were included in one but not both House and Senate versions of this block grant were deleted as well, including grants for child welfare, foster care, child abuse prevention, and runaway children. This left the final SSBG program smaller and narrower than either the House or Senate versions—and not very different from the existing Title XX social services block grant apart from substantial budget cuts.[44] Similarly, when it emerged from conference, the low-income energy assistance block grant consolidated only a single existing program.

In education, few restrictive modifications were adopted in conference, primarily because neither chamber had passed an expansive block grant to begin with. Both rejected the administration's proposal that the two largest federal education programs—which provided grants for teaching handicapped and educationally disadvantaged children—be included in a separate local education block grant. As a result, the conference focused on similar plans for consolidating thirty-seven mostly small discretionary federal grants into a modest state education block grant.

Despite these modifications, it would be a mistake to conclude that the president failed in his quest for block grants. Senate supporters of the president claimed that he had won 70–80 percent of his initial budget requests.[45] As table 8-6 shows, Congress consolidated seventy-seven categorical programs into nine new or revised block grants, which was not too far off the president's goal of consolidating eighty-five programs into seven grants. Compared with earlier block grant efforts, this alone was a spectacular achievement. In one year, in a single law, the Reagan administration had obtained the enactment of more block grants and the consolidation of more programs than had been accomplished in the preceding twenty-five years of grant reform initiatives. Despite the fact that outlays for block grants in fiscal 1982 were 15 percent below fiscal 1981 spending levels, the proportion of the federal aid budget devoted to "broad-based" assistance—mainly block grants—rose by more than one-fifth under Ronald Reagan, going from 11.3 percent in 1981 to 14 percent by 1987.

Post-1981 Politics

These successes were never repeated. Only one additional block grant was enacted after 1981, the Job Training Partnership Act of 1982, which revised and restructured the existing CETA block grant. Even this modest achievement was counterbalanced in 1985 by the repeal of the primary care block grant, which eliminated the little-used block grant option provided for states under the community health centers program.

This decline in fortunes was not for want of trying on the president's part. In the five years after 1981 the Reagan administration issued twenty-four additional block grant proposals, several of which were recommended to Congress on repeated occasions (table 8-6). Yet few were seriously considered. Some failed even to obtain a sponsor to introduce

TABLE 8-6. Reagan Administration Proposals for New or Expanded Block Grants, Fiscal Years 1983–87

Block grant proposal	Number of programs proposed for consolidation
1983	
Child welfare block grant	4
Rental rehabilitation grants	2
Combined welfare administration	3
Vocational and adult education	3
Handicapped education	2
Rehabilitation services	3
Primary care block grant	3
Maternal and child health	1
1984	
Indian community development and housing	1
Indian housing	1
General nutrition assistance	3
Older Americans programs	3
Primary care block grant	3
State fiscal assistance block grant	22
Local fiscal assistance block grant	2
Transportation block grant	6
Rural housing block grant	4
1985	
Science and math education	1
Older Americans programs	4
Non-school nutrition programs	2
Primary care block grant	3
1986	
Primary care block grant	3
1987	
Pollution control block grant	7
Highway and transit block grant	6
Primary care block grant	3

SOURCE: Based on Sandra S. Osbourn, "Block Grants: Inventory and Funding History," CRS, November 21, 1986.

them in Congress.[46] Since then the number of new block grant proposals sent to Congress declined as the chronic failure to advance consolidation legislation appeared to dampen even this administration's enthusiasm for the block grant device.

There were several reasons, both substantive and political, for this reversal of fortunes. Substantively, many of the most obvious and politically tenable candidates for consolidation were folded into block grants in 1981. Several of the remaining programs proposed for subsequent consolidation—such as family planning and migrant health grants—had already been considered and firmly rejected by Congress. In other instances, the administration simply failed to present a convincing case. It proposed consolidating the women, infants, and children (WIC) nutrition program into the maternal and child health block grant, even though this promised at least temporary dislocations in what was widely considered to be one of the most successful of all federal aid programs.[47] Similarly, a proposal to consolidate funding for the regionally targeted black lung health clinics into a nationally distributed primary care block grant clearly spelled the termination of a unique program rather than a structural change in its administration.

Several political factors made matters even more difficult for block grants. To begin with, the administration used block grants to obtain budget cuts in 1981, and, as George Peterson has pointed out, "Subsequent proposals . . . failed in large part because they [became] identified politically as instruments of domestic budget cutting."[48] Consequently, block grants were no longer considered management-oriented devices deserving of bipartisan support but were perceived as a political and budgetary tool of conservatives. Therefore, traditional supporters of block grants among state and local officials grew wary of further administration proposals. Governors like Jerry Brown of California complained that the Reagan approach to block grants was part of "a shell game" designed to "shift the burden to state and local governments."[49] Local officials, including Republicans like Indianapolis Mayor Willam Hudnut, condemned the administration's strong bias toward block grants to states rather than local governments. "We do not want to be administrative provinces of either the federal government or the states," he declared.[50]

In addition the president had fewer political resources available in subsequent years. Although reconciliation continued to be an integral part of the budget process, Congress refused to use it again for authorizing such wholesale changes in legislation. Even during 1981, Democrats condemned it as the most "brutal and blunt instrument . . . since Nixon used impoundment," while Republicans confessed that "nobody is particularly happy about this procedure."[51] A top Budget Committee aide said simply, "I don't think we'll do it again. Period."[52] Moreover, as noted in chapter 7, the president's voting strength in Congress declined after 1981 because conservative Democrats returned to their party fold on key votes and moderate Republicans increased their willingness to support existing federal aid programs. The loss of twenty-six Republican House seats in the 1982 election further weakened the president's political support in that chamber. Individually any one of these factors might have been sufficient to erode what was a very narrow margin of support for block grants in the Congress to begin with. In combination, they proved simply overwhelming.

The only departure from this pattern of post 1981 defeats—the Job Training Partnership Act of 1982 (JTPA)—was an exception that proved the rule. Unlike the president's 1981 block grants or subsequent proposals, JPTA was enacted in an atmosphere of consensual, bipartisan block grant politics reminiscent of the early 1970s.

Much as Nixon's block grants reflected dissatisfaction with earlier Great Society programs, the new job training block grant stemmed from widespread disillusionment with CETA. Ironically, of course, CETA was considered a major achievement of Nixon's original New Federalism when it was first enacted in 1973. It had consolidated seventeen highly fragmented categorical programs into a single job training block grant, created a new program of public service employment, and established a new system for delivering job training services at the local level. During the 1974–75 recession, a large additional public service employment title was added.

Although CETA provided jobs for more than a million unemployed persons and job training and work experience for thousands more, by 1978 the program had become a "dirty four letter word" in the eyes of many. Stories of corruption and mismanagement—directed mainly at CETA's public employment titles—undermined support for the entire legislation. Moreover, careful evaluations of CETA training programs often failed to detect substantial improvements in the future earnings of trainees.[53] In response to these problems, Congress substantially amended the program in 1978, tightening up program controls and eligibility and reducing funding. In 1981 Congress returned again to CETA and terminated the public employment titles of the legislation. These changes helped curb the most flagrant abuses and direct more employment assistance to the neediest clients, but they also dampened support for the program among both clients and local governments.

Against this backdrop of disillusionment with CETA, which in any case was scheduled to expire on September 30, 1982, three major replacements were introduced in Congress in 1982. The bills all featured improved linkages between the private sector and government training programs and less reliance on public employment. But they differed widely on other issues, from funding levels to how services would be delivered.

The administration's bill contained sharply reduced funding for training programs and a much narrower range of services and eligible clients. At the same time, the measure gave the states and private industry councils a much larger role in designing and delivering training services. Only localities with populations in excess of 400,000 (compared with 100,000 under CETA) would have been permitted to operate their own programs under this bill.

At the other extreme was H.R. 5320, sponsored by Augustus Hawkins, chairman of the House Employment Opportunities Subcommittee. This proposal retained many CETA services and much of the existing operating structure. It also raised authorizations for training programs above 1982 levels and included a new $1 billion public jobs program for areas with high unemployment.

The bipartisan Senate bill, S. 2036, sponsored jointly by Senators Dan Quayle of Indiana and Edward M. Kennedy of Massachusetts, occupied a middle ground. Eligibility for local designation as a service delivery area was increased only to 200,000, and a roughly equal partnership between industry councils and local elected officials was established. Although stipends and wages were retained as allowable local expenditures, support services and administration were limited to 30 percent of program costs and some of the least efficient uses of training funds were restricted or prohibited.

The new law was largely patterned after this bipartisan compromise. In deference to the administration, subsidies and allowances for trainees were sharply reduced, and the roles of state governments and the private sector were expanded. Other provisions followed the Senate bill to a large extent:

—CETA's system of local prime sponsors was abolished and instead local units of government with populations above 200,000 were designated as service delivery areas (SDAs).

—New private industry councils were established in each SDA to develop a training plan and to determine the use of training funds, subject to approval by the local chief elected official of the SDA. In cases of disagreement, governors were given power to arbitrate.

—The level of funding was upward of $3 billion a year, of which 78 percent was distributed to state and local governments on the basis of unemployment and poverty; the Senate limit of 30 percent on administration and support services was retained.

—The transition year for phasing out CETA and phasing in the new block grant was to be 1983.

Conclusion

When Ronald Reagan entered the White House, he and his entourage of close aides brought with them a radical intergovernmental agenda cloaked in continuities from the past. The continuities were readily apparent. In the realm of intergovernmental spending, for example, Ronald Reagan's budgets did not mark an absolute reversal of past policies; rather, they rapidly accelerated the downward trends in the growth and relative significance of federal aid that had begun during the Carter administration. With respect to policy instruments, Reagan relied even more heavily than Nixon on block grants to promote his New Federalism. However, these continuities disguised fundamental differences with the policies of the past, not only of the Great Society but of the first New Federalism as well.

That Reagan's budgets should conduct a frontal assault on the programmatic heritage of Lyndon Johnson should come as no surprise. Reagan's hostility to programs like community action and legal services went back to his days as governor of California. The extent of his attack was less predictable, however, particularly for state and local governments and their associations in Washington.

At the core of the Great Society was the service strategy, which the Reagan administration frowned upon in virtually all respects. Both the traditionalist and libertarian factions of modern conservatism opposed the service strategy because they believed that it drained public resources and sponsored dependency on government by establishing elite cadres of social engineers who reject traditional social values. The greatest impact of the administration's numerous initiatives to reverse or eliminate such policies was felt by state and local governments. With their large educational and social service bureaucracies, state and local governments had become the foot soldiers of the service strategy. They suffered accordingly when federal grants for education, training, and social services were reduced by as much as 33 percent between 1980 and 1985, which is far in excess of the cuts incurred by all federal aid or domestic spending in those years.

State and local government lobbies suffered just as much. Thanks in large part to the policies of the Nixon administration, they were unusually dependent on federal contracts and subsidies for staff and resources. Although the Reagan administration sometimes worked with them as allies, it was far more apt to view these organizations as "just another interest group." Indeed, to some extent, their dependency was all the more objectionable because it symbolized their decline from proud and independent "co-sovereigns" to submissive supplicants of federal aid. When the administration moved aggressively to "defund the left" and reduce or eliminate direct subsidies to social lobbying associations, state and local government associations as a whole received the largest cuts of all, which forced them to reduce their staffs and operations drastically.

Other programs with roots in the Nixon administration suffered sizable and sometimes startling cuts as well. General revenue sharing was reduced, then capped, and then finally abolished. Welfare benefits for the working poor were cut back sharply. Perhaps even more than the attacks on the Great Society, these departures from policies adopted in the Nixon administration reveal the extent to which Reagan intended to break with the past.

Through block grants, in particular, the president sought to achieve a new and radical objective: to eliminate federal participation altogether in a vast array of domestic activities. Since this goal was not immediately realizable in many instances, block grants constituted a politically viable "halfway house" to termination, with the first installment represented by cuts of 25 percent in block grant budgets.

The irony of Reagan's radical approach was that it was more ambitious than Nixon's approach yet initially it was more successful. This paradox can be explained by the very different political strategy with which Reagan pursued his block grants. Rather than build a consensus for reform on each affected issue, the Reagan administration hitched consolidation proposals to the high stakes and polarized politics of his budget policies.

This tactic produced striking results in the short term but at the expense of long-term gains. In essence, the polarization of block grant politics poisoned the well for future consolidations, as was evident from the rapidly diminishing returns reaped by this strategy once the unusually propitious political circumstances of 1981 evaporated. After 1981 only one additional block grant was enacted out of twenty-four new proposals. This was the Job Training Partnership Act of 1982, which reflected the more consensual style of block grant politics that had reached its zenith under Richard Nixon. However, the conflictual strategy of 1981 superseded this tradition and put it, perhaps permanently, to rest.

9

Comprehensive Federalism Reform: The Missing Chapter

THE MOST dramatic intergovernmental reform proposal of the Reagan presidency was the federalism initiative of 1982, which recommended a comprehensive restructuring of the federal government's relationships with states and localities in "a single bold sweep." Reagan's plan, as outlined in his State of the Union address, was to nationalize health care financing for the poor, terminate the federal role in welfare, and turn back forty-three major federal grant programs to the states along with $28 billion in federal excise tax sources to pay for them. One respected scholar predicted that, if fully implemented, this initiative would return intergovernmental fiscal relations to the days before the New Deal.[1]

Although it was the centerpiece of the president's 1982 agenda, this initiative was never introduced as legislation in Congress. Anticipating strong resistance from Congress, the administration was reluctant to proceed with the plan without the support of state and local governments. The nation's governors conducted negotiations with the White House on a joint proposal, but the policy differences between them could not be overcome. Moreover, important sources within the administration opposed the plan as well. David Stockman, in particular, had accepted it at first only as a means toward deficit reduction. Once the governors made clear they would support it only on a revenue-positive or neutral basis, OMB and eventually the White House backed away from the proposal, and a compromise was never reached.

Although the federalism initiative was central to the president's 1982 budget and its outlines were largely crafted by OMB, it was never mentioned in David Stockman's memoirs of his five years at the agency. His book skips from the events of 1981 directly to those of 1983. The bold federalism plan also left surprisingly little trace in subsequent Reagan budgets or legislative proposals. When presidential assistant Richard Williamson departed from the White House in 1983 soon after the plan's demise, even most of the personnel closely associated with it were gone. Thus in substance as well as literary treatment, the president's bold initiative may be considered the "missing chapter" in Reagan federalism.

The Origins of the "Sorting Out" Plan

Although it represented a bold departure from existing policy, President Reagan's plan for sorting out governmental functions rested on a substantial intellectual base that had been developed in a series of explicit policy proposals over the previous thirteen years. To this foundation the president added his own long-held views about the proper assignment of functions in a federal system.

Public finance economists had long maintained that governmental functions could be divided among the different levels of government in a rational and systematic fashion.[2] For example, services and activities that command the resources of the nation as a whole, such as management of the economy, belong clearly to the federal government. So, too, do those policies that concern public goods involving substantial geographic "externalities," where policy effects spill over across state and local boundaries and affect citizens in other jurisdictions. Economists usually assign responsibility for income redistribution to the national level as well. They reason that public and private resources vary widely among the states, and an optimum level of redistribution is unlikely to be achieved at the state level owing to interstate tax competition and recipient migration.

By the same token, economic logic suggests that other governmental activities should be placed at the state and local levels. Most other policies are "allocational" and reflect differences in local tastes for publicly provided goods. Because local decisions on these policies do not affect citizens in other jurisdictions, they can be safely left to local discretion. At the same time, overall public welfare can be maximized because mobile citizens can shop for a community offering a preferred mix of public goods and taxation. Most developmental policies are also deemed to be properly subnational. Because they are designed to promote economic growth within a single state or local community, these jurisdictions have the incentive to pursue such policies independently, to the extent supported by local residents.[3]

One of the first serious contemporary proposals for implementing such concepts and rationally sorting out governmental responsibilities was developed by the U.S. Advisory Commission on Intergovernmental Relations. In 1969 the ACIR recommended that the national government assume full financial responsibility for public assistance programs—including medicaid and general assistance. It also recommended that state governments assume greater fiscal responsibility for local education.[4] The commission reaffirmed these positions eight years later and then expanded upon them in 1981.[5] At that time it recommended a comprehensive realignment of state and federal roles in the governmental system, including federal assumption of financial responsibility for income maintenance programs and the reduction or termination of federal involvement in areas of primary concern to state and local governments.

Similar recommendations were advanced by other organizations as well. Following ACIR's lead, the National Governors' Conference endorsed greater federal funding of welfare programs in 1969. In 1980 and 1981 the governors again endorsed full federal assumption of financial responsibility for income maintenance programs, but they called upon states to assume more responsibility for public safety, education, and transportation programs.[6] Also in 1980 President Carter's Commission on a National Agenda for the Eighties called for "clarification of the present confused division of labor in the federal system" and endorsed reforms along the lines advocated by the ACIR and state officials.[7] The following year the governors stepped up their reform efforts, joining with the National Conference of State Legislatures on a shared sorting out strategy. Following the 1981 budget and tax reductions, they called upon the administration to negotiate on a more rational division of governmental resources and responsibilities.

All these recommendations sprang from similar policy concerns. Initially, the focus was on the advantages of nationalizing income maintenance programs. The ACIR, most state officials, and many policy analysts believed such a move would narrow interstate disparities in benefit levels; reduce incentives for migration *to* high-benefit states and *away* from high-tax states; take into account the high correlation between poverty rates and national economic conditions; and reduce income disparities through the progressive federal income tax.[8] These arguments were reinforced in the late 1970s by the growing dysfunctions in the intergovernmental system. By 1980 many intergovernmental analysts had come to believe that the performance of the federal aid system was earning poor marks on all counts: efficiency, effectiveness, equity, and accountability. Thus the ACIR concluded that the intergovernmental system had grown "more pervasive, more intrusive, more unmanageable, more ineffective, more costly, and above all, more unaccountable." [9] The president later used these very words in his State of the Union address.

The idea of sorting out governmental functions also held a strong personal appeal for the president. However, he did not take this to mean simply rationalizing intergovernmental responsibilities. To Reagan sorting out meant returning to the states most existing federal domestic responsibilities—including welfare. Indeed, in his race against Gerald Ford for the 1976 Republican presidential nomination, he announced that the central feature of his domestic policy platform was an ambitious plan to return to the states $90 billion in federal programs.

Complaining that the "crushing weight of central government" had turned states and localities into "little more than administrative districts, subdivisions of Big Brother government in Washington," Reagan urged a "systematic transfer of authority and resources to the states." [10] Specifically, he argued that eliminating federal programs for "welfare, education, housing, food stamps, Medicaid, community and regional development, and revenue sharing, to name a few," would reduce federal spending by up to $90 billion annually. These savings, he urged, could be put to use in balancing the federal budget, retiring a portion of the national debt, and reducing personal income taxes by 23 percent—thus creating "tax room" for states and localities to pick up the terminated programs if they so desired.

The Reagan plan was aggressively attacked by Gerald Ford, who called the mass transfer of programs "unrealistic" and "irresponsible." [11] Because the plan appeared to require state tax increases, it was particularly controversial in tax-conscious New Hampshire, where it contributed to Reagan's unexpected defeat in the presidential primary there. Although Reagan subsequently backed off from the plan, veteran Reagan watcher Lou Cannon concluded that it "prevented Reagan from winning the Republican presidential nomination of 1976." [12] Owing in part to this inauspicious attempt, the concept was not taken up again until 1982, and then it was done almost haphazardly.

Developing the Federalism Initiative

As is often the case with major presidential initiatives designed around a State of the Union address—including Nixon's 1971 New Federalism proposals—the Reagan administration's proposal emerged late amidst White House confusion. Other options, ranging from a major new tax and budget package to a welfare block grant, had been explored by various administration officials in the second half of 1981, but with few tangible results. By one account the administration's planning process was in "disarray" by mid-November.[13] By that point decisionmaking options were becoming more limited because of worsening economic conditions, gloomy budgetary projections, and growing restlessness among state and local officials, some of whom were calling for a "domestic summit" with the president in December to head off a feared second round of massive domestic budget cuts. Since the president did not endorse even the general thrust of his federalism proposal until December 23, 1981, it is not surprising that the plan was viewed as a "last minute addition" to the president's agenda for 1982.[14]

Work on a federalism component for Reagan's 1982 domestic agenda had actually begun in the summer of 1981. In August word was leaked to the press that the administration was seriously considering a block grant for AFDC and possibly medicaid, and thus following through on a long-term goal of the president and his White House aide Robert Carleson. In his outgoing address as president of the National Governors' Association (NGA), Governor George Busbee of Georgia announced that, after dealing with the White House, he was "convinced a major effort will be made . . . to transfer responsibility for income maintenance programs to the states," and he declared the NGA "should serve notice that we will oppose block grants for AFDC or Medicaid."[15] Two days later Carleson confirmed that a "general decision" had been made to convert AFDC to a block grant but that "the timing and form depend a lot on the budgetary situation and they are very important."[16] Within a month, however, strong opposition from the states and from Congress combined with budgetary obstacles to waylay the block grant proposal. "It's not dead," observed one White House official, "but it's very, very much on the back burner."[17]

Work on a broader federalism reform proposal continued behind the scenes under the auspices of White House intergovernmental assistant Richard Williamson and policy adviser Martin Anderson. However, this work "went slowly and failed to produce a plan that seemed both viable and sufficiently ambitious."[18] The focus of attention for new initiatives shifted largely to budgetary and tax policy. Stockman reports that he and other top administration aides met with the president throughout much of early November 1981 in an attempt to hammer out a comprehensive plan of further budget cuts and excise tax increases that would reduce the deficit by approximately $100 billion by fiscal 1984.[19] However, the president, backed by Treasury Secretary Donald Regan, rejected any effort to raise taxes. Any remaining hope that the 1982 agenda could be fashioned around an aggressive program of deficit reduction disappeared on December 4 when the president "stubbornly" rejected a final appeal by White House Chief of Staff James Baker and OMB director David Stockman to include a tax increase in the new budget. Following this incident, the president lamented to close aide Michael Deaver, "I just don't think that some of my people believe in my program the way I do." [20]

Thus by the end of the year the president's 1982 agenda was, in Richard Darman's words, in serious "disarray." Faced with serious economic and budgetary issues in the year ahead but with little hope of being able to meet them head-on, Darman argued in a memo to the Communications Strategy Group that the administration needed a coherent and positive initiative to "advance right through the '82 elections." [21] Seeking an agenda that combined "low cost/high payoff initiatives" with "the lift of a driving dream," Darman recommended a program of small stimulative federal grants that would promote "states as laboratories" of policy innovations. As Laurence Barrett explains, "that idea died because one of [New] Federalism's real goals was to reduce government activity . . . at all levels, not to stimulate it." [22] But the proposal helped to refocus White House attention on federalism as a positive issue around which different factions in the administration could coalesce and one that they could adapt to their own ends. Williamson recalls that "Darman became persuaded that if we were going to make the cuts we were agreeing to in the budget meetings, we had to have some major budget initiative so it didn't look like the president was just scorching the earth." [23]

Over the next month, a small group of White House staff worked on developing a comprehensive federalism proposal, restructuring program responsibilities among the federal government and the states. Given Reagan's long-held interest in the concept, they knew that the president would not only endorse this agenda but enthusiastically support it. For the president, Meese, and Carleson it provided an opportunity for going beyond a welfare block grant and returning responsibility for AFDC entirely to the states. Although Carleson resisted the political price of such a turnback—namely, nationalizing certain other programs—he had little opportunity to say so. "After his bull shit at the Governors' Conference [announcing a welfare block grant], he was called out to California and told he could no longer make public statements," said Williamson. "Carleson first read about [the federalism initiative] in the papers, though some of his ideas were included." [24] For his part, Williamson believed from dealing with the governors that they might accept the welfare trade as part of a balanced swap. The governors had already publicly proposed a fiscally neutral exchange of program responsibilities and a return of federal tax sources to the states, and Governors Bruce Babbitt (Democrat of Arizona) and Lamar Alexander (Republican of Tennessee) had already made a similar proposal to Williamson in private.

Stockman was quick to see the potential fiscal dividends of such a plan in his campaign to reduce the deficit. Like block grants, a structural reform concept attractive to the states could be used as a vehicle for budget cuts that they would otherwise resist. At the same time the president might buy tax increases tied to a desirable goal like an excise tax trust fund to be returned to the states. Finally a bold federalism initiative would meet James Baker and Michael Deaver's requirement that the administration's political momentum be maintained and "jazz up an otherwise grim State of the Union Message." "It's important," said one, "that we have something to say besides budget cuts, budget cuts, and more budget cuts."[25]

With OMB resources at his disposal, Stockman assumed major responsibility for translating the concept of a federalism initiative into a workable proposal. With the help of the Treasury Department and White House staff, OMB worked in almost total secrecy on the plan, and there were surprisingly few leaks to the press about it. Cabinet members were excluded, and even within OMB only a handful of career staff participated in designing the plan.[26]

From the input of this small group Stockman and Williamson distilled a sweeping plan with two main components. First, they proposed a $20 billion program "swap" in which the federal government would return to the states full responsibility for funding AFDC and food stamps in exchange for federal assumption of state contributions to medicaid. Second, the plan included a temporary $28 billion trust fund or "super revenue sharing" program to replace approximately forty-three federal aid programs for education, health, social services, community develpment, and transportation (see tables 9-1 and 9-2). Initially each state was to have the choice of retaining specific programs in categorical form or accepting unrestricted monies from the trust fund in their place. After four years, however, both the trust fund and the federal taxes supporting it were to begin phasing out, leaving states the option of replacing federal taxes with their own and continuing the terminated programs or allowing both to cease altogether.

As expected the president approved the general thrust of this plan when it was first presented to him on December 22 and 23, 1981.[27] At that time Stockman had convinced other principal administration aides—James Baker, Edwin Meese, and Donald Regan—that the trust

TABLE 9-1. Original Design of Reagan's 1982 Federalism Initiative for Fiscal Year 1984
Billions of dollars

Federal responsibilities	Cost	State responsibilities	Cost
	Swap component		
Assume state share of medicaid	19.1	Assume federal costs of AFDC and food stamps	16.5
	Turnback component		
Establish federalism trust fund Windfall profit tax on oil	16.7	. . .	. . .
Excise taxes from alcohol, tobacco, gasoline, and telephones	11.3	Assume responsibility for 43 federal programs returned to states	30.2
TOTAL	47.1	TOTAL	46.7

SOURCE: Executive Office of the President, "The President's Federalism Initiative: A Basic Framework," press release, January 26, 1982, pp. 3, 10.

fund portion of the plan could be financed by doubling federal excise taxes for gasoline, alcohol, telephones, and tobacco. By raising these taxes immediately but not "returning" them to the states for four years, the administration could obtain the additional revenues Stockman sought in a way that appeared integral to the plan's success. When Reagan endorsed this plan in December, including the tax increase, OMB proceeded to develop and refine the programmatic and fiscal details.

One month later, however, just days before the State of the Union address was to be delivered, the proposed tax increase brought on yet another crisis. When a more detailed version of the plan was presented to Reagan for final approval on January 20, 1982, White House conservatives expressed reservations about raising any form of taxes through the plan. The president reduced or eliminated some of the proposed excise tax increases, but agreed to replace them with other increases on luxury goods and corporations.[28] When word of this decision leaked the following day, the increases were bitterly attacked by the Chamber of Commerce and key House conservatives like Congressmen Jack Kemp and Trent Lott. The next day Reagan reversed his decision to include any tax increase, telling close aides that "I haven't been able to sleep because of this. I just can't do it. I just let you think I agreed with you so you'd leave me alone."[29] Thus only five days before presenting his plan to Congress and the country, the president eliminated over $16 billion in revenues

TABLE 9-2. Programs Slated for Turnback to States under
Reagan's Federalism Initiative
Billions of dollars

Programs by category	Estimated 1984 expenditure
Education and training	3.3
Vocational rehabilitation	
Vocational and adult education	
State education block grants	
CETA	
Work incentive and training	
Low-income energy assistance block grant	1.3
Social, health, and nutrition services	8.0
Child nutrition, child welfare	
Adoption assistance	
Foster care, runaway youth,	
Child abuse, legal services,	
Social services block grant	
Community services block grant	
Preventive health block grant	
Primary care block grant	
Maternal and child health block grant	
Alcohol, drug abuse, and mental health block grant	
Black lung clinics, family planning	
Migrant health centers,	
Women, infants, and children nutrition program	
Transportation	6.4
Airport grants	
All noninterstate highways	
Interstate transfer	
Appalachian highways	
Urban mass transit grants	
Community development and facilities	6.4
Water and sewer grants and loans	
Community facilities loans	
Community development block grant	
Urban development action grants	
Wastewater treatment grants	
General revenue sharing	4.8
Estimated total for 43 programs	30.2

SOURCES: Executive Office of the President, "The President's Federalism Initiative: Basic Framework," press release, January 26, 1982, p. 8; and "Fact Sheet: Federalism Initiative," press release, January 27, 1982.

from it and forced OMB to scramble to make the plan add up. In the end this was done by placing $16.7 billion in corporate energy taxes—the temporary windfall profits tax—into the trust fund to make up the difference.

With this version in hand the president went before Congress and the country proposing to comprehensively restructure the intergovernmental system in "a single bold stroke." He condemned the existing "maze of interlocking jurisdictions and levels of government" and the "jungle of grants-in-aid" and promised to "make government again accountable to the people, to make our system of federalism work again." Acknowledging that his complex proposal was still incomplete, however, he declared that "its full details will . . . [be] worked out only after close consultation with congressional, State, and local officials." [30]

Political Reactions to the Federalism Initiative

If the administration expected to dominate the 1982 agenda with its bold proposal, it was soon disappointed. The reactions of both the press and public officials to the president's speech varied greatly. Many governors and state legislators approved of the idea of sorting out governmental functions and spent much of the year negotiating with the administration on a mutually acceptable proposal. Reactions from other quarters were generally less favorable. Many local officials expressed concern about the reduction in federal aid and the severity of federal ties called for by the plan. Members of Congress and affected interest groups objected to turning back the specific programs covered by the trust fund. Virtually all those concerned raised questions about reducing the federal role in welfare. Looming ominously in the background were the lengthening shadows of a recession and ballooning budget deficits. As the federalism plan became bogged down in secret and protracted negotiations with the governors, these economic conditions swept it from public attention and eventually dominated the election year agenda.

Responses from the States

Most state officials—Republicans and Democrats alike—approved of the overall intent of the president's plan but questioned its specific provisions. Governor Richard Snelling of Vermont, then chairman of the National Governors' Association, said the president "deserves enormous praise for putting the subject on the table," and Governor Bruce Babbitt of Arizona called the proposal "elegant and imaginative." [31] At the same time, both governors raised some serious questions about appropriate federal-state roles. Governor Hugh Carey of New York was less positive, calling the proposal "hastily conceived and poorly designed." [32]

Much of the controversy surrounding the president's initiative had to do with its welfare provisions. As already mentioned, giving states full responsibility for aid to families with dependent children was a long-standing goal of the president and several of his advisers. As he declared in his 1975 federalism speech, "If there is one area of social policy that should be at the most local level of government possible, it is welfare. It should not be nationalized—it should be localized." [33] Seven years later, in his 1982 State of the Union address, he reiterated this position, arguing that full state responsibility for AFDC and food stamps "will make welfare less costly and more responsive to genuine need, because it'll be designed and administered closer to the grassroots and the people it serves." [34] In supporting this claim, the administration pointed to welfare reforms implemented in California in the early 1970s as an example of what could be accomplished by the states. This experience led Robert Carleson, who had been director of the California Department of Social Welfare under Reagan, to comment, "With federal regulations eliminated, the states would be able to provide relief to the taxpayer and, at the same time, would increase benefits to those who are truly in need." [35]

Knowing that the president was firmly committed to reducing the federal role in welfare, administration officials argued that the federalism initiative made a major concession to the states by offering to assume the full costs of medicaid. This move would benefit states, they said, because medicaid costs were rising much faster than AFDC expenses. Moreover, because medicaid served large numbers of elderly patients, the move would also benefit program users by consolidating federal responsibility for programs aiding senior citizens. [36]

State officials strongly supported federalizing medicaid financing, but they objected to picking up the full costs of AFDC and food stamps. As Governor William Winter of Mississippi declared, "True federalism in this enlightened time must recognize that . . . we cannot split ourselves up into 50 states, contending regions, rich and poor, skilled and unskilled, white and black." [37] State officials argued that some form of national public assistance program had been advanced by every recent president of either party, including Nixon, Ford, and Carter. Finally, they questioned the rationale for dividing responsibilities for welfare and medical assistance to the poor. According to Wisconsin State Representative Tom Loftus, this would mean that "you would be an American when you are poor and sick, but a Texan when you're just poor." [38] States were especially concerned about termination of the federal food stamp program because it significantly narrowed disparities in welfare benefits among the states.

Against the backdrop of worsening economic conditions and resulting state budget shortfalls, the fiscal aspects of New Federalism became an added concern for state officials. In fiscal 1982 and 1983, state year-end budget balances averaged only 2.1 percent of state general fund expenditures compared with an average of 7.7 percent for the previous four years.[39] Certain states had even more difficult problems. Despite balanced budget requirements in virtually all states, nine ran budget deficits in one or both of those fiscal years, whereas only four states had done so during the entire period from 1978 to 1981. Many others found that to avoid such problems they had to raise taxes and reduce government services in the midst of the recession. Thus even some potential supporters feared that the president's plan had come "at the worst possible time." "We may all be so anemic by the end of the year that the states won't be able to function as partners," said Governor Scott Matheson of Utah. California legislator John Vasconcellos added, "We are in the red, on the verge of bankruptcy, and there's nothing we could pick up."[40]

Although the president described his initiative as a financially equal swap, many state officials feared that it would cost them extra money in the long run, and growing fiscal problems left little room in which to accommodate additional expenses. Ironically the administration had worked hard to make sure that its proposal minimized financial winners and losers among states. In some states, the costs of assuming the federal contribution for food stamps and AFDC would outweigh the savings from the federal assumption of medicaid. Other states, however, would gain from this exchange. These disparities were to be evened out by contributions from the federalism trust fund. States gaining from the welfare-medicaid swap would have their trust fund allocations reduced by that amount. Loser states would receive additional allotments from the fund to compensate. The administration claimed that eventually most states would gain slightly from the federalism initiative because medicaid costs were projected to rise faster than welfare costs.

Despite assurances that there would be no "winners or losers," many state officials remained leery of the fiscal consequences of the plan. To begin with, the administration assumed that AFDC and food stamps should and would be scaled back by Congress as proposed in its fiscal 1983 budget, before the states assumed those programs. Without these reductions, the Congressional Budget Office estimated that states as a whole would initially pay $1.5 billion more to assume welfare programs than they would save from the federalization of medicaid.[41] States also raised questions about the medicaid portion of the swap. Medicaid benefits varied enormously from state to state. A totally national program would presumably have more uniform benefit levels—higher than those in low-benefit states but lower than in high-benefit states. Some states in the latter category would have felt compelled to continue supplementing federal medicaid payments, thereby reducing any fiscal dividend for them because of the swap.

State officials were also concerned about the trust fund portion of the initiative. Using CBO baseline figures, Governor Carey maintained that the cost of the programs to be included in the trust fund would total $37 billion by fiscal 1984, not $30 billion as calculated by OMB.[42] The administration's figure was based on the assumption that the substantial budget cuts recommended for those programs would be adopted before the federalism plan was implemented. Moreover, both the trust fund and the federal excise taxes supporting it were to begin phasing out in fiscal 1988. Although states would have the option of assuming these tax sources themselves, the distribution of "tax room" would not be uniform throughout the country. Per capita revenues from cigarette excise taxes would be much smaller in Utah than in neighboring Nevada, for example, and only a fraction of states would have access to revenues from the windfall profits tax on oil. For these reasons the Governors' Association and the National Conference of State Legislatures (NCSL) argued for a financing system that would provide general federal revenues and some degree of equalization among states with differing needs and taxing capacities.

Other Reactions

State officials were hardly alone in questioning the details of the federalism initiative. Although public opinion polls showed considerable support for the New Federalism concept,[43] the plan itself encountered a barrage of criticism from members of Congress, local governments, affected interest groups, and the press. Like state officials, other groups objected most to the "swap" elements of the plan.

The plan had barely been announced in the State of the Union address before it was criticized in newspaper editorials. The *New York Times* likened it to "turning back the clock." Although the paper acknowledged the need for some sorting out of functions, it questioned: "Where is the logic in Federalizing one poverty program but turning back others? Do poor people get equally sick in different places but unequally hungry?"

Columnist Joseph Kraft called it "a smoke screen obscuring the sinking economy" and concluded that the only rationale for its inconsistencies was the president's "well-known animus toward social programs." [44]

To no one's surprise, many advocates of social programs felt threatened by the plan. The AFL-CIO charged that the New Federalism initiative would "cripple facilities and services on which all Americans depend and jeopardize the health and welfare of millions of the poor." [45] "The worst thing you can do," according to Andrew Mott of the Coalition on Block Grants and Human Needs, is to decentralize "responsibilities you know will be neglected because of lack of political will." [46]

Local officials were also wary. Many local governments were deeply suspicious of turning major program responsibilities over to the states and thereby severing their direct funding link to Washington. "The pass-through [issue] is the number 1 problem," said one urban representative of the president's plan.[47] A state legislator from New York observed that county governments in his state were "clearly afraid of being bankrupted in the name of the new federalism." [48]

All of these opposing views were fully represented in Congress, where one observer reported that the "long knives are out," ready to kill the initiative if introduced.[49] Governor James Thompson of Illinois, who had been invited to the Capitol to hear the president's State of the Union address, reported afterward that "at least two members of my congressional delegation turned around [during the speech] and said to me: 'Over our dead bodies.' "[50]

Even some strong congressional supporters of the sorting out concept were troubled by specific features of the president's plan. Senator David F. Durenberger of Minnesota, chairman of the Senate Intergovernmental Relations Subcommittee, openly questioned the programmatic logic of the swap initiative, even after the administration agreed in April to retain food stamps at the federal level: "I am not happy with the outcome. . . . What sense does it make to have Social Security, Medicare, Medicaid, Food Stamps, and housing assistance all at the federal level and leave dependent children with the states?" [51] Besides supporting full federal responsibility for basic income maintenance programs, the senator proposed allocating trust fund revenues on an equalizing basis. "It is time for the federal government to recognize a responsibility for equalizing the fiscal capacity of places," he observed.[52]

But the most serious political obstacle confronting the federalism initiative may well have been the worsening economic conditions. Many members of Congress simply dismissed the proposal as a diversion from more pressing economic problems, or they perceived it as a backdoor means of cutting social programs. Within days of the president's address, a congressional newsletter reported that the federalism plan was "sinking into a sea of economic problems of greater importance." A few months later the *New York Times* reported that the proposal had "become entangled in the [budget] stalemate." "Budgetary problems are taking more and more of Congress' attention, and elections are coming on," agreed one administration adviser.[53] With the fate of the economy affecting almost every federal, state, and local official and distorting the spending estimates on which the federalism plan was based, the timing of the plan became a hurdle in itself.

Negotiations on Federalism

Initial negative reactions and hostile economic conditions notwithstanding, the administration proceeded to negotiate with state and local officials on a specific legislative proposal. From the beginning, the president had indicated that the details of his federalism initiative were tentative and that representatives of state and local governments would be consulted about changes. The strong disagreements sparked by the federalism initiative made it all the more necessary to present a united front before Congress and drove the administration and state officials to seek a joint legislative proposal on federalism reform. Although they were ultimately unsuccessful, the nature and intensity of these negotiations and the scope of the issues at stake were unprecedented in the history of intergovernmental relations.

In late February, before these formal negotiations started up, the governors attempted to redefine their position on sorting out while making some concessions to the president's position. They dropped their bid for the immediate nationalization of all income maintenance programs, suggesting instead that consideration of changes in AFDC and food stamps be deferred. They announced support for the creation of a federalism trust fund and their willingness to negotiate over the president's list of programs to be included in it. They also emphasized their support for the federal assumption of medicaid costs. But the governors differed with the president on several points. They wanted to remove AFDC and food stamps from the plan and have a much smaller trust fund component. In addition they urged that trust fund allocations be made on the basis of state fiscal capacity.[54]

In order to deal with the substantial number of points still at issue, the White House, states, and localities established negotiating teams to resolve differences and produce a compromise proposal. The administration team was headed up by top White House aides Richard Williamson, James Baker, Edwin Meese, and David Stockman, backed up by an eleven-member technical working group drawn from the major domestic departments, OMB, and the Executive Office of the President. Both the governors and state legislators appointed bipartisan negotiating teams with six members each, while local governments were represented by a single group of eleven mayors, county officials, and one township representative.[55]

During late February and March, following the governors' winter conference, high administration officials, often including the president, held eight major meetings with these state and local officials in an effort to resolve their remaining differences. These high-level meetings were supplemented by "dozens" of additional meetings between Williamson and other members of the White House Intergovernmental Affairs Office and the staffs of state and local public interest groups in Washington.[56] Both sides hoped that these meetings would produce a specific legislative proposal by early April 1982.

When the target date passed without an agreement being announced, there was a flurry of reports indicating that the negotiations were in danger of collapsing.[57] The administration and the states remained at loggerheads over the assignment of welfare responsibilities, while local governments opposed any plan lacking safeguards for direct federal-local grants returned to the states. Fear of outright failure prompted renewed bargaining, however, and all sides began making major concessions. On April 14 the administration agreed to retain food stamps as a federal responsibility but continued to insist that AFDC be turned over to the states. The governors accepted this basic formulation, with some further revisions, and in early May, Governor Snelling announced that "a compromise has been engineered, but not approved formally by either side."[58] According to Snelling, the governors believed that the administration had agreed to support a minimum national floor for state AFDC benefits, to establish a "safety net supplemental" fund for states suffering temporary economic crisis or chronically low fiscal capacity, and to refrain from making automatic downward readjustments in food stamp benefits when state welfare payments increased. In return, the states were prepared to accept full responsibility for AFDC and to include additional categorical programs in the federalism trust fund to pay for the above concessions. The major remaining issue to be decided, said Snelling, was the level of federal medicaid benefits under a nationally financed program. Many states were concerned that added costs would be imposed on states with high benefits if national benefits were set too low.

Despite this hint of success, succeeding weeks brought conflicting trends of further progress in some areas and deadlock and backpedaling in others. In late May the National League of Cities gave new momentum to the initiative by reversing its earlier position and endorsing state assumption of AFDC under conditions similar to those that the governors were proposing. Again there were rumors that a joint legislative proposal would shortly be sent to Capitol Hill.[59] An agreement seemed close, but it was never joined. The treatment of medicaid proved more difficult to resolve than expected, and with the prolonged negotiations shaky agreements began to unravel. For example, Williamson reports that by May OMB was engaged in "active resistance" to the medicaid provisions of the initiative: "The critics' charge that this was Stockman's Trojan Horse for cuts had a ring of truth to it. There was a constant effort by OMB at that time to stall. They didn't want to do it. It had become an albatross. I had to get the president to personally call Stockman twice. Dave would say, 'yes Mr. President' and then not do anything."[60] Other opposition resurfaced in the White House from Robert Carleson, who reemphasized his basic philosophical objections to any increase in federal responsibilities.[61] By the time that senior White House officials met with state negotiators on June 23, the administration had backed off from earlier concessions or clarified its opposition to several of the items that the governors had previously thought were settled, including the "unhitching" of AFDC and food stamps.[62]

When the state and local governments saw that the administration was only becoming more disorganized and inflexible, their enthusiasm dwindled. Hoping that an endorsement of the new initiative would give it renewed momentum, the president described the outlines of a modified administration proposal in a July speech to the National Association of Counties. Although the plan contained several key concessions to state and local interests, support for it was so weak that a resolution endorsing the general concept had to be withdrawn for fear that it would fail.[63] Similarly a report from the state legislative negotiating team to the NCSL executive committee in late July was distinctly cool, noting that "at no time have we either endorsed or approved the initiative as a whole" and that, should a proposal be sent to Congress at the conclusion of negotiations, "normal policy procedures will be followed by NCSL to determine the formal NCSL response."[64]

The strongest rejection came from the governors, at their annual summer conference. Disappointed that no final agreement had yet been reached and frustrated because the fast approaching midterm congressional elections precluded sending a proposal to Congress in 1982, the governors more or less gave up. They formally resolved to focus their future efforts on developing an independent federalism initiative rather than attempting to settle remaining differences with the White House. As Governor Snelling, the outgoing chairman of the NGA, reported to the organization's executive committee: "it no longer seems prudent to pin our hopes for a new federalism on the outcome of any negotiations with the White House." [65] He laid much of the blame for the failure to reach a final agreement on remaining differences over how to implement the federal takeover of medicaid.

In a formal sense, this gubernatorial revolt was short-lived. Following a "White House power play" two days after the position was adopted, the governors reversed themselves and agreed to continue discussions with the administration while developing their own proposal.[66] Nevertheless, by this stage the handwriting for a joint proposal on federalism was clearly on the wall.

After a final meeting with the president in late September, which sought to identify areas of agreement for the future, the two sides went their separate ways. In a letter to the president on November 19, 1982, the Executive Committee of the NGA outlined the governors' operating position on federalism reform. As they had done ten months earlier, the governors proposed deferring action on AFDC and food stamps. They suggested, instead, that attention focus first on medicaid and that the federal government assume full responsibility for the program in exchange for state assumption of up to eighteen existing federal grant programs. In order to ease passage of this proposal, the governors suggested that medicaid be divided into three components: acute care for the federally aided elderly poor, acute care for AFDC-eligible recipients, and long-term care. The federal government could choose to assume any or all of the components, turning back a specific group of federal programs with each component. A revolving fund for balancing winning and losing states was also proposed, but no method for dealing with long-term fiscal disparities was indicated.[67]

For its part, the administration concentrated on developing a fiscal 1984 budget proposal with four megablock grants, which together would have consolidated thirty-four major federal aid programs totaling $21 billion. Specifically, it proposed consolidating twenty-two education, social service, and health service programs into a massive block grant to states; two programs (revenue sharing and CDBG) into a large local block grant; six highway and transit grants into a transportation block grant; and four programs into a rural housing block grant. None was ever seriously considered by Congress or the states. By December, before the budget was even announced, the governors had rejected the concept of megablocks and declared that the president's federalism initiative was "dead."[68] The new agenda for the states, declared NGA chairman Scott Matheson, would be "budget, budget, budget."[69]

Both sides conceded that the negotiations had failed primarily because of the income maintenance issue. Even after it was agreed that food stamps would remain a federal responsibility, three welfare-related issues stalled the bargaining: the fiscal relationship between federal food stamp and state AFDC benefits; the provision of a "safety net fund" to ensure adequate AFDC benefits in poor states; and the treatment of "medically needy" people under medicaid, whose high medical bills would bring their incomes close to welfare levels.[70] As Richard Williamson later observed, "Each side . . . misjudged its ability to find common ground on income maintenance. Neither side appreciated how firmly committed the other was to its position."[71]

Administration disunity was another complicating factor. From the beginning some members of the White House staff, like Robert Carleson, were philosophically uncomfortable with the idea of federalizing any income maintenance responsibilities, and as the pressure to do so mounted during negotiations with the states they began to object to the way that the plan was evolving. Others, like Stockman and to some extent Baker, originally bought into the federalism initiative because it had the potential to reduce the federal deficit. They lost enthusiasm and even became obstructionist when the president removed all tax increases from the federalism trust fund and the negotiating process made clear that state and local governments would not allow other parts of the plan to become a vehicle for hidden budget cuts.

These concerns about the fiscal effects of the federalism initiative also contributed to the plan's demise. For both the federal government and the states, uncertainty about the long-term fiscal implications of the proposal was heightened by the immediate budgetary shortfalls stemming from the 1982 recession. In the end, these basic considerations left both sides unwilling to forge a compromise.

Conclusion

The failure of the federalism initiative—when considered in the context of Reagan's other policy decisions—illustrates the limits of the president's own commitment to federalism reform, even though he had placed it at the top of his policy agenda and seemed willing to negotiate on certain points in order to gain acceptance of his proposal. Throughout his presidency, Reagan demonstrated an underlying ambivalence toward his goal of strengthening federalism—even as he defined it. Although his many policy objectives were frequently compatible, whenever Reagan had to choose between the goals of his federalism agenda and competing budgetary and philosophical objectives, he consistently fell short of his federalism aims.

Nowhere was this clearer than in his reaction to budgetary issues associated with the sorting out plan. Initially the president proposed a plan that appeared to be revenue neutral, although it presupposed substantial reductions in federal aid to state and local governments. The president's "obsession over short-term budget considerations" immediately put state and local governments on guard and initially slowed the negotiations.[72] Moreover, it fortified suspicions that the president had agreed to federalize medicaid merely to gain the control he needed to reduce the program. Although the administration's concern over the federal deficit was certainly understandable, it was never an obstacle to other costly initiatives in defense, supply-side tax policy, or even urban enterprise zones. There is little doubt that Reagan could have achieved an agreement with the governors on a common federalism plan if he had been willing to devote additional federal resources to their concerns, just as Nixon had done before him. Although some important concessions were made, notably on food stamps, the president could not bring himself to sacrifice either his budgetary or his welfare goals for the sake of federalism reform: "As much as the president wanted to strike a deal with the governors, and walk in step with them to Capitol Hill, the philosophical gap proved to be too wide. To move state and local officials, the president needed a bigger carrot than in good faith he felt he could offer."[73]

In the final analysis, this ambivalence was the real "missing chapter" in the story of the 1982 initiative. It contributed greatly to the president's failure, although other serious obstacles would have been waiting in the Congress even if the intergovernmental negotiations had been successful. Moreover, the story was repeated in other areas of the president's agenda, especially regulation.

10

Regulatory Federalism under Reagan

DEREGULATION was an important plank in Ronald Reagan's New Federalism program. According to an early report by the president's Task Force on Regulatory Relief, "Regulatory relief is a major part of the President's efforts to revitalize federalism. As we ... return many of the responsibilities currently held by the Federal Government to state and local government, reduction in bureaucratic red tape and the unduly burdensome regulations is a key component."[1] This high-level attention to the regulatory dimensions of federal-state-local relations was unprecedented, and it signaled a major change in the nature of intergovernmental relations.

Until the 1970s intergovernmental relations meant, for all practical purposes, a complex administrative network for the disbursement of federal grants-in-aid to state and local governments. In the context of federalism, the purpose of federal regulations was to ensure that federal aid was properly planned, budgeted, and accounted for. Whenever the question of federal aid reform arose, it was usually because of the need to ameliorate the negative side effects imposed by grant restrictions and to deal with the consequences of multiple and competing funding sources.

As discussed in chapter 5, this one-dimensional framework changed dramatically in the 1960s and 1970s with the proliferation of new and more intrusive types of intergovernmental regulations, along with the rapid growth of tax subsidies for state and local governments. Some of the new regulatory devices continued to be attached to grants, which were handy vehicles for new forms of federal influence, whereas others were independent of federal aid. However, they all differed from traditional administrative requirements in their techniques and intensity of influence (see table 10-1), and they differed from the more traditional forms of economic and social regulation in their uniquely intergovern-

TABLE 10-1. Typology of Intergovernmental Regulatory Programs

Program type	Description	Major policy areas
Direct orders	Mandates state or local actions under the threat of criminal or civil penalties	Public employment, environmental protection
Cross-cutting requirements	Applies to all or many federal assistance programs to ensure broad coverage	Nondiscrimination, environmental protection, public employment, grants management
Crossover sanctions	Threatens to terminate aid provided under one or more specified programs unless the requirements of another program are satisfied	Highway safety and beautification, environmental protection, health planning, handicapped education
Partial preemptions	Establishes federal standards, but delegates administration to states if they adopt standards equivalent to national minimum requirements	Environmental protection, natural resources, occupational safety and health, meat and poultry inspection

SOURCE: Advisory Commission on Intergovernmental Regulations, *Regulatory Federalism: Policy, Process, Impact, and Reform*, A-95 (GPO, 1984), p. 8.

mental focus. The new devices regulate state and local governments directly or enlist them as agents to regulate the private sector.

The politics of these new regulatory instruments often differed as well. Many originated in congressional committees outside the traditional funding sources for state and local governments, or they were the products of new, symbolically driven forms of intergovernmental politics.[2] Collectively, the new regulatory federalism implied a very different model of intergovernmental interaction, and it added considerable complexity to intergovernmental relations.

These differences were not fully recognized until the early 1980s, although a few questions had begun to arise in the late 1970s. The first to note the intrusiveness of federal regulations were state and local government officials; even liberal Democratic mayors found themselves publicly denouncing the pernicious effects of the federal government's "mandate millstone."[3] Anecdotes about seemingly absurd cases of federal regulatory burdens were frequently exposed by the news media.

Although both regulatory burdens and regulatory reform became matters of heightened public interest and presidential activity starting with the Nixon administration, such reform efforts focused on the economic impact of regulation, particularly on private business and individuals. Before the 1980s few people recognized that state and local governments were often the explicit targets of federal regulations or that they were key participants in their implementation. Furthermore few saw the implications of this situation for both federalism and regulatory reform. This appeared to change with the election of Ronald Reagan, who made regulatory reform a central plank of both his economic and New Federalism programs.

This chapter explores three dimensions of Reagan's regulatory policy. The discussion first turns to the administration's explicit program for intergovernmental deregulation. It developed two strategies for this purpose, administrative and legislative. Substantive changes in pending regulations were studied and in some cases implemented administratively through the president's Task Force on Regulatory Relief. In addition some administration-proposed changes in intergovernmental legislation also had regulatory implications, particularly those covering the 1981 block grants.

Second, it is important to recognize the intergovernmental implications of the administration's broader deregulatory program. Although the administration had established a centralized regulatory review process in the Office of Management and Budget, sensitivity to the unique character of intergovernmental regulation appeared to be missing within OMB. The consequences of this omission far outweighed those of the president's modest agenda for intergovernmental regulatory reform.

The third point to consider is the nature of regulatory expansion under Ronald Reagan. Such expansion had two sources: Congress and the administration. During the president's first term, his administration attempted to persuade Congress to roll back existing regulatory statutes. Yet it succeeded only in preventing the enactment of major new additions to the existing pool of regulatory statutes during this period. That stalemate began to break down after 1985, when the Ninety-ninth Congress adopted important and costly new requirements affecting state and local governments, mainly in the field of environmental protection.

More telling has been the administration's own willingness to support expansions of federal regulatory authority over state and local governments when such authority was consistent with its broader economic and ideological aims. Federal regulatory expansion has been advocated or endorsed by the administration in areas such as trucking, state workfare, national product liability insurance, coastal zone management, local taxicab and affirmative action policies, and the nationwide minimum drinking age.

Thus in regulation as elsewhere the Reagan administration has left a complex but often disappointing legacy when measured against its original objectives. Although the administration recognized the intergovernmental impact of federal regulation early on, its long-term commitment to this goal proved surprisingly superficial and its deregulatory accomplishments did not extend beyond its first two years in office. Furthermore, an intergovernmental perspective was never incorporated into the principal regulatory review process established in the Executive Office of the President. On the contrary, this administration, like previous administrations, found it difficult to resist the temptation to establish new intergovernmental regulations when such requirements provided a convenient method of achieving the president's social and economic goals.

Substantive Deregulation and the New Federalism

When Ronald Reagan entered office in 1981, deregulation was a major concern. In order to defuse what David Stockman identified as a "ticking regulatory time bomb,"[4] the administration launched a series of far-reaching regulatory initiatives: it immediately froze hundreds of pending rules and regulations; created a presidential task force to review these regulations and recommend cost-cutting modifications; formed a strict regulatory review and clearance process within OMB, on a par with the agency's existing budget and legislative clearance functions; and systematically placed staunch, antiregulation conservatives in key positions within federal regulatory agencies.

These initiatives were designed to curb the growth in federal regulatory activities that occurred in the 1960s and 1970s. Most available indicators of regulatory activity—especially the number of federal regulatory agencies, federal spending on regulatory activities, and pages of rules published in the Federal Register—showed rapid increases in the 1970s (see table 10-2). Although less precise, estimates of the economic costs imposed on business and society by such regulations also showed rapid growth. As a result, federal regulatory expansion had become a national concern by the time Reagan was elected. Although new requirements continued to be added throughout the 1970s, Nixon, Ford, and Carter launched increasingly sophisticated efforts to improve the analysis of all regulatory costs imposed on society and to coordinate the regulatory initiatives of federal agencies.

This expansion of federal regulatory activity was paralleled by the development and expansion of regulations aimed specifically at state and local governments (see chapter 5). The ACIR identified new and more intrusive types of federal regulation that were designed to regulate state and local governments directly or enlist them as federal agents to regulate private individuals or businesses. Significantly, these new types supplemented the more traditional federal grant requirements, which also be-

TABLE 10-2. Growth in Federal Regulation, 1970–78

Expenditures in millions of current dollars

Year	Number of major regulatory agencies	Federal expenditures on economic regulations	Federal expenditures on "social" regulations	Pages in federal register
1970	20	166	1,449	20,036
1971	23	196	1,882	25,447
1972	23	246	2,247	28,924
1973	26	298	2,773	35,592
1974	27	304	3,860	45,422
1975	28	427	4,251	60,221
1976	28	489	5,028	57,072
1977	28	544	6,383	65,603
1978	28	608	7,576	77,497
Addendum Percent increase, 1970–78	25	266	425	267

SOURCE: "Regulatory Policy: The First Three Waves of Rules," document prepared for the Regulatory Policy Seminar, Federal Executive Seminar Center, Kings Point, N.Y., March 1986.

came more numerous, more detailed, and more specific during this period.[5]

According to David Beam, the number of intergovernmental regulations increased from ten to thirty-six in the 1970s.[6] The cumulative costs of just six of these regulations in seven jurisdictions accounted for almost 20 percent of all federal aid received by these communities.[7] Thus it is not surprising that more than two-thirds of the nation's mayors in 1981 considered it "urgent" or "important" for the federal government to reduce regulatory burdens in at least seven program areas, from environmental protection to access for the handicapped. A majority of mayors agreed that in "most or all cases," standards mandated by the federal government were "unrealistic" or overly specific.[8]

By the early 1980s careful observers of intergovernmental regulation had concluded that "during the 1960s and 1970s, state and local governments for the first time were brought under extensive federal regulatory controls," and that "these . . . have altered the terms of a long-standing intergovernmental partnership."[9] As one scholar pointed out,

The federal government . . . has vastly extended its control over the states and cities through a large—but largely unnoticed—system of public sector regulation. Federal regulations have grown to define not only who should benefit from government programs but how states and cities must run those programs: what accounting standards they must follow, what environmental effects they must measure, who can be hired under the programs, and how much they must be paid.[10]

Early Intergovernmental Responses

The Reagan administration tried to tackle this problem in its earliest deregulation initiatives. Thus deregulation was one of four items (the other three were federal budget reductions, tax cuts, and block grants) given top priority in Reagan's original New Federalism program.[11] Murray Weidenbaum, chairman of the president's Council of Economic Advisers, wrote in 1981,

> Our policy of regulatory reform is designed to strengthen the federal system. The elimination of ineffective regulations and insistence on sound justification for all regulatory actions will substantially reduce burdens on state and local budgets. . . . Regulatory reform will also . . . increase the discretion—and the responsibility—of states and local governments.[12]

The administration adopted two broad strategies to provide substantive relief from specific regulatory burdens. One consisted of administrative actions that could be taken unilaterally by the executive branch. It was supplemented by proposals for changes in regulatory statutes. Both had important implications for intergovernmental relations.

Administrative Responses

The president took the first administrative action in this direction on his second day in office, when he established the Presidential Task Force on Regulatory Relief. To give the group visibility and influence within the executive branch, Reagan appointed Vice-President George Bush as chairman and called upon high-ranking officials from the White House and the cabinet to serve as members. The group was asked to study the possible impact on the economy of federal rules that were still in the proposal stage, to review existing rules identified as particularly burdensome, and to propose changes in regulatory statutes where appropriate. More generally the task force was to "provid[e] leadership" in regulatory matters and to serve as a "court of appeals" in agency disputes with OMB in the newly created regulatory review process.[13]

The group's first act was to obtain a presidential order freezing pending federal regulations for at least sixty days and block the issuance of new regulations for a similar time period. The order was designed to prevent the implementation of the so-called midnight regulations promulgated by the Carter administration on the eve of Reagan's inauguration. This gave the new administration time to subject the regulations to a cost-benefit analysis. Although many of the affected rules were not intergovernmental, as a result of this process the administration withdrew the proposed federal rules for expanding bilingual education, prohibiting discrimination in the dress code of local schools, and requiring that states and public utilities provide certain fixed services in the performance of residential energy audits.[14]

Then in March 1981 the Bush task force invited state and local governments and the private sector to identify problems created by existing federal regulations. The major governmental associations surveyed their members and presented the task forces with nearly 500 recommendations for changes in federal rules and regulations.[15] The task force subsequently selected 111 rules for intensive review and modification, of which one-quarter were intergovernmental in character. Significant actions providing regulatory relief to state and local governments included revisions in the so-called Davis-Bacon regulations, which were designed to give local governments more flexibility in the calculation of "prevailing wages" paid in federally supported construction projects; changes in the regulations governing public transportation of the handicapped to give local authorities greater freedom to provide less costly means of access; and reductions in the reporting and accounting requirements in the national school lunch program. The task force estimated that these and the remaining twenty-four regulatory actions it undertook would reduce the regulatory compliance burden on state and local governments by 11.8 million work hours a year. These actions were also said to save approximately $2 billion dollars a year in recurring costs and $4 to $6 billion in one-time capital costs.[16]

Other administrative actions with substantial intergovernmental implications occurred in the "partial preemption" programs, which are now common in the areas of environmental regulation, public health, and occupational safety. Under such programs the federal government legally preempts the right to regulate an area that has traditionally been a state responsibility and to establish minimum federal standards therein. However, states may remain active by assuming the responsibility for enforcing federal standards and by supplementing them, if they wish, with stricter state requirements. Typically, some states choose to participate as intergovernmental agents of the federal government, whereas others prefer to let the federal government administer the program directly with its own administrative apparatus.

During Reagan's first term, the federal government's formal delegation of regulatory authority to states increased rapidly in several partial preemption programs, and federal oversight of state performance was relaxed. For example, the Reagan administration was responsible for 78 percent of the federal approvals for the first phase of state hazardous waste programs and for more than half of the state surface mining programs receiving final or conditional approval by the federal government.[17] This led some analysts to conclude that state and local governments were "the big winners" under deregulation.[18] "State and local governments quietly captured some of the most important and enduring victories of the president's regulatory relief campaign," argued the author of one major study.[19] In the Clean Air Act, for example, the administration implemented new policies that gave states more power to make minor changes in their state implementation plans without detailed federal oversight and review.

Despite the bold claims about winning big, many of these program delegations appeared to be a normal part of program life cycles and had little to do with the administration in office. Similar bursts of delegation had occurred under other administrations at similar stages in program operations as states acquired the experience and resources needed to handle regulatory programs themselves. Indeed, Fix acknowledges that the approvals in the Resource Conservation and Recovery Act "represented a continuation of policies set in motion under the Carter administration."[20] Moreover, in areas like surface mining and occupational safety and health, cutbacks in personnel and inspections in federally operated programs were so severe under Reagan that the delegation of greater authority to state-run programs may have produced more regulatory activity in some states.[21]

Legislative Responses

Although administrative deregulation was favored because it could be implemented quickly and unilaterally, the Reagan administration discovered early on that there were limits to what it could accomplish through administrative means. The Clean Air Act is a case in point. This statute is hundreds of pages long and, like many other intergovernmental regulatory statutes, is highly detailed in many key areas. As a result the Reagan administration originally planned to supplement its strategy of administrative deregulation with proposals for altering the legislative basis of regulatory programs. With the exception of its 1981 block grants, however, the administration proved unable to develop specific legislative proposals or encountered stiff resistance from Congress and affected interest groups.

These failures were highlighted by the administration's ill-fated attempts to rewrite the nation's environmental statutes. This was initially a high priority of the new administration, and the prospects for success seemed bolstered by strong support from the business and labor communities and by the fact that the Clean Air Act was to expire in 1982. Despite considerable efforts the administration was unable to develop a specific legislative proposal for congressional consideration. Instead it submitted to Congress a list of eleven general principles to be considered in revising clean air laws. The administration's credibility with respect to environmental issues was further undermined by scandals at the Environmental Protection Agency and by highly publicized gaffes by Interior Secretary James Watt. Since Congress itself was deeply divided on the question of relaxing environmental regulations, the administration's disorganization merely ensured that the legislative stalemate on the issue would continue throughout Reagan's first term.[22]

In regulation, as in many other areas, the major exception to this pattern of legislative failure was a product of the 1981 Reconciliation Act and the creation of nine new block grants. Although these grants did not affect the newer forms of intergovernmental regulation, they gave the administration an opportunity to condense and simplify the traditional grant requirements attached to the seventy-seven programs consolidated into the block grants—and the administration took full advantage of it. In education, for example, the merger of thirty-three separate programs into a single block grant allowed the administration to replace 667 pages of regulations in governing the old programs with a single, 20-page set of requirements affecting the new block grant.[23] Reductions in other block grants were equally dramatic. The regulations covering the implementation of the new health care block grants filled just six pages in each case and did little more than restate the limited conditions placed on the use of these funds in the statutes themselves. Overall, OMB estimated that the 1981 block grants reduced the paperwork imposed on state and local governments by 5.9 million work hours, or 91 percent.[24] The administration estimated that the seven block grants under the jurisdiction of the Department of Health and Human Services alone saved the states $52 million in paperwork costs.

Deregulation through Procedural Reforms

The Reagan administration also introduced reforms designed to alter the content of federal regulations by changing the processes that produce them. The new procedures and institutions established in the Executive Office of the President to oversee the rule-making process quickly became the focus of Reagan's deregulation effort.

The most important procedural reform, Executive Order 12291, was instituted in February 1981. This order required that, where laws permit, agencies must identify and adopt the most cost-effective methods of regulation when considering new regulatory actions; they must select alternatives in which the social benefits outweigh the social costs; and they must submit proposed regulations to OMB for review and comment before they are issued or published in the Federal Register. This last development constituted a major expansion of presidential authority over executive branch decisionmaking, on a par with OMB's budget review and legislative clearance functions. OMB created a new unit with a sizable staff of economists and lawyers—the Office of Information and Regulatory Affairs (OIRA)—to accommodate its new oversight responsibilities. To ensure that OMB's regulatory analysts could have input into the design of new regulations at a sufficiently early stage, the administration supplemented the review process by Executive Order 12492, requiring that agencies publish a calendar of the rules that they expected to propose during the coming year and that they act only on the regulations so identified.

The new OMB review process quickly became a highly controversial part of the Reagan deregulation effort. OMB statistics show that 13 percent of all regulations submitted to OMB for review in 1981 were revised and that by 1986 this proportion had risen to almost 32 percent.[25] According to OMB, many of the changes—approximately one-third—were needed to correct minor grammatical problems or to clarify sentences here and there. Others—such as those affecting cotton dust standards of the Occupational Safety and Health Administration (OSHA)—were substantial. In addition, OMB delayed some rules for long periods of time, and never even completed its review of others.[26] Partly as a result, the number of proposed rules has declined by 2,000 since 1980 and the number of final rules issued has declined by 3,000 over the same period. This means that the number of pages published in the Federal Register each year during this time span fell by 46 percent—or over 39,000 pages.[27]

The number of rules issued and pages published in the Federal Register are at best imprecise indicators of changes in regulatory policymaking. Conceivably, fewer but broader rules could have greater scope and impact. Nonetheless, most observers believe that the OMB review function has altered the regulatory process in fundamental ways. Indeed, some charge that OMB reviews now provide a secret channel through which industry can exert influence on federal regulation.[28] Agency officials have also begun to anticipate OMB's reactions when developing new regulatory proposals and thus try to soften proposed rules before submitting them to OIRA. As one official of the Environmental Protection Agency (EPA) has admitted, "Staff people start to say 'we shouldn't do this rule because we'll never get it through OMB.' It happens on a regular basis."[29] As a result, many scholars and members of Congress believe that the new procedures are responsible for a large and possibly unprecedented expansion of presidential authority over the regulatory process, which some consider unconstitutional and thus are seeking to change through the courts or legislation.

Inasmuch as the OMB review process plays an important role in the administration's regulatory relief program and deregulation is a central element of the administration's New Federalism, it is noteworthy that intergovernmental issues have by and large been overlooked within the OMB process. One comprehensive study of the Reagan administration's regulatory relief effort concluded that OMB review has been of marginal benefit to state and local governments.[30] Some cynics have suggested that the OMB process has been designed primarily to protect the administration's constituencies in the business community and that issues of federalism are at best incidental and often in conflict with such concerns. As one intergovernmental lobbyist observed, "When our problems are business's problems, then we get action. By the same token, when we are business's problem, we feel the heat."[31]

This tendency to give considerable attention to private sector concerns in the regulatory process, as explained in more detail later in this chapter, has been reinforced by certain aspects of the OMB's professional culture. The OMB's Office of Information and Regulatory Affairs is staffed largely by economists, whose professional training leads them to treat regulation in terms of economic efficiency and to focus their energies on traditional economic regulation. They are often unaware of and uninterested in the unique institutional issues connected with regulations that are applied to state and local governments or for which they act as agents or coregulators. Thus, when one OMB staffer was asked to identify which intergovernmental rules his superiors were most interested in, his response was: "They don't know what intergovernmental regulation is."[32]

Deregulation and Intergovernmental Management

Structural and procedural changes within OMB have also drawn attention away from the intergovernmental dimensions of much federal regulation. Organizational units and institutional processes within OMB that dealt with intergovernmental coordination and management in the past have been reorganized or abolished under Reagan, so that the agency now has little institutional capacity for handling issues in these areas. The Nixon administration had established virtually all of these structures and procedures to improve intergovernmental management. By eliminating and downgrading them, Reagan signaled a thoroughly different orientation toward federalism and intergovernmental relations.

The Reagan administration wasted little time in getting the reorientation under way. The system of standardized Federal Regional Councils established in 1969 to coordinate and simplify the diverse regional operations of different federal departments and agencies was first pared down and then abolished in 1983. The Intergovernmental Affairs division in OMB was also abolished in 1983, after its personnel and functions had been allowed to dwindle for two years. The division's remaining responsibilities—streamlining administrative operations in the field, overseeing auditing and financial management practices in federal grants, and monitoring implementation of the formal intergovernmental consultation process—were divided among three disparate units remaining within OMB. According to one analysis of OMB's diminishing role in intergovernmental management, "The traditional activities of OMB in intergovernmental management have been overshadowed, if not superseded, by . . . a new and very different intergovernmental agenda. Vestiges of the old OMB intergovernmental management functions and structure are still in place, but it is not clear that they are significant any more." [33]

The relationship between deregulation and OMB's changing intergovernmental role can be seen in the transformation of the "A-95" process of intergovernmental consultation. This process was established in 1969 to implement provisions of the Demonstration Cities Act of 1966 and the Intergovernmental Cooperation Act of 1968. The latter law was passed in response to state and local complaints about the proliferation of Great Society grant-in-aid programs. States and localities maintained that the federal government was establishing new programs in their jurisdictions unbeknownst to elected officials, and in many cases was giving them to different local agencies or nonprofit organizations for competing or overlapping purposes. To remedy this situation and improve coordination, the budget office issued OMB Management Circular A-95, which required that state, regional, and local governments be notified and allowed to comment on applications for federal aid within their jurisdictions, and that governors be allowed to review state plans required under federal programs. A system of regional and statewide "clearinghouses" was established throughout the country, and federal agencies were instructed to comply with the notification and review procedures.

After a time serious questions arose concerning the usefulness of the procedure and some state and local governments proposed that its operations be modified. Yet almost all intergovernmental observers were surprised when the Reagan administration proposed to abolish the process as part of its regulatory relief program. The administration claimed that the consultation process, created to assist state and local governments, now constituted a major regulatory burden imposed by the federal government. It was replaced with a vague new process that left virtually all procedural and implementation issues up to the discretion of the individual states. Few outside the administration judged the new process to be an improvement over the past one.[34]

Interestingly, administration officials have proudly termed the A-95 revision "the most sweeping change made in federal government philosophy and procedures in regulating the intergovernmental system."[35] Yet the process touted as the best of Reagan's New Federalism has been responsible for the elimination of the very organizational structures and personnel in the Executive Office of the President that can contribute an intergovernmental perspective to federal policymaking. Moreover, as a purely administrative change, it leaves untouched existing statutes that require regional coordination in federal programs. The result here as elsewhere has been confusion as to the differences between the new administrative procedures and established law. Indeed, the A-95 changes epitomize the Reagan administration's disdain for the administrative methods of intergovernmental reform favored by the Nixon administration.

Regulatory Expansion

Despite the presidential rhetoric indicating that regulatory relief was to be one of the main pillars of the New Federalism, the new regulatory review process and organizational changes within OMB hinted that intergovernmental concerns would have lower priority than the administration had intimated. This point is well illustrated by the regulatory expansion that took place in several areas during Reagan's first six years in office.

In some areas—especially environmental regulation—the expansion was clearly initiated by Congress. After several years of stalemate between the White House and Capitol Hill, the Clean Water and Safe Drinking Water acts were reauthorized by the Ninety-ninth Congress. These renewals imposed substantial new regulatory burdens on state and local governments. For example, municipalities are now required to monitor "nonpoint" pollution from thousands of storm sewers and to implement costly testing for seventy-seven additional chemicals in municipal water supplies.[36] Similarly, local school districts are required first to identify asbestos hazards and then to remove them from local schools at an estimated cost of hundreds of millions of dollars.[37]

Apart from indicating the bipartisan revival of support for new environmental regulations in Congress, these congressional initiatives say little that is new about the politics of regulatory expansion. They simply show that scientific advances have made it possible to identify new environmental hazards and that Congress is willing to translate political concerns about such hazards into legislation that imposes high costs onto third parties that are required to deal with them. In contrast, the cases in which Reagan has supported the expansion or retention of federal regulatory authority over state and local governments have some interesting implications. The administration has consistently avoided devolution whenever this policy has conflicted with the competing administration goals of reducing regulatory burdens on the private sector or advancing its conservative social policy agenda.

The designers of the administration's deregulation program foresaw that this policy might conflict with the devolutionary goals of New Federalism. Murray Weidenbaum pointed out in 1981, "Shifting regulatory responsibility to states and localities is rarely welcomed by business, because of their concern over the diversity of regulatory requirements, restraints, and prohibitions that can result."[38] As Weidenbaum suggests, when it comes to regulation business generally prefers not only fewer requirements to more, but uniformity to diversity. Yet in recent years the states—like the federal government—have become increasingly active regulators in more and more policy areas, from consumer and environmental protection to occupational and product safety. Often such activity is built upon federal regulatory foundations, as in the case of environmental programs in which the states are required or strongly encouraged to enforce federal minimum regulatory standards but are permitted to supplement or exceed them. In other cases, states have chosen to develop their own regulatory activities. In either case, private industry has sought repeatedly to have the federal government restrict state regulatory activities beyond the minimum national standards or to preempt state regulatory authority in a given field entirely. According to one business spokesman, the "national interest cannot be subjected to the parochial interest of localities." [39]

Such concerns have not been ignored by the Reagan administration, which has sided again and again with business interests. In a recent study of proposed federal preemptions, the administration was found to have "supported moves to take regulatory powers from the states" in nine out of the twelve cases studied.[40] A similar finding was reported in an analysis of Reagan administration briefs to the Supreme Court:

> The Administration . . . doesn't hesitate to give states' rights a back seat. . . . In each instance [examined], the issue, broadly framed, concerned states' rights, and . . . the Administration argued that Federal regulation should prevail. . . . Cynics might suggest that . . . the Administration's preference for big business is so strong that it will override conflicting concerns for federalism.[41]

Several cases involving transportation, social policy, and product liability regulation also illustrate this point.

Product Liability

Reagan administration support for national product liability legislation has been described as a case in which "result oriented reformers [in the administration] won out over those who would have adhered to . . . the [federalist] principles of the framers." [42] Historically, manufacturers' liability for injuries resulting from defective products has been governed by state laws. In recent years, however, mounting concern has been voiced by business spokesmen about the difficulties resulting from differing and often increasingly stringent state laws in this area, and many have called for preemptive federal legislation to correct these problems.

Backed by the Product Liability Alliance—a coalition of more than 200 trade and business organizations—legislation to this effect was introduced in Congress in 1982 by Senator Robert Kasten (Republican of Wisconsin). The Kasten bill would supersede state product liability laws but, in order to avoid overloading already crowded federal court dockets, would retain state court jurisdiction to try liability cases and interpret federal law. Thus, in the words of one analyst, the bill "represent[s] a new approach to centralization that borders on state conscription."[43]

Confronted with a difficult choice between the concerns of manufacturing interests and its own federalism proclivities, the Reagan administration "agonized" for several months over whether to support national product liability legislation. The strongest support for national legislation came from Commerce Secretary Malcolm Baldridge and from regulatory reform advocates in the administration. As one supporter of preemption in the administration wrote, conflicting state liability laws have created "significant burdens on interstate commerce" and "tremendous uncertainty for manufacturers."[44] However, others in the administration, including Attorney General William French Smith and Labor Secretary Raymond Donovan, argued that such a position was hardly consistent with the president's recently announced federalism initiative. Moreover, opponents pointed to practical difficulties in the Kasten approach. For example, denying federal courts jurisdiction to resolve likely differences in statutory interpretations by fifty different state judicial systems was hardly the way to guarantee uniformity in the domain of product liability. Nevertheless, when the issue was put to the president for resolution, "Reagan overrode the objections . . . that any endorsement of federal legislation would run counter to the administration's 'federalism' drive" and agreed to support the preemptive Kasten bill.[45]

Federal Trucking and Drinking Age Standards

Two new and highly visible federal regulations affecting transportation were also enacted with the support and encouragement of the Reagan administration. Like several other pioneering intergovernmental regulations enacted in the 1960s and 1970s, both requirements threatened to reduce federal highway aid so as to force states to adopt uniform federal standards on truck size and a minimum drinking age.

The trucking industry had long hoped to preempt state restrictions on truck length, width, and weight and by this means to expand the use of highly efficient double trailer trucks. Although such trucks were permitted in most areas of the country by 1982, they were still prohibited by fourteen states and the District of Columbia because of concerns about their safety and their destructive effects on highways.[46] Against a backdrop of concerns about crumbling infrastructure and deteriorating highways, the Reagan administration launched an initiative to alter this situation in May 1982. To help fund additional highway renovation, Secretary of Transportation Drew Lewis proposed increasing the federal and local governments to court. Such a litigatory approach was not entirely without precedent as the administration had already used it when trying to enforce handicapped infants' rights. In addition, the Federal Trade Commission had campaigned to eliminate local government restrictions on the taxicab industry. Indeed, many of the affirmative action plans in question were originally imposed on municipalities by lawsuits undertaken by earlier administrations. Yet by the mid-1980s these policies were accepted by most of the cities involved and by their employees, who resented yet another wave of federal intervention.

This controversy stemmed from the U.S. Supreme Court's ruling in *Firefighters Local Union 1784* v. *Stotts*. In this 1984 decision, the Court ruled that contractually established seniority rights assumed precedence, in making layoffs, over the rights of black employees hired later through a court-ordered affirmative action plan. Since then lower courts have interpreted the Stotts ruling narrowly, in part because it was a statutory interpretation of the Civil Rights Act of 1964 and not a constitutional interpretation.

Rather than wait for further clarification and stronger constitutional footing before challenging locally supported plans, the Reagan Justice Department took Stotts to be a mandate against "quotas" and reverse discrimination.[53] It sought reversal of consent decrees in fifty-six localities and, meeting strong resistance from many of these, it took Indianapolis to court. To the Republican mayor of that city, and many less involved observers, such actions appeared inconsistent with the president's New Federalism. In the words of columnist Neal Peirce: "By initiating expensive legal action, Justice also makes something of a joke of the 'New Federalism' ideal of returning power to the grassroots."[54]

Conclusion

The Reagan administration came into office proclaiming that deregulation was a critical component in its comprehensive federalism reform strategy. Despite the bold beginnings, this promise has not been realized where state and local governments are concerned. Its explicit program of intergovernmental deregulation—implemented administratively through the President's Task Force on Regulatory Relief and legislatively through the 1981 block grant regulations—was forcefully pursued only in the first two years of the administration and has since largely fallen from sight. Within its ongoing regulatory relief apparatus and procedures, the administration's commitment to addressing intergovernmental regulatory issues has often been lukewarm and haphazard. It succeeded in tempering Congress's appetite for new regulations only temporarily, and the politics of budgetary stringency appears to be promoting greater congressional interest in regulation as a relative low-cost method for financing new program initiatives.

Most important, given its federalism and regulatory reform rhetoric, the Reagan administration has itself been a surprisingly important source of new intergovernmental regulatory initiatives. This underscores the degree to which Reagan's views on federalism serve to advance other, more deeply held values. In each case of regulatory expansion examined in this chapter, the administration has been confronted with difficult policy decisions. Forced to choose between policies supportive of its federalist objectives (devolution, enhanced state autonomy, and balanced intergovernmental relationships) and those supportive of other presidential priorities (such as easing regulatory burdens on the private sector and pursuing conservative social policy objectives), the administration decided to pursue a course that was openly or implicitly contrary to its stated intergovernmental goals.

To be sure, some of these decisions were reached reluctantly. Some may have been the product of bureaucratic momentum and political compromise more than calculated strategy. Also, certain cases have gone the other way: in 1983 the Department of Transportation declined to preempt local airport noise restrictions despite calls for uniformity from the airline industry; although it ultimately relented, the administration long resisted legislative efforts to preempt state pesticide regulations; and in 1986, the president supported western demands that the federal 55-mile speed limit on rural highways be raised. Nonetheless, in the truly difficult decisions the overall thrust of this administration's regulatory policy seemed to bear little resemblance to the president's rhetoric on intergovernmental reform.

In part this pattern of regulation is the natural expression of power and position. As former Nixon economic aide Herbert Stein has written: "Even conservative governments when in office do not want to limit their own powers." [55] Yet it also has deeper implications for our understanding of Reagan's view of federalism. For Reagan strengthening federalism is an instrument rather than a policy objective in itself. In this respect he resembles his more liberal predecessors—perhaps more closely than either would care to admit—by his willingness to sacrifice his federalism goals whenever they conflict with his other deeply held policy objectives.

11

Reagan Federalism and the Future of Reform

EDERALISM is under siege. That has been the underlying premise of the sweeping reform proposals examined in this book. Proponents of federalism as a system of representation, as a method of administration, and as a structure for policymaking have voiced repeated and even strident concerns in recent decades about the health and viability of the federal system. In one sense the New Federalism reforms of presidents Nixon and Reagan can be viewed as barometers of the perceived strength of these pressures on the system. At the same time, changing views about the long-term vitality and resilience of contemporary federalism may mean that we have seen the last of such grand reform schemes for the time being, at least in forms as dramatic as those pursued by these two Republican presidents.

Previous chapters have also demonstrated that the Nixon and Reagan reform agendas, although shaped by common concerns, were quite different in both their aims and their political outcomes. Those differences are important because they chart the shifting course of conservative ideology over the past two decades and reflect broader changes in the structure of American politics.

The New Federalism and Conservative Ideology

Richard Nixon was an "activist conservative" president who was fully at ease with the idea of an energetic government, and this orientation thoroughly colored his intergovernmental reform initiatives. Nixon's principal concern was how this governmental energy should be channeled and where the wellsprings of activism should reside.

Nixon's New Federalism agenda was a coherent strategy designed to address these questions. Nixon proposed a more rational sorting out of the functional responsibilities of the various governmental levels in order to make government "leaner, but in a sense . . . stronger."[1] This was a decentralizing approach, but it was not intended to be antigovernment per se. It was viewed as a "positive Republican alternative to running things out of Washington . . . something to be *for*."[2] Rather than simply "getting government off the backs of the people," Nixon believed that a properly designed decentralization program would make government more effective and creative. As he wrote in the margin of one memorandum: "Decentralization is not an excuse for inaction, but a key to action."[3] In the words of one former aide,

> The notion was to have the Federal Government do what it does best (levy taxes) and to have state and local governments do what they do best (administer local spending). That was intended to result in a kind of "national localism." . . . The Feds would say to the locals "do it your way," adding gently but firmly "but do it."[4]

This activist orientation was evident in specific features of the administration's reform proposals. Complex "capacity building" schedules were included in certain block grants, and additional funding for block grants and revenue sharing was provided to entice congressional support. The general revenue sharing formula rewarded the most active spenders at the state level by factoring in a measure of "tax effort." Uniform national benefits for welfare were proposed, and entitlement spending and intergovernmental regulations were expanded at unprecedented rates. Although some of these elements were concessions to congressional demands and were in keeping with the liberal temper of the times, there is no question that the activist thrust of Nixon's New Federalism was consistent with the president's general philosophy of government, which guided his decisions from foreign policy to executive branch reorganization.

In sharp contrast, Ronald Reagan has been far more skeptical about domestic governmental activism. Indeed the theme underlying his policies seems to be a "fundamental opposition to the modern welfare state" itself.[5] Reagan's discomfort with the welfare state extends even to the bedrock social insurance programs of the 1930s, although he has been understandably reluctant to challenge these programs directly. This discomfort emerges most clearly in some of his broad philosophical statements, such as those that appeared in his first economic report to the Congress:

*We should leave to private initiative all the functions that individuals can perform privately.

*We should use the level of government closest to the community involved for all the public functions it can handle. . . .

*Federal Government action should be reserved for those needed functions that only the national government can undertake.[6]

When asked subsequently by reporters which "domestic" functions he would assign to for the last category, Reagan could think of only one: national security![7] Even at the local level, his positive vision of private communal action leaves little room for government of any kind. Rather, he emphasizes volunteerism as "an essential part of our plan to give government back to the people."[8]

Reagan's New Federalism was an expression of this broader philosophy of government. Far from diffusing activism throughout all governmental jurisdictions, Reagan's federalism would constrain it at every level. Reagan openly rejected Nixon's managerial approach to federalism reform during his 1976 presidential campaign: "It isn't good enough to approach this tangle of confusion by saying we will try to make it more efficient or 'responsive.' . . . The problem must be attacked at its source. . . . We can and must *reverse* the flow of power to Washington; not simply slow it or paper over the problem."[9] The alternative he proposed was the radical "$90 billion plan" designed to eliminate practically all federal aid programs and to slash federal taxes by 23 percent. In this way Reagan hoped to redress what he saw as the major flaw in the existing intergovernmental aid system—the failure to "tie the spending and taxing functions together." Of course this very "flaw" lay at the heart of Nixon's New Federalism. In Reagan's view, however, this separation of functions was responsible for the government's uncontrolled growth and spending, which "blurs the difference between wasteful states and prudent ones, and . . . destroys incentives toward economy." Citizens in fiscally conservative states, he argued, are "called upon to pay in federal taxes and inflation for other states that don't curb their spending." In short, because the root of the problem was profligacy at all levels of government, an intergovernmental solution was needed. To "put an effective lid on spending," it was necessary to dismantle stimulative federal programs and return "tax room" to the states. "When tax increases are proposed in state assemblies and city councils," Reagan explained, "the average citizen is better able to resist and to make his influence felt." [10]

Although Reagan never returned to this specific plan once he took office and in fact toned down his subsequent proposals and rhetoric somewhat, his federalism reform initiatives continued to reflect this general hostility to governmental activism at all levels. The strategy outlined above was implemented in part through the administration's domestic spending program, which singled out federal grants for state and local government services for the deepest cuts among all the major budget categories. In contrast to Nixon, Reagan did not use block grants to harness the federal fisc to state and local priorities. Instead the president and his top assistants considered these grants "a step toward total withdrawal of the Federal Government from education, health and social services programs which . . . are properly the responsibility of state and local governments." [11] This withdrawal strategy was pursued even further in the ill-fated federalism initiative of 1982, which did propose "turning back" to states over $30 billion in federal aid programs, along with AFDC and food stamps. The administration opened yet another avenue of attack on the funding base of state and local governments in its proposals to eliminate the major indirect subsidies provided through the tax code.

In short, from program structure to budget to tax policy, the Reagan administration waged a comprehensive assault on the intergovernmental dimensions of public sector activism. Even the few exceptions to this pattern have been instructive. Reagan's proposal to nationalize medicaid funding in 1982 was clearly a political concession required to advance his long-held goals of denationalizing AFDC and turning back other domestic programs. Even at that, administration support for the concept withered once it became clear that the plan could not be used as a vehicle for further budget reductions. Moreover, in regulatory policy, from interstate trucking standards to product liability insurance, the administration consistently favored federal over state and local authority whenever the former has been more supportive of free markets or private sector interests. Indeed, federalist rhetoric notwithstanding, the administration even took local governments to court when they implemented objectionable policies regarding affirmative action or taxing cab licensing. It is this tension between intergovernmental deference, implied by the president's devolutionary rhetoric, and the logical imperatives that flow from the president's broader philosophy of government that gives rise to Reagan's unique brand of instrumental federalism.

Paradoxical Politics

The political responses to the reform initiatives of Nixon and Reagan and the political coalitions both administrations constructed to achieve their goals differed as much as their objectives. Paradoxically, the activist and nationally oriented Nixon was overwhelmed by the centrifugal parochialism and fragmentation of the 1970s. In contrast, Reagan, the antigovernment crusader, won crucial victories through his mastery of national politics.

Nixon proposed a coherent and internally consistent program of federalism reform. Nonetheless, Congress addressed the proposals in a segmented and individualized fashion, as can be seen in the treatment of Nixon's block grants. The political responses to these proposals were based principally on the attitudes and interests within each policy subsystem. The pattern of idiosyncratic politics was repeated across the entire range of Nixon's reform agenda. General revenue sharing, for example, failed to arouse the kind of congressional unanimity that greeted most of the president's block grant proposals within each policy area. Rather, GRS caused sharp divisions within Congress that cut across party lines. As Beer has shown, it generated its own unique coalitions, structured by the "categorical phalanx" on the one side and the pressures of "distributive localism" on the other.[12] The politics of the family assistance plan were different again, although cross-party cleavages were present here too. In the House, FAP attracted broad bipartisan support, largely in deference to the president and the influential chairman and ranking member of the Ways and Means Committee. In the Senate, however, FAP twice collapsed when conservatives and liberals joined forces to fight its provisions for precisely the opposite reasons.

The politics of Reagan's New Federalism evolved in two distinct phases, each characterized by a far higher degree of policy interdependence than was evident in the the 1970s. The first phase was marked by the president's budget and tax victories of 1981. In that single year, the fragmented subsystem politics that colored Nixon's reform efforts gave way to a highly visible, majoritarian style of presidential policy leadership as Reagan successfully constructed a partisan-conservative phalanx that pushed much of his fiscal policy through Congress more or less intact. The highly polarized and unified partisan coalitions in Congress proved critical in key votes on the president's program, and the overall levels of party voting in Congress remained high throughout the 1980s. This greater degree of political interdependence was reinforced by new budgetary procedures that served to integrate diverse spending and authorization issues on the president's terms. As a result, some analysts have argued that Reagan has attempted to govern "in a style more typical of parliamentary democracies . . . as the leader of an unchecked majority party." [13]

This pattern did not continue past 1981, for several reasons. With the control of Congress divided between the Democrats in the House and Republicans in the Senate, Reagan lacked the political resources needed to build majority coalitions on a strictly partisan basis, and the situation merely grew worse after the 1982 elections. Moreover, Congress had arguably made the "easiest" fiscal decisions in 1981, so that the president found it far more difficult to hold his coalition together when the highly controversial proposals of subsequent years came up for debate.

In addition, that coalition itself was unstable. Although the party-building activities of the Republicans in the late 1970s contributed to the president's victory, their new-found strength was short-lived, even in the Senate. To complicate matters, the president's first-year success in the House was due in part to the very atomization that characterized Congress in the late 1970s. As Steven Smith has argued, the policymaking implications of Congress's fragmentation into semiautonomous committees and subcommittees are quite different from those of extreme individualization, even though legislative decentralization is being promoted in both cases.[14] Depending on the degree of subcommittee proliferation and autonomy, the politics within this committee framework retains elements of the functional insulation and stability that characterized the earlier, oligarchical Congress. In contrast, as many observers from Aristotle to modern analysts of mass society have pointed out, a highly individualized system of government is volatile and subject to sudden and sharp swings between stalemate and stampede, depending upon a leader's capacity for symbolic manipulation. Ironically, it was this volatile and disconnected policy environment in the House, born of the extreme individualism of the 1970s, that contributed to Reagan's temporary victory in 1981.

Although Reagan's majoritarian style of leadership lost effectiveness after 1981, intergovernmental policymaking did not return to the fragmented patterns of the 1970s. Rather, by institutionalizing a "new politics of deficits," [15] the fiscal policies adopted in 1981 ushered in a new phase of rationalizing politics, as the domestic policy agenda became preoccupied with the fiscal, institutional, and policy consequences of the 1981 initiatives. Opportunities and incentives for new entrepreneurial initiatives were reduced and redirected as zero-sum budgeting created new patterns of policy interdependence. The numbers of new laws introduced and passed declined, and those proposed and adopted have been restructured by the new policymaking environment.

The Ironies of Reform

The New Federalism initiatives of Nixon and Reagan both left ironic legacies that changed the direction not only of the federal system but also of American politics and policy in general. Richard Nixon sought to simplify and streamline intergovernmental relations and to produce a more decentralized and rationalized federal system than the one he inherited. Yet he left behind a system of massive intergovernmental interdependence and institutionalized new and higher levels of federal fiscal and regulatory dominance. Ronald Reagan enjoyed more success in his efforts to refocus the policy agenda and accomplish desired changes in policy direction. Yet he, too, will leave behind a legacy of support for governmental activism nationwide.

In his efforts to reduce the size and activity of the welfare state, Reagan has accomplished more than most analysts thought likely when he entered office. Federal spending priorities, popular expectations, and the federal policymaking environment have all been substantially altered during the Reagan presidency. Since 1980 nondefense discretionary spending has declined by 29 percent as a proportion of GNP, and general federal revenues are down 13 percent. Entitlement growth as a percentage of GNP has been limited to just 5 percent during this period, and federal aid to state and local governments has been reduced by one-fourth. As a result, federal grants as a percentage of total federal outlays and as a percent of state and local outlays have declined in importance (see table 8-4).

In some respects, however, the welfare state is stronger today as a result. Just as the New Deal helped save capitalism from its own worst excesses, so Reagan's agenda has trimmed questionable programs and answered concerns about governability and uncontrolled governmental growth. As a result, the underpinnings of popular support for the welfare state are in some ways stronger today than when Ronald Reagan took office. Americans have always been ambivalent toward governmental activism. At one level, they hold the views of "ideological conservatives" who are suspicious of governmental authority in the abstract, while at another level they are "operational liberals" who pragmatically support a broad range of government programs to address social problems.[16] According to opinion polls, the first set of conservative attitudes gained ascendancy in the early 1980s, thereby generating the plausible if simplistic belief that Reagan had received a popular mandate for his domestic policies. By 1986, however, American public opinion had reverted to older patterns of broad support for governmental spending, and polls indicated that Americans no longer supported substantial budget cuts in virtually any area of domestic policy. Indeed, recent research on Americans' confidence in public and private institutions indicates that, thanks in large part to Ronald Reagan, confidence in the federal government has rebounded more strongly than for any other major institution in society.[17]

Thus, depending on uncertainties surrounding the economy and a viable deficit reduction process, Reagan has apparently squeezed much of what is likely to be extracted from the American welfare state, producing at best a stable and somewhat lower public sector share of the economy. Much of what remains is now firmly institutionalized.[18] Given politicians' relentless search for new and creative program initiatives to deal with contemporary problems, however, even this achievement may ultimately prove to be only a temporary interregnum in the long-term growth of American government.

The End of (New) Federalism?

Given the failure of two very different federalism reform plans, what is the future of New Federalism? Have we witnessed the last of such grand schemes, now that Ronald Reagan is preparing to leave office?

The answer, of course, will depend on a variety of factors, from the personality and objectives of the next president to unforeseen developments and events. Yet much also depends on the fate of the federal system itself. Two scenarios about the future of American federalism are commonly advanced today.

State Renaissance

The most widely accepted scenario suggests that there will be no need for dramatic reforms in the foreseeable future. The federal system is remarkably healthy, according to this interpretation, and all the obituaries of recent years were premature. Indeed, the real story concerning federalism since 1960 is that it has remained resilient and adaptable in the face of dramatic and repeated changes in federal policy. This resilience is evident in the burst of state and local policy innovation, in the declining dependence of states and localities on federal assistance, and in the new era of cooperative federalism that characterizes the administration of remaining federal aid programs.

Despite Reagan's intentions and policies to the contrary, the welfare state remains alive and well—not only in Washington but also subnationally. Indeed, state governmental activism has flourished during the 1980s as state after state has aggressively addressed issues of educational reform, economic development, and welfare dependency. For example, two education scholars recently noted that "the last two years have witnessed the greatest and most concentrated surge of educational reform in the nation's history. . . . The most surprising aspect of the 'tidal wave' of reform is that it came from state governments. . . . State governments responded with new legislation, policy initiatives, and funding." [19] The specific reforms themselves are too numerous to list, but they range from enhanced funding and curricular changes nationwide, to the wholesale reform of educational systems in Mississippi and Arkansas, to bold innovations in personnel and enrollment systems in Tennessee and Minnesota.

Apart from education, states like Massachusetts and New Jersey in the east and California in the West have taken the lead in work-related welfare reform, an approach that is now being considered in Washington. Midwestern states have far outstripped the federal government in the breadth of their policy responses to the 1980s agricultural depression, adopting dozens of programs to expand agricultural markets and to provide social and financial counseling and support services.[20] Health care, insurance reform, and higher education have been priorities for innovation in other states.

Nor is this burst of state activism considered to be a temporary response to Reagan administration policies. Looking over the broad range of state and local policy innovations in recent years, one seasoned observer of subnational governments has concluded that this "new sense of independence from the federal government . . . promises to be both more profound and more permanent than most people have recognized." [21]

To some extent, this state renaissance is an outgrowth of earlier federal policies that stimulated considerable state capacity building, both institutionally and politically.[22] At the same time, heavy reliance on federal funding threatened to create a degree of dependency and inertia among states over the long run. Coming on the heels of policies that established an infrastructure for state activism, both real and anticipated federal aid cuts under Reagan prompted greater state and local self-reliance, which in time supplemented the capacity for independent policy innovation with the desire to utilize it. This change in outlook was particularly evident in state responses to federal aid cuts during the Reagan era. After two decades of unprecedented federal intergovernmental intervention, most states moved aggressively to replace federal grant funding in areas of traditional state competence lost through block grants and other program reductions.[23] This state response in the face of adversity is an indication of the underlying resilience of the federal system.

There is no question that state and local governments are now less financially dependent on the federal government. In a process some have called "de facto New Federalism" federal aid has declined 22 percent since 1978 as a percentage of state and local revenues. During this same period intergovernmental aid has dropped 33 percent as a proportion of the entire federal budget and as a percentage of GNP.[24] Direct federal-local fiscal relations have been especially hard hit. With the elimination of general revenue sharing and the state-oriented structuring of the Reagan block grants, many localities that used to receive direct federal funding through Great Society programs and Nixon's New Federalism now receive no direct assistance from the federal government.

Despite real reductions in federal assistance, state and local government expenditures have actually increased during the 1980s. Higher tax collections, broadened tax bases, and additional user fees in these jurisdictions have more than made up for declines in federal funding. Nor are these trends toward greater state and local fiscal independence expected to be short lived, inasmuch as the existing constraints on the federal budget began before Reagan and show signs of continuing for many years. Given the vulnerability of federal aid compared with entitlements and other domestic priorities, even a Democratic president after 1988 may be unable to reverse these trends, particularly if the threat of a balanced budget amendment returns if conservatives lose the White House.

Changes have also taken place in the way that the remaining federal programs are implemented. Recent studies of federal program administration have emphasized "when federalism works" rather than the problems of complexity, duplication, and conflict.[25] Longitudinal analyses of federal initiatives have stressed that federal, state, and local governments are capable of resolving implementation problems and improving program performance over time.[26] These changes can be likened to the gradual refinement of New Deal programs, which by the 1950s led to an intergovernmental era often dubbed "cooperative federalism."

According to the logic of this rosy scenario, bold federalism reforms of the type proposed by Nixon and Reagan are a thing of the past. If ever they were appropriate, they are now clearly obsolete responses to intergovernmental problems that no longer exist. "No one expects a return to the days of overwhelming federal dominance," writes John Herbers.[27] Instead, we can look forward to a dynamic state and local sector flourishing in a new age of cooperative federalism.

Co-optive Federalism

A less cheerful scenario for the future of federalism would allow federalism reform back on the agenda. Although less fashionable today, this scenario draws attention to both new and lingering challenges to the long-term vitality of state and local governments which may sustain interest in federalism reform schemes of some kind. According to David Walker, "The systemic position of state and local governments, while operationally powerful, is weak constitutionally and politically. . . . Reagan federalism . . . has done little to . . . place the American states on a par with their counterparts in . . . other federal systems." [28] Although this situation may not pose an immediate threat to the health of the federal system, problems may result from the "tyranny of small decisions," as Laurence Tribe has put it: "No one expects Congress to obliterate the states, at least in one fell swoop. If there is any danger, it lies in the tyranny of small decisions—in the prospect that Congress will nibble away at state sovereignty, bit by bit, until someday essentially nothing is left but a gutted shell." [29]

Such a scenario rests, first, on the assumption that states and localities are legally vulnerable under contemporary judicial interpretations of the Constitution. Traditionally, the Supreme Court provided the ultimate definition of federal and state roles in the federal system, using such provisions as the Tenth Amendment and the commerce clause to carve out separate spheres of sovereignty for each level of government. Indeed, until the 1950s, most accepted definitions of federalism referred to just such a judicially policed system of "dual federalism." [30]

This system of constitutionally defined spheres of state autonomy began to erode during the twentieth century, particularly after the New Deal. By 1942 the Court proclaimed the Tenth Amendment to be no more than a "truism," and it established the legal framework for virtually unlimited federal intervention in state affairs through the spending power and commerce clause.[31] In 1976 the Supreme Court made a brief attempt to reinterpret the Tenth Amendment as a limitation on Congress's jurisdiction under the commerce clause, but the complex test established in *N.L.C.* v. *Usery* to protect "integral" and "traditional" state functions from federal intrusion proved unworkable. Within a decade the Court had thrown up its collective hands and overturned the *N.L.C.* decision, relying instead upon "the effectiveness of the federal political process in preserving the States' interests." Indeed, the Court majority stated emphatically that it would no longer adjudicate disputes pitting Congress's power to regulate interstate commerce against state sovereignty claims: "State sovereign interests . . . are more properly protected by procedural safeguards inherent in the structure of the federal system than by judicially created limitations on federal power." [32]

Ironically, the Court may have abandoned state and local governments to the political fray at the very time that their ability to defend their interests effectively in Washington had reached a low point. The relative weakness of decentralized party organizations; the rise of nationally oriented media, electoral resources, and interest groups; and observed behavior in Congress all raise questions about the Court's logic. "One wonders why," writes Martha Derthick, "if the states' interests are so well protected by the political branches, the issue [decided in *Garcia*] reached the Supreme Court at all." [33]

The basis for the Court's reasoning in the *Garcia* case goes back to arguments developed in the 1950s, when both legal scholars and political scientists began to theorize that the states and localities protect their interests in the federal system principally through structural and political means. Legal experts argued that the structural features of the constitutional system—such as the electoral college and equal state representation in the Senate—ensure that state interests are represented in Congress and the Executive Branch. [34] Political scientists often questioned the importance of such structural features, noting that the presidency (since the 1930s) and the Senate (since the 1960s) have most often been the source of federal activism and extensions of federal authority. [35] They pointed, instead, to the critical role played by the political parties, which "are responsible for both the existence and form of the considerable measure of decentralization that exists in the United States." [36]

Since the 1950s and 1960s, however, the electoral system in the United States has been transformed. The locus of innovation and leadership has shifted from local organizations, many of which are now practically moribund, to the formerly weak and episodic national parties. Although party modernization is taking place in many states and localities today, it is often the direct result of stimulation by the national party organizations. [37]

At the same time, political parties as a whole have lost the near monopoly they once enjoyed over most elements of the electoral system, including candidate nominations, electoral communications, campaign resources and financing, and voter mobilization. In most cases, these ac-

tivities have become dominated by competing nationally oriented institutions. State and local party leaders and activists no longer make independent judgments about presidential candidates at national party
conventions but rather ratify decisions made earlier by primary elector-
ates and caucuses. Independent campaign consultants resemble modern
political nomads marketing their expertise in congressional campaigns
from coast to coast. Many congressional candidates today are reluctant
or unable to raise campaign funds from their own constituents and thus
spend more and more time trying to raise funds from political action committees in Washington and money centers in California and
New York. Meanwhile candidates increasingly communicate with voters
through nonparty means, including independently styled and financed
direct-mail appeals and advertising in the more or less homogenized
mass media—particularly television. As a result, scholars suggest that
both the president and members of Congress have become far less dependent on state and local politicians for their political success. "The development of national issue-oriented followings by Presidential candidates
seeking nomination," writes Leon Epstein, "has largely replaced . . . state
and local party leaders, acting through the old confederative structure." [38] Similarly in the legislative branch, "representatives and senators,
once in office, feel little sense of obligation to their state and local parties,
and the parties lack significant influence on the behavior of legislators in
the halls of Congress." [39]

To be sure, state and local influence in Washington is not felt solely
through political parties and elections. Over the past three decades, state
and local governments have greatly increased the size and sophistication
of their lobbying presence in the nation's capital. Over the years, this
intergovernmental lobby has had its share of important victories, from
enacting general revenue sharing to funding medicaid. Yet the need to
develop such a representational presence, in part to compensate for the
political changes described above, may well be a sign of weakness rather
than strength. Given the explosion of interest groups in Washington since
1960, the state and local sector has, at best, only kept pace with its functional competitors. [40]

Thus it may be no accident that general revenue sharing and CETA
were virtually the only large programs that the Reagan administration
successfully eliminated, or that grants-in-aid have suffered a dispropor-
tionate share of budget cuts over the past eight years, or that grants to
governments were left relatively unprotected by Congress from across-
the-board cuts under the Gramm-Rudman process. Even the exceptions
to this pattern can be informative. Most, though not all, of the state and

local income tax deduction was preserved during the bitter battle over tax reform. Yet this victory was achieved only after great effort, on an issue supported by three-quarters of the American people, for which the principal beneficiaries are taxpayers in the higher income brackets, thanks to the lobbying campaign organized and funded by New York real estate interests and organized labor.

According to the pessimistic scenario, the very perception that intergovernmental interdependence has declined under contemporary federalism is fanciful. In many ways, the levels of government are more interdependent than ever. To be sure, Reagan's New Federalism sought to reduce the complexity of existing intergovernmental arrangements and to move the federal system back in the direction of neatly separated functions reminiscent of nineteenth century "dual federalism"—although on its own strongly decentralizing terms. And there is no question that federal aid has declined as a percentage of state and local revenues, and will probably continue to do so.

Yet the 1980s have also witnessed the institutionalization of new interdependencies in intergovernmental relations that have reduced the relative significance of federal aid flows. Until the 1970s intergovernmental relations meant essentially the expenditure and administration of federal grant funds. In the 1970s and 1980s this federal aid dimension was supplemented by a great many new forms of federal regulatory and tax policy. Despite—but also because of—tax and regulatory reform, both policy areas are now firmly entrenched on the intergovernmental agenda. This means that henceforth state and local governments will have to face a more complex environment in Washington. Rather than being solely concerned with what federal funding is available and how to obtain or retain it, they must now watch closely for new and intrusive federal regulations while they seek to protect their remaining benefits in the federal tax code. The chief lobbyist for the National Governors' Association recently lamented, "The intergovernmental agenda is getting so long it would take all my time just to keep up the list of issues. We can't begin to respond to them all." [41]

Such tax and regulatory issues are likely to remain of interest to federal policymakers precisely because of continuing fiscal constraints. As the policy platforms of the 1988 presidential candidates make clear, modern politicians—and the people who elect them—still believe that their role is to "do something" about the endless and changing list of problems confronting contemporary society. Unable to devote substantial public funds to the pursuit of new priorities, policymakers are apt to accelerate the pattern already established in recent years—by imposing new regulatory burdens on states and localities while competing with them over tax revenues. According to Martha Derthick,

> In particular, there is a danger that Congress, in striving to close the gap between its desire to define large goals and its unwillingness to provide the administrative means to achieve them, will try to conscript the states. That is, it will give orders to them as if they were administrative agents of the national government, while expecting state officials and electorates to bear whatever costs ensue.[42]

Such regulatory conscription, first developed in the 1970s, has been used with renewed frequency during Reagan's second term to control nonpoint water pollution in urban areas, to preserve groundwater, and to extend civil rights protections in the use of federal aid funds. Similarly, virtually every federal tax bill enacted by Congress since 1978 has contained provisions inhibiting state and local governments from generating revenue in some manner. The federal government has increased its competition with states for "tax room" by raising gasoline and excise taxes. It has relentlessly attempted—often successfully—to place restrictions on tax-exempt municipal bonds. And it has eliminated the federal income tax deductions for state excise, sales, and personal property taxes.

To be sure, the new complexity of the intergovernmental agenda affects all levels of government. Just as the federal government has involved itself in what were traditionally state and local responsibilities, so many national issues are becoming more and more localized.[43] In the words of a prominent rural sociologist, "World politics are now local politics."[44] He was speaking about the impact of third world debt financing and international trade on midwestern agriculture. But his subject could just as easily have been the proliferation of local "nuclear free zones," state and local antiapartheid policies, state-federal conflicts over the foreign military assignments of state national guardsmen, or increasingly aggressive state efforts both to attract foreign investment and to promote the marketing of state products and commodities around the world.

The proliferation of such issues in itself reflects changes in traditional ideas about the legitimate boundaries of federal, state, and local responsibilities. Of course, there are significant practical and constitutional constraints limiting the capacity of state and local governments to effect independent policies in these areas of national concern. The long-term problem for states and localities is that the reverse may not be true of the federal government. The federal government is and will remain dependent on subnational governments for the administration of most domestic policies. The terms of that dependence are the crux of the problem. Given the prevailing constitutional, political, and fiscal trends, states and localities risk experiencing the worst of all possible worlds. In the past they were legally protected from excessive federal incursions, and federal influence came mostly in the form of federal grants and subsidies. Now that their political and legal defenses are being eroded, even as federal budget constraints are multiplying, their future may be filled with federal mandates and preemption.

Even the new cooperative federalism described in recent implementation studies may prove to be more akin to "co-optive" federalism. Evidence from recent case studies suggests that a key factor helping to improve intergovernmental administration has been the co-optation of local decisionmaking processes by cadres of federally inspired interest groups and professionals, rather than bargaining between levels of government.[45] However harmonious such a process becomes, state and local resources directed toward federal priorities will not be available for alternative state and local priorities. And, after all, the fact that smaller, territorially organized constituencies have different kinds of policy priorities is one of the basic rationales for a federal system in the first place. Moreover, the resulting administrative pattern of vertically organized, functionally fragmented spheres of authority is akin to the very system of "picket-fence" federalism that frustrated generalist officials and gave rise to Nixon's New Federalism to begin with.

Conclusion

Should such a scenario continue to evolve, it may well be that comprehensive federalism reform can be expected to continue.[46] Because the structure of intergovernmental relations is changing, however, future reforms will probably not be patterned on either the Nixon or the Reagan model. The targets of reform will change as the intergovernmental system evolves. In any case, the political track record of these two presidents leaves much to be desired. The highly rationalized approach of the Nixon administration was incapable of generating sufficient passion and commitment to gain enactment. The strongly ideological agenda of the Reagan administration is passionately advocated, but only a minority of Americans support its stance against the welfare state.

Whatever the political approach, the future of federalism reform—and of federalism in general—will ultimately depend on the values that Americans hold in highest esteem. If federalism continues to be considered as an institution that embodies important political values in American society, then its future should be secure. Even though the functions of the federal system and the nature of the commitment to it may change over time, the system continues to promote certain unique principles of government. For example, federalism provides for multiple arenas of collective decisionmaking and preserves local diversity within a framework of nationally shared values. Although these functions are hardly new, Nathan and Doolittle suggest that liberals have gained a new appreciation of federalism's segmented policymaking system during the Reagan years.[47] Without doubt, since the 1960s the federal system has proved itself capable of supplementing functional representation in federal policy with territorially based patterns of representation.[48] Policy studies have repeatedly shown the value of combining the often lofty and abstract perspective on policymaking in Washington with the more practical perspectives gained from "street level" service delivery.[49] In the end, federalism reform efforts will most likely recur whenever the political system's capacity to preserve such values is endangered or impaired.

Notes

Introduction

1. *McCulloch* v. *Maryland,* 4 Wheaton 316,421 (1819).

2. U.S. Commission on Intergovernmental Relations, Meyer Kestnbaum, chairman, *A Report to the President for Transmittal to Congress* (Washington, D.C., 1955), pp. 6, 59–68.

3. *Report of the Joint Federal-State Action Committee to the President of the United States and to the Chairman of the Governor's Conference* (Washington, D.C., 1958). See the discussion in Deil S. Wright, *Understanding Intergovernmental Relations,* 2d ed. (Pacific Grove, Calif.: Brooks-Cole, 1982), pp. 53–56.

4. See Samuel H. Beer, "Political Overload and Federalism," *Polity: The Journal of the Northeastern Political Science Association,* vol. 10 (Fall 1977), pp. 6–7.

5. See Samuel H. Beer, "The Adoption of General Revenue Sharing: A Case Study in Public Sector Politics," *Public Policy,* vol. 24 (Spring 1976), pp. 132–41. Quotation from p. 139.

6. Interview of President Reagan with representatives of the Washington press, November 19, 1981.

7. David A. Stockman, "The Social Pork Barrel," *Public Interest,* no. 39 (Spring 1975), pp. 3–30.

8. James Bryce, *The American Commonwealth* (New York: Macmillan, 1893), vol. 2, pp. 358–59.

9. Paul Pierson, "Cutting Against the Grain: The Politics of Welfare State Retrenchment in Britain and the United States" (Yale University, 1988), p. 2. Among the many comparisons of the Thatcher and Reagan reactions against the welfare state, I find Pierson's the most comprehensive and balanced and have relied on it heavily in the following discussion of the question.

10. In July 1986 the seasonally adjusted unemployment rate for Britain, which had been rising since 1981, reached "the highest level ever," at 3.2 million people, according to the *Daily Telegraph,* July 18, 1986. The U.K. average of unemployment was 10.3 percent a year during the period 1979–84, as against 5.3 percent during the period 1974–79. Peter Hall, *Governing the Economy: The Politics of State Intervention in Britain and France* (Cambridge, Eng.: Polity Press, 1986), p. 120.

11. See Beer, *Britain Against Itself: The Political Contradictions of Collectivism* (Norton 1982), pp. 37–47.

12. *Action Not Words* (London: Conservative and Unionist Central Office, 1966). Similarly, in preparation for the general election of 1970, Heath "concentrated many of his policy enquiries on improving the methods and structure of government activity; he thereby aimed at lessening the scope of public interference without reducing its benefits." David Butler and Michael Pinto-Duschinsky, *The British General Election of 1970* (London: Macmillan, 1971), p. 68.

13. Pierson, "Cutting Against the Grain."

14. John Kincaid, "The State of American Federalism, 1986," *Publius*, vol. 17 (Summer 1987), pp. 24–25, 32.

15. See, for example, Timothy J. Conlan, "Alternative Perspectives on Federalism," in U.S. Advisory Commission on Intergovernmental Relations, *The Condition of Contemporary Federalism: Conflicting Theories and Collapsing Constraints* (Washington, D.C., 1981), chap. 1; and David R. Beam, Timothy J. Conlan, and David B. Walker, "Federalism: The Challenge of Conflicting Theories and Contemporary Practice," in Ada W. Finifter, ed., *Political Science: The State of the Discipline* (Washington, D.C.: American Political Science Association, 1983), p. 18.

16. Bryce, *American Commonwealth*, vol. 1, p. 253.

Chapter One

1. See U.S. Advisory Commission on Intergovernmental Relations (ACIR), *The Condition of Contemporary Federalism: Conflicting Theories and Collapsing Constraints*, A-78 (Government Printing Office, 1981), chap. 3.

2. V. O. Key, Jr., *The Responsible Electorate* (Harvard University Press, 1966), p. 31.

3. ACIR, *Significant Features of Fiscal Federalism, 1985–86 Edition*, M-146 (GPO, 1986), pp. 6, 16.

4. Ibid. See also David B. Walker, *Toward a Functioning Federalism* (Cambridge, Mass.: Winthrop, 1981).

5. ACIR, *Fiscal Balance in the American Federal System*, A-31 (GPO, 1967), p. 260.

6. Executive Office of the President, Bureau of the Budget, "Creative Federalism: Report on Field Surveys of Problems in Administering Intergovernmental Programs," quoted in ACIR, *Improving Federal Grants Management: The Intergovernmental Grant System—An Assessment and Proposed Policies*, A-53 (GPO, 1977), pp. 11, 12.

7. Charles L. Schultze, *The Politics and Economics of Public Spending* (Brookings, 1968), p. 105.

8. Quoted in James L. Sundquist and David Davis, *Making Federalism Work* (Brookings, 1969), p. 15.

9. ACIR, *An Agenda for American Federalism: Restoring Confidence and Competence*, A-86 (GPO, 1981), p. 101.

10. Ronald Reagan, "National Conference of State Legislatures, Remarks at

the Annual Convention," July 30, 1981, in *Weekly Compilation of Presidential Documents,* April 3, 1981, p. 834.

11. See Samuel H. Beer, "In Search of A New Public Philosophy," in Anthony King, ed., *The New American Political System* (Washington, D.C.: American Enterprise Institute, 1978), p. 5; and Everett Carll Ladd, Jr., and Charles D. Hadley, *Transformations of the American Party System: Political Coalitions from the New Deal to the 1970s* (Norton, 1975).

12. Ladd and Hadley, *Transformations of the American Party System;* James L. Sundquist, *Dynamics of the Party System: Alignment and Realignment of Political Parties in the United States* (Brookings, 1973); and Sidney Verba and Gary Orren, *Equality in America: The View from the Top* (Harvard University Press, 1985), pp. 128–30.

13. Herbert McCloskey, Paul V. Hoffman, and Rosemary O'Hara, "Issue Conflict and Consensus among Party Leaders and Followers," *American Political Science Review,* vol. 54 (June 1960), pp. 406–27.

14. Samuel H. Beer, "The Adoption of General Revenue Sharing: A Case Study in Public Sector Politics," *Public Policy,* vol. 24 (Spring 1976), p. 160.

15. See Richard E. Dawson, *Public Opinion and Contemporary Disarray* (Harper and Row, 1973).

16. See Walter Dean Burnham, *Critical Elections and the Mainsprings of American Politics* (Norton, 1970); and Ladd and Hadley, *Transformations of the American Party System.*

17. Quoted by Garnett O. Horner, "Nixon Looks Ahead: 'A New Feeling of Responsibility . . . of Self Discipline,'" *Washington Star-News,* September 9, 1972; reprinted in Richard P. Nathan, *The Plot That Failed: Nixon and the Administrative Presidency* (John Wiley, 1975), pp. 166, 168.

18. Ronald Reagan, *The Creative Society* (New York: Devon-Adair, 1968), p. 19.

19. See Herbert Croly, *The Promise of American Life* (Jersey City, N.J.: Da Capo Press, 1986).

20. "Address to the Congress on the State of the Union, January 22, 1971," *Public Papers of the Presidents: Richard M. Nixon, 1971* (GPO, 1972), pp. 53–55.

21. Reagan quoted in William A. Schambra, "Progressive Liberalism and American 'Community,'" *Public Interest,* vol. 80 (Summer 1985), p. 47; and Reagan, "National Conference of State Legislatures," pp. 836–87.

22. Statement on signing the State and Local Fiscal Assistance Act, October 20, 1972. Quoted in "Nixon Goal: A Leaner but Stronger Government," *National Journal,* December 16, 1972, p. 1911.

23. Interview with the *Evening Star* and *Washington Daily News,* November 9, 1972, in ibid.

24. Ibid.

25. Quoted in "New Federalism II: Philosophy—Great Society Failures, Conservative Approach to Government Underlie New Federalism Drive," *National Journal,* December 16, 1972, p. 1916.

26. Reagan, "National Conference of State Legislatures," pp. 834–35.

27. See Ronald Reagan, fund-raising letter on behalf of the Republican Governors Association/Republican National Committee, n.d., p. 3.

28. This literature is reviewed in Daphne Kenyon, "Interjurisdictional Tax and Policy Competition: Good or Bad for the Federal System?" paper submitted to the ACIR, November 3, 1987.

29. Quoted in Schambra, "Progressive Liberalism," p. 47.

30. Anthony King, "The American Polity in the Late 1970s: Building Coalitions in the Sand," in Anthony King, ed., *The New American Political System* (American Enterprise Institute, 1978), p. 371.

31. See Lawrence C. Dodd and Bruce I. Oppenheimer, *Congress Reconsidered,* 3d ed. (Congressional Quarterly Press, 1985); James L. Sundquist, *The Decline and Resurgence of Congress* (Brookings, 1981); Gary Orfield, *Congressional Power: Congress and Social Change* (Harcourt Brace Jovanovich, 1975); and ACIR, *An Agenda for American Federalism: Restoring Confidence and Competence,* A–86 (GPO, 1981).

32. David Broder, *The Party's Over: The Failure of Politics in America* (Harper and Row, 1972).

33. Calculated from Kay Lehman Schlozman and John T. Tierney, *Organized Interests and American Democracy* (Harper and Row, 1985), p. 75.

34. Jack L. Walker, "The Origins and Maintenance of Interest Groups in America," *American Political Science Review,* vol. 77 (Spring 1983), pp. 390–406.

35. For the most original and detailed analysis of this process of "rationalizing politics," see Lawrence D. Brown, *New Policies, New Politics: Government's Response to Government's Growth* (Brookings, 1983). See also Beer, "Adoption of General Revenue Sharing."

Chapter Two

1. Lawrence D. Brown, *New Policies, New Politics: Government's Response to Government's Growth* (Brookings, 1983), p. 45.

2. Edwin Harper, quoted in "New Federalism I: Return of Power to States and Cities Looms as Theme of Second-term Domestic Policy," *National Journal,* December 16, 1972, p. 1909.

3. See James L. Sundquist, *Politics and Policy: The Eisenhower, Kennedy, and Johnson Years* (Brookings, 1968), p. 137.

4. Most of these initiatives are described in detail in U. S. Advisory Commission on Intergovernmental Relations, *Improving Federal Grants Management* (GPO, 1977).

5. Paul Studenski, "Federal Grants in Aid," *National Tax Journal,* vol. 2 (September 1949), p. 211.

6. Commission on the Organization of the Executive Branch, *A Report to Congress on Federal-State Relations* (GPO, 1949), pp. 31–32.

7. This view was expressed by the Kestnbaum Commission. See Commission on Intergovernmental Relations, *A Report to the President* (GPO, 1955), p. 122.

8. See Deil Wright, *Federal Grants in Aid: Perspectives and Alternatives*

(Washington, D.C.: American Enterprise Institute, 1968), pp. 11, 131; Selma Mushkin and John F. Cotton, *Sharing Federal Funds for State and Local Needs* (Praeger, 1967), p. 182; and James Maxwell, *Financing State and Local Governments*, rev. ed. (Brookings, 1969), pp. 58–59.

9. ACIR, *The Comprehensive Employment and Training Act: Early Readings from a Hybrid Block Grant*, A-58 (GPO, 1977), pp. 5, 19.

10. Sar A. Levitan and Joyce K. Zickler, *The Quest for a Federal Manpower Partnership* (Harvard University Press, 1974), p. 6.

11. Personal interview, August 17, 1978.

12. Testimony of Mayor John Reading, *Manpower Development and Training Legislation, 1970*, Hearings before the Subcommittee on Employment, Manpower, and Poverty of the Senate Committee on Labor and Public Welfare, 91 Cong. 2 sess. (GPO, 1970), p. 2006.

13. James L. Sundquist and David Davis, *Making Federalism Work* (Brookings, 1969), p. 7.

14. Quoted in Deil Wright, *Understanding Intergovernmental Relations* (North Scituate, Mass.: Duxbury Press, 1978), p. 57.

15. Walter Heller, *New Dimensions of Political Economy* (Harvard University Press, 1967), p. 142.

16. Quoted in Harry Scheiber, "American Federalism and the Diffusion of Power: Historical and Contemporary Perspectives," *University of Toledo Law Review*, vol. 9 (1978), p. 661.

17. Lawrence Kirsch, "Block Grants: Methods and Implications," Budget Bureau staff paper, Washington, D.C., December 1968.

18. "Address to the Nation on Domestic Programs, 8 August 1969," *Public Papers of the Presidents: Richard M. Nixon, 1969* (GPO, 1970), p. 643.

19. See Heller, *New Dimensions of Political Economy*; and James M. Buchanan, *Fiscal Theory and Political Economy: Selected Essays* (University of North Carolina Press, 1960).

20. Paul R. Dommel, *The Politics of Revenue Sharing* (University of Indiana Press, 1974), pp. 42–52.

21. Heller, *New Dimensions of Political Economy*, pp. 169, 170.

22. Wright, *Federal Grants in Aid*, p. 11.

23. Richard M. Nixon, quoted in Richard P. Nathan, *The Plot That Failed: Nixon and the Administrative Presidency* (John Wiley and Sons, 1975), p. 102.

24. *The Intergovernmental Revenue Act of 1969 and Related Legislation*, Hearings before the Subcommittee on Intergovernmental Relations of the Senate Committee on Government Operations, 91 Cong. 1 sess. (GPO, 1970), p. 155.

25. Milton Friedman, *Capitalism and Freedom* (University of Chicago Press, 1962), chap. 12.

26. Nixon, "Address to the Nation on Domestic Programs," p. 638.

27. Nathan, *The Plot That Failed*, p. 31.

28. Vincent J. Burke and Vee Burke, *Nixon's Good Deed* (Columbia University Press, 1974), p. 67.

29. Richard P. Nathan, "Special Revenue Sharing: Simple, Neat, and Correct," Washington, D.C., May 5, 1971, p. 2.

30. Memorandum, John Ehrlichman, director, Domestic Council, to Ed Harper, "OMB Staff Recommendations, January 6," January 9, 1971.

31. Dommel, *The Politics of Revenue Sharing*, pp. 107–08.

32. Office of Management and Budget, Revenue Sharing Working Group, "Initial Report of the OMB Working Group on a F.Y. 72 Revenue Sharing Program," December 1, 1970, p. 2.

33. Interview with Richard P. Nathan, June 5, 1978.

34. George Shultz, director, Office of Management and Budget, "Memorandum for the President on Revenue Sharing," December 18, 1970.

Chapter Three

1. Quoted in Jonathan Cottin, "Wide-Ranging Interests Oppose Administration's Proposals," *National Journal,* April 10, 1971, p. 773.

2. Interview with Richard P. Nathan, Washington, D.C., June 5, 1978.

3. Quoted in Timothy B. Clark and others, "Drive to Return Power to Local Governments Faces Hill Struggle over Control of Programs," *National Journal* (December 16, 1972), p. 1928.

4. Congressman Carl Perkins, quoted in Karen DeWitt, "Administration Revenue Sharing Plan Unlikely to Get Passing Grade from Congress," *National Journal,* March 24, 1973, p. 421.

5. Interview with Congressman Albert Quie, May 25, 1978.

6. Quoted in Gary Orfield, *Congressional Power: Congress and Social Change* (Harcourt Brace Jovanovich, 1975), p. 169.

7. David Mayhew, *Congress: The Electoral Connection* (Yale University Press, 1974), pp. 49, 52, 53.

8. Ibid., pp. 128, 129.

9. Morris P. Fiorina, *Congress: Keystone of the Washington Establishment* (Yale University Press, 1977), p. 48.

10. Ibid., pp. 73, 74.

11. Douglass Cater, *Power in Washington* (Random House, 1964), p. 17.

12. Hugh Heclo, "Issue Networks and the Executive Establishment," in Anthony King, ed., *The New American Political System* (Washington, D.C.: American Enterprise Institute, 1978), pp. 88, 102–03.

13. For a similar analysis of the deep degree of subsystem autonomy and fragmentation in the transportation field, see John W. Kingdon, *Agendas, Alternatives, and Public Policies* (Little, Brown, 1984), pp. 124–26.

14. See Arthur Maass, *Congress and the Common Good* (Basic Books, 1983); Martha Derthick and Paul Quirk, *The Politics of Deregulation* (Brookings, 1985); and Kingdon, *Agendas, Alternatives, and Public Policies.*

15. Garth Mangum, *The Emergence of Manpower Policy* (Holt, Rinehart, and Winston, 1969), pp. 70–75.

16. Ibid., pp. 80, 81.

17. See James L. Sundquist and David Davis, *Making Federalism Work* (Brookings, 1969); and J. David Greenstone and Paul E. Peterson, *Race and*

Authority in Urban Politics: Community Participation and the War on Poverty (New York: Russell Sage Foundation, 1973).

18. See Henry Aaron, *Politics and the Professors: The Great Society in Perspective* (Brookings, 1978).

19. Sar A. Levitan and Joyce K. Zickler, *The Quest for a Federal Manpower Partnership* (Harvard University Press, 1974), p. 50.

20. National Manpower Policy Task Force, "Improving the Nation's Manpower Effort," undated policy paper, reprinted in *The Manpower Act of 1969*, Hearings before the Select Subcommittee on Labor of the House Education and Labor Committee, 91 Cong. 2 sess. (GPO, 1970), pp. 107–09.

21. "Statement of the United States Conference of Mayors and the National League of Cities," *Manpower Development and Training Legislation, 1970*, Hearings before the Subcommittee on Employment, Manpower, and Poverty of the Senate Labor and Public Welfare Committee, 91 Cong. 2 sess. (GPO, 1970), p. 3027.

22. Martin Anderson, *The Federal Bulldozer* (MIT Press, 1964), p. 228.

23. Bernard Frieden and Marshall Kaplan, *The Politics of Neglect: Urban Aid from Model Cities to Revenue Sharing* (MIT Press, 1977), pp. 126, 192.

24. Interview with Edward Silverman, National Association of Housing and Redevelopment Officials, August 16, 1977.

25. Quoted in "The Changing Model Cities Concept," *Nation's Cities*, vol. 8 (November 1970), p. 29.

26. William Lilley III, "Both Parties Ready to Scrap Grant Programs in Favor of 'City Strategy' Package of Aid," *National Journal*, July 3, 1971, p. 2701.

27. William Lilley III, "Capitol Hill Activists Work on Plan to Snare Policy Role from HUD," *National Journal*, January 9, 1971, p. 59.

28. *Housing and the Urban Environment*, Report and Recommendations of the Subcommittee on Housing of the House Committee on Banking and Currency, Committee Print, 92 Cong. 1 sess. (GPO, 1971), pp. 39, 41.

29. Interview with George Gross, counsel, House Subcommittee on Housing, April 1, 1978.

30. Interview with Nancy Remine, National Association of Counties, August 17, 1978.

31. Interview with William Langbehn, chief, Division of Legislation and Program Development, Employment and Training Administration, U.S. Department of Labor, August 15, 1978.

32. Memorandum, Edwin Harper to John Ehrlichman and George Shultz, "Urban Revenue Sharing and the Basic Sewer and Water Problem," April 22, 1971.

33. Memorandum, Dick Eckfield, National League of Cities, to Allen Pritchard and John Gunther, "Saving Model Cities in the Community Development Bill," February 28, 1974.

34. Interview with George Gross; emphasis in the original.

35. "Additional Views of Senator Taft," in *Housing and Community Development Act of 1974*, S. Rept. 693 to Accompany S. 3066, 93 Cong. 2 sess. (GPO, 1974), p. 744.

36. Testimony of Percy Moore, in *Manpower Development and Training Legislation, 1970,* Hearings, pt. 3, p. 2060.

37. Ibid., pt. 1, p. 117.

38. *Congressional Quarterly Almanac, 1973* (Washington, D.C.: CQ, 1974), p. 7-A.

39. Quoted in *Housing Affairs Letter,* vol. 73-3 (January 19, 1973), p. 4.

40. *Congressional Quarterly Almanac, 1970* (CQ, 1971), p. 51-S.

41. Dennis Fargas, quoted in Charles Culhane, "Mayors, Labor Leaders Add Political Muscle to Hill Challenge of Manpower-Training Cuts," *National Journal,* April 7, 1973, p. 499.

42. Interview with John Murphy, National Association of Counties, August 23, 1977.

43. Interview with David Garrison, National League of Cities and U.S. Conference of Mayors, August 23, 1977.

44. Interview with John Sasso, National Community Development Association, August 25, 1977.

45. Interview with John Murphy.

46. Interview with William Langbehn.

47. John L. Moore, "Congress Gathers Wide Support for Reshaping Administration's Community Development Bill," *National Journal,* June 2, 1973, p. 797.

48. Interview with Anthony Valanzano, minority counsel, House Subcommittee on Housing, August 9, 1977.

49. Interview with Congressman Albert Quie.

50. William Mirengoff and Lester Rindler, *CETA: Manpower Programs Under Local Control* (Washington, D.C.: National Academy of Sciences, 1978), p. 19.

51. Interview with David Garrison.

Chapter Four

1. Paul R. Dommel, *The Politics of Revenue Sharing* (Indiana University Press, 1974), p. 95.

2. Ibid., p. 105.

3. Douglas Ayers, "A City Visits Washington," *Nation's Cities Weekly,* vol. 9 (January 1971), pp. 24, 25.

4. Donald H. Haider, *When Governments Come to Washington: Governors, Mayors, and Intergovernmental Lobbying* (Macmillan, 1974), pp. 252, 253.

5. Dommel, *Politics of Revenue Sharing,* p. 114.

6. Quoted in Samuel H. Beer, "The Adoption of General Revenue Sharing: A Case Study in Public Sector Politics," *Public Policy,* vol. 24 (Spring 1976), p. 181.

7. Ibid., p. 171.

8. Dommel, *Politics of Revenue Sharing,* pp. 162–66. See also Martha Derthick, *Uncontrollable Spending for Social Services Grants* (Brookings, 1975).

9. Beer, "Adoption of General Revenue Sharing," p. 187.

10. Ibid.

11. Ibid., p. 188.

Chapter Five

1. Vincent J. Burke and Vee Burke, *Nixon's Good Deed: Welfare Reform* (Columbia University Press, 1974), p. 52. This section relies heavily on their excellent account of the politics of the family assistance plan.

2. Ibid., p. 69.

3. Daniel Patrick Moynihan, *The Politics of a Guaranteed Income: The Nixon Administration and the Family Assistance Plan* (Random House, 1973), pp. 130–36.

4. Ibid., chap. 3.

5. Burke and Burke, *Nixon's Good Deed*, p. 92.

6. Ibid., p. 67.

7. Richard Nixon, "Address to the Nation on Domestic Programs, August 8, 1969," *Public Papers of the Presidents: Richard Nixon, 1969* (GPO, 1970), p. 638.

8. Ibid., pp. 640, 639.

9. Congressional Quarterly, *Congress and the Nation*, vol. 3: 1969–1972 (Washington, D.C.: CQ, 1973), p. 623.

10. "Remarks at the White House Conference on Food, Nutrition, and Health, December 2, 1969," *Public Papers: Nixon, 1972*, p. 981.

11. Moynihan, *Politics of a Guaranteed Income*, p. 437.

12. Congressman Philip Landrum, quoted in Burke and Burke, *Nixon's Good Deed*, p. 147.

13. Ibid., p. 165.

14. U.S. Advisory Commission on Intergovernmental Relations, *Public Assistance: The Growth of a Federal Function*, A-79 (GPO, 1981), pp. 79–82.

15. "Poverty in the United States: Where Do We Stand Now?" *IRP Focus*, vol. 7 (Winter 1984), p. 6.

16. Congressional Quarterly, *Congress and the Nation*, pp. 619–20.

17. ACIR, *Regulatory Federalism: Policy, Process, Impact, and Reform*, A-95 (GPO, 1984), p. 245.

18. This regulatory typology was first devised and elaborated in David R. Beam, "Washington's Regulation of States and Localities: Origins and Issues," *Intergovernmental Perspective*, vol. 7 (Summer 1981), pp. 8–18.

19. Donald F. Kettl, *The Regulation of American Federalism* (Louisiana State University Press, 1983), p. 34.

20. This was true of both Title IX of the Education Amendments of 1972, which prohibited discrimination against women in educational programs, and section 504 of the Rehabilitation Act of 1973, which prohibited discrimination against the handicapped.

21. Congressional Quarterly, *Congress and the Nation*, p. 756.

22. Mel Dubnick and Alan Gitelson, "Nationalizing State Policies," in Je-

rome Hanus, ed., *The Nationalization of State Government* (Lexington, Mass.: D. C. Heath, 1981), pp. 56–57.

23. See Alfred A. Marcus, *Promise and Performance: Choosing and Implementing an Environmental Policy* (Westport, Conn.: Greenwood Press, 1980), chap. 2.

24. Charles O. Jones, *Clean Air: The Policies and Politics of Pollution Control* (University of Pittsburgh Press, 1975), pp. 203–05.

25. ACIR, *Protecting the Environment: Politics, Pollution, and Federal Policy,* A-83 (GPO, 1981), pp. 24–31.

26. J. Clarence Davies III and Barbara S. Davies, *The Politics of Pollution,* 2d ed. (Indianapolis: Bobbs-Merrill, 1975), p. 193.

27. Thomas J. Madden, "The Law of Federal Grants," in ACIR, *Awakening the Slumbering Giant: Intergovernmental Relations and Federal Grant Law,* M-122 (GPO, 1980), p. 17.

28. ACIR, *Regulatory Federalism,* pp. 80–81.

29. Ibid., p. 81.

30. Calculated from table 8-3, "Party Unity Votes in Congress, 1953–1986," in Norman J. Ornstein, Thomas E. Mann, and Michael J. Malbin, *Vital Statistics on Congress, 1987–1988* (Washington, D.C.: CQ Press, 1987), p. 208.

Chapter Six

1. Ralph Widner, "State Growth and Federal Politics," *State Government,* no. 47 (Spring 1974), p. 90.

2. U.S. Advisory Commission on Intergovernmental Relations, *Federalism in 1974: The Tension of Interdependence,* M-89 (GPO, 1975), p. 16.

3. William Mirengoff and Lester Rindler, *CETA: Manpower Programs Under Local Control* (Washington, D.C.: National Academy of Sciences, 1978), p. 19.

4. Donald F. Kettl, "Regulating the Cities," *Publius,* vol. 11 (Spring 1981), p. 123.

5. ACIR, *Catalogue of Federal Grants-in-Aid,* M-139 (GPO, 1984), p. 2.

6. James Q. Wilson, *American Government: Institutions and Policies* (Lexington, Mass.: D. C. Heath, 1986), p. 349. See also Joel Havemann, "Carter's Reorganization Plans—Scrambling for Turf," *National Journal,* May 20, 1978, pp. 788–94.

7. David S. Broder, "Reshuffling the Chaos," reprinted in *County News,* April 3, 1978, p. 4.

8. Quoted in David Rosenbaum, "President Delays Urban-Aid Rise," *New York Times,* December 18, 1977.

9. See Kay Lehman Scholzman and John T. Tierney, *Organized Interests and American Democracy* (Harper and Row, 1986), p. 326.

10. ACIR, *An Agenda for American Federalism: Restoring Confidence and Competence,* A-86 (GPO, 1981), p. 101.

11. See Theodore J. Lowi, "Europeanization of America? From United States to United State," in Theodore J. Lowi and Alan Stone, eds., *Nationalizing Government: Public Policies in America* (Beverly Hills, Calif.: Sage, 1978), pp. 15–

enue Sharing: Case Study in Public Sector Politics," *Public Policy,* vol. 24 (Spring 1976), pp. 127–96.

42. Interview with William Langbehn, former chief, Division of Legislation and Program Development, Employment and Training Administration, U.S. Department of Labor, August 15, 1978.

43. See James Q. Wilson, "American Politics, Then and Now," *Commentary,* vol. 67 (February 1979), pp. 41–46.

44. Quoted in Sawhill and Stone, "The Economy," p. 72.

45. Richard S. Williamson, "The Self-Government Balancing Act: A View from the White House," *National Civic Review,* vol. 71 (January 1982), p. 19.

46. "National Conference of State Legislatures: Remarks at the Annual Convention, July 30, 1981," in *Weekly Compilation of Presidential Documents,* August 3, 1981, p. 834.

47. Eugene Eidenberg, "Federalism," in Hawkins, ed., *American Federalism,* p. 112.

48. Governors Jerry Brown and Harry Hughes, quoted in Adam Clymer, "Governors Split over Reagan Proposals," *New York Times,* January 28, 1982.

49. See Reagan, "National Conference of State Legislatures," pp. 834–35.

Chapter Seven

1. Executive Office of the President, *Federalism: The First Ten Months—A Report from the President* (Washington, D.C.: EOP, November 1981), p. 28.

2. *Congressional Quarterly Almanac, 1981* (Washington, D.C.: CQ, 1982), p. 19E.

3. Dale Tate, "New Federalism No Panacea for State and Local Governments," *Congressional Quarterly Weekly Reports,* April 25, 1981, p. 709.

4. John L. Palmer and Gregory B. Mills, "Budget Policy," in John L. Palmer and Isabel V. Sawhill, eds., *The Reagan Experiment* (Washington, D.C.: Urban Institute Press, 1982), p. 81.

5. David B. Walker, Albert J. Richter, and Cynthia Colella, "The First Ten Months: Grant-in-Aid, Regulatory, and Other Changes," *Intergovernmental Perspective,* vol. 8 (Winter 1982), pp. 7–9.

6. James R. Storey, "Income Security," in Palmer and Sawhill, eds., *Reagan Experiment,* p. 376.

7. John Shannon, "Federal and State-Local Spenders Go Their Separate Ways," in Robert Jay Dilger, ed., *American Intergovernmental Relations Today: Perspectives and Controversies* (Englewood Cliffs, N.J.: Prentice Hall, 1986), pp. 169–83.

8. Martin Tolchin, "Reagan Used Legislative Shortcut to Slash Budget: Stockman's Plan Bore Fruit," *New York Times,* June 28, 1981.

9. Richard P. Nathan, "Retrenchment in Washington Ripples Across Country," *Public/Private,* vol. 1 (November 1982), p. 43.

10. Hedrick Smith, "President Attains Mastery at the Capitol," *New York Times,* July 30, 1981.

11. Congressman James Jones, quoted in *Congressional Quarterly Almanac,*

1981, p. 256. See also Dennis Farney and Leonard M. Apcar, "Budget Triumph Seen Giving Ronald Reagan Firmer Grip on Economic Policy, Added Political Momentum," *Wall Street Journal*, June 29, 1981.

12. Robert Fulton, "Federal Budget Making in 1981: A Watershed Year in Federal Domestic Policy," *New England Journal of Human Services*, vol. 1 (Fall 1981), p. 26.

13. Data on this and the following three votes are taken from ibid., p. 28, and from *Congressional Quarterly Almanac, 1981*, pp. 245, 257.

14. Fulton, "Federal Budget Making in 1981," pp. 29–30.

15. See Dale Tate, "Reconciliation Conferees Face Slim Choices," *Congressional Quarterly Weekly Reports*, July 4, 1981, pp. 1167–69.

16. Quoted in Naomi Caiden, "The Politics of Subtraction," in Allen Schick, ed., *Making Economic Policy in Congress* (Washington, D.C.: American Enterprise Institute, 1983), p. 117.

17. Bill Peterson, "Billions in Days: Frenzy on the Hill," *Washington Post*, June 28, 1981.

18. Russell Baker, "The New Deal: It Was Time for It to Die," *Minneapolis Tribune*, August 4, 1981.

19. See, for example, Arthur H. Miller, "What Mandate for Change?" *Public Welfare*, vol. 40 (Spring 1982), pp. 9, 13; and Everett C. Ladd, "The Brittle Mandate: Electoral Dealignment and the 1980 Presidential Election," *Political Science Quarterly*, vol. 96 (Spring 1981), pp. 1–25.

20. Thomas E. Mann and Norman J. Ornstein, "Sending a Message: Voters and Congress in 1982," in Mann and Ornstein, eds., *The American Elections of 1982* (American Enterprise Institute, 1983), pp. 135–37.

21. See Lawrence C. Dodd and Bruce I. Oppenheimer, "The House in Transition," in Dodd and Oppenheimer, eds., *Congress Reconsidered* (Praeger, 1977), pp. 21–53; and Barbara Sinclair, "Coping with Uncertainty: Building Coalitions in the House and Senate," in Thomas E. Mann and Norman J. Ornstein, eds., *The New Congress* (American Enterprise Institute, 1981), p. 220.

22. See Sinclair, "Coping with Uncertainty," pp. 204, 216; James Singer, "Labor and Congress: New Isn't Necessarily Better," *National Journal*, March 14, 1978, p. 352; and "Special Interest Lobbies Cultivate the 'Grass Roots' to Influence Capitol Hill," *Congressional Quarterly Weekly Reports*, September 12, 1981, pp. 1739–42.

23. *Congressional Quarterly Almanac, 1981*, pp. 36C, 19C.

24. Lou Cannon, *Reagan* (Perigee Books, 1982), p. 331.

25. *Congressional Quarterly Almanac, 1981*, pp. 30C, 10C.

26. Quoted in John White, "The Speaker Speaks: A Talk with 'Tip,'" *Party Line*, vol. 11 (November 1982), p. 7.

27. Demetrios Caraley and Yvette R. Schlussel, "Congress and Reagan's New Federalism," *Publius*, vol. 16 (Winter 1986), p. 61.

28. See Gary C. Jacobson, "Congressional Campaign Finance and the Revival of the Republican Party," in Dennis Hale, ed., *The United States Congress: Proceeding of the Thomas P. O'Neill, Jr. Symposium on the U.S. Congress* (Leominster, Mass.: Eusey Press, 1982), p. 318.

29. See Jacobson, "Congressional Campaign Finance"; Cornelius P. Cotter and John F. Bibby, "Institutional Development of Parties and the Thesis of Party Decline," *Political Science Quarterly,* vol. 95 (Spring 1980), pp. 1–27; and Alan Ehrenhalt, "Campaign Committees: Focus of Party Revival," *Congressional Quarterly Weekly Reports,* July 2, 1981, p. 1345.

30. Jacobson, "Congressional Campaign Finance," p. 319.

31. Bill Keller, "Coalitions and Associations Transform Strategy, Methods of Lobbying in Washington," *Congressional Quarterly Weekly Reports,* January 23, 1982, p. 123.

32. Hedrick Smith, "Taking Charge of Congress," *New York Times Magazine,* August 9, 1981, pp. 47, 48.

33. Bill Keller, "Special Interest Lobbyists Cultivate the 'Grass Roots' to Influence Capitol Hill," *Congressional Quarterly Weekly Reports,* September 12, 1981, pp. 1739–42.

34. See Aaron Wildavsky, *The Politics of the Budgetary Process* (Boston: Little, Brown, 1964); and Caiden, "Politics of Subtraction," pp. 102–03.

35. Norman J. Ornstein, Thomas E. Mann, and Michael J. Malbin, *Vital Statistics on Congress, 1987–1988* (CQ Press), p. 204.

36. Because comparable data on the House are available only for the five years shown, identical years were selected for table 7-6 for the Senate. However, complete data have been compiled for the Senate from 1975 to 1986, and the averages for the years shown in the table are representative of the time periods selected.

37. Helen Dewar, "Reagan's Themes, Deficits Alter Course of Democratic Mainstream," *Washington Post,* March 9, 1987.

38. Congressman Al Swift, quoted in David Maraniss, "Leaders Tailor Panels for Productivity," *Washington Post,* May 22, 1983.

39. Kay Lehman Schlozman and John T. Tierney, *Organized Interests and American Democracy* (Harper and Row, 1986), p. 155.

40. Quoted in Ward Sinclair, "Farm Relief Bill Gathers No Moss," *Washington Post,* April 23, 1987.

41. Both Foley and Kennedy are quoted in Dewar, "Reagan's Themes, Deficits Alter Course."

42. *Governors Bulletin,* December 20, 1985, p. 3.

43. Author's interview with Gerald Miller, executive director, National Association of State Budget Officers, Washington, D.C., April 3, 1987.

44. See Caiden, "Politics of Subtraction"; Allen Schick, "The Distributive Congress," in Allen Schick, ed., *Making Economic Policy in Congress,* pp. 100–30, 257–74; and John Ellwood, "The Great Exception: The Congressional Budget Process in an Age of Decentralization," in Lawrence C. Dodd and Bruce I. Oppenheimer, eds., *Congress Reconsidered,* 3d ed. (Congressional Quarterly, 1985), pp. 315–42.

45. William Schneider, quoted in Dewar, "Reagan's Themes, Deficits Alter Course."

46. Charles Hulton and June O'Neill, "Tax Policy," in Palmer and Sawhill, eds., *Reagan Experiment,* p. 113.

47. Joseph A. Pechman, ed., *Tax Reform and the U.S. Economy* (Brookings, 1987), p. 1.

48. Hon. Ted Weiss, "Legislation to Repeal Gramm-Rudman," Extensions of Remarks, *Congressional Record,* daily edition, January 7, 1987, p. E31. See also statement of Sen. Daniel Patrick Moynihan, *Congressional Record,* daily edition, April 24, 1986, p. S.4792.

49. David A. Stockman, *The Triumph of Politics: Why the Reagan Revolution Failed* (Harper and Row, 1986), pp. 53, 297.

50. John Shannon and Susannah Calkins, "Financing Federal Growth: Changing Aspects of Fiscal Constraints," in ACIR, *The Condition of Contemporary Federalism: Conflicting Theories and Collapsing Constraints* (GPO, 1981), p. 143.

51. See Cannon, *Reagan,* p. 324; and Stockman, *Triumph of Politics,* p. 229.

52. John C. Witte, *The Politics and Development of the Federal Income Tax* (University of Wisconsin Press, 1985), p. 128.

53. Ronald Reagan, *Weekly Compilation of Presidential Documents,* August 17, 1981, p. 868.

54. Stockman, *Triumph of Politics,* pp. 229–34; and Lawrence I. Barrett, *Gambling with History: Reagan in the White House* (Penguin, 1984), pp. 14, 55.

55. *Congressional Quarterly Almanac, 1981,* p. 91.

56. William Greider, *The Education of David Stockman and Other Americans* (Dutton, 1982), p. 50.

57. Stockman, *Triumph of Politics,* p. 239.

58. Witte, *Politics and Development of the Income Tax,* p. 228.

59. Barrett, *Gambling with History,* p. 169.

60. *Congressional Quarterly Almanac, 1981,* p. 100.

61. Quoted in Greider, *Education of David Stockman,* p. 58.

62. Catherine E. Rudder, "Tax Policy: Structure and Choice," in *Making Economic Policy in Congress,* p. 206.

63. Stockman, *Triumph of Politics,* p. 262.

64. Ibid., p. 263; and Keller, "Special Interest Lobbyists Cultivate the 'Grass Roots,'" pp. 1739–42.

65. Witte, *Politics and Development of the Federal Income Tax,* p. 229.

66. Susan B. Hanson, "The Politics of Federal Tax Policy," in James P. Pfiffner, ed., *The President and Economic Policy* (Institute for the Study of Human Issues, 1986), p. 197.

67. Witte, *Politics and Development of the Federal Income Tax,* p. 230.

68. Stockman, *Triumph of Politics,* p. 262.

69. Ellwood, "Great Exception," p. 332.

70. Rudder, "Tax Policy" p. 207.

71. Interview with Donald Susswein, August 14, 1986.

72. Ibid.

73. *Congressional Quarterly Almanac, 1984,* p.143.

74. See Joseph T. Minarik, *Making Tax Choices* (Urban Institute Press, 1985); and Henry Aaron and Harvey Galper, *Assessing Tax Reform* (Brookings, 1985).

75. Interviews with Treasury Secretary James A. Baker III, March 20, 1987; and former Assistant Treasury Secretary Ronald Pearlman, August 28, 1986.

76. "Interview with Presidential Assistant Mitchell Daniels," *First Monday,* vol. 15 (July 1985), p. 20.

77. Stockman, *Triumph of Politics,* p. 362.

78. Ronald Reagan, "Tax Reform: Message to Congress Transmitting Proposed Legislation, May 29, 1988," *Weekly Compilation of Presidential Documents,* June 3, 1985, p. 708.

79. "Interview with Treasury Secretary James Baker," *First Monday,* vol. 15 (July 1985), p. 18.

80. "Remarks to Citizens' Groups, May 29, 1985," *Weekly Compilation of Presidential Documents,* June 3, 1985, p. 712.

81. Senator Robert Dole, "Foreword," in Donald B. Susswein, *How to Understand and Survive the Coming Tax Reforms* (New York: American Management Association, 1985), p. 7.

82. Quoted in "Taxes behind Closed Doors," *Frontline #411,* transcript of Public Broadcasting System broadcast, April 15, 1986, p. 3.

83. For example, Bradley theorist Joseph Minarik argued that tax reform was a necessary precondition for a general tax increase.

84. George Peterson, "Federalism and the States: An Experiment in Decentralization," in John L. Palmer and Isabel V. Sawhill, eds., *The Reagan Record* (Urban Institute Press, 1984), p. 228.

85. Government Finance Officers' Association, "GFOA Opposes the Administration's Tax-Exempt Bond Provisions," position statement, June 21, 1985, Washington D.C., p. 1.

86. Executive Office of the President, *The President's Tax Proposals to the Congress for Fairness, Growth, and Simplicity* (GPO, May 1985), app. C.

87. See remarks of Congressman Robert Matsui, in Timothy B. Clark, "The Tax Reform Spotlight Is Falling on State and Local Tax Deduction," *National Journal,* June 29, 1985, p. 1511.

88. Quoted in "State Tax Deduction: Why and Why Not," *Tax Notes,* December 24, 1984, p. 1167.

89. Ronald Reagan, fund-raising letter on behalf of the Republican Governors Association/Republican National Committee, n.d., p. 3.

90. "National Conference of State Legislatures: Remarks at the Annual Convention in Atlanta, July 30, 1981," *Weekly Compilation of Presidential Documents,* August 3, 1981, p. 834.

Chapter Eight

1. Quoted in Claude E. Barfield, *Rethinking Federalism: Block Grants and Federal, State, and Local Responsibilities* (Washington, D.C.: American Enterprise Institute, 1981), p. 61.

2. Richard P. Nathan and Fred C. Dolittle, "The Untold Story of Ronald Reagan's 'New Federalism'" *Public Interest,* no. 77 (Fall 1984), p. 97.

3. See David B. Walker, "The Condition and Course of the System," in Lewis

G. Bender and James Stever, eds., *Administering the New Federalism* (Boulder, Colo.: Westview, 1986), pp. 329–47.

4. See remarks of Donald Moran, associate director of OMB for Human Resources, in Barfield, *Rethinking Federalism,* pp. 23, 24.

5. Jerry Turem, "Social Service Managers and Budget Cuts," *New England Journal of Human Services,* vol. 2 (Winter 1982), p. 19.

6. Congressional Research Service, "The Impact of Legislative Changes on Major Programs Administered by the Department of Education, FY 1980–1986," Report 85-551-EPW, Washington, D.C., January 31, 1986.

7. Samuel H. Beer, "The Adoption of General Revenue Sharing: A Case Study in Public Sector Politics," *Public Policy,* vol. 24 (Spring 1976), pp. 160, 162.

8. Ronald Reagan, "Conservative Blueprint for the 1970s," Speech to the Executive Club of Chicago, September 26, 1975, as reprinted in *Congressional Record,* October 1, 1975, p. 31184.

9. Ronald Reagan, *The Creative Society* (Devin-Adair, 1968), pp. 17, 20, 14.

10. Rochelle L. Stanfield, "'Defunding the Left' May Remain Just Another Fond Dream of Conservatives," *National Journal,* August 1, 1981, p. 1374.

11. Quoted in Steven V. Roberts, "Budget Axe Becomes Tool of Social Change," *New York Times,* June 21, 1981.

12. Howard J. Phillips, quoted in Stanfield, "'Defunding the Left,'" p. 1374.

13. Harold Wolman and Fred Teitlebaum, "Interest Groups and the Reagan Presidency," in Lester M. Salamon and Michael S. Lund, eds., *The Reagan Presidency and the Governing of America* (Washington, D.C.: Urban Institute Press, 1985), pp. 315–16.

14. See 1982 HUD Urban Policy Report, and "Statement of David A. Stockman before the Committee on Governmental Affairs, United States Senate," press release, February 4, 1982.

15. Ibid. See also Stanfield, "'Defunding the Left,'" pp. 1376–78.

16. See, for example, Jo Ann Boyd, "Despite Setbacks, Reagan's Assault on Legal Services Corp. Bears Fruit," *National Journal,* March 12, 1983, pp. 562–64.

17. Quoted in Barfield, *Rethinking Federalism,* p. 24.

18. Quoted in Rochelle L. Stanfield, "Block Grants Look Fine to States; It's the Money That's the Problem," *National Journal,* May 9, 1981, p. 830.

19. Quoted in Roberts, "Budget Axe," p. 2.

20. Robert Carleson, as quoted in Barfield, *Rethinking Federalism,* p. 26.

21. "National Conference of State Legislatures: Remarks at the Annual Convention in Atlanta, Georgia, July 30, 1981," *Weekly Compilation of Presidential Documents,* August 3, 1981, p. 835.

22. For more details on these proposals, see David R. Beam, "New Federalism, Old Realities: The Reagan Administration and Intergovernmental Reform," in Salamon and Lund, eds., *Reagan Presidency,* pp. 431–32.

23. *Budget of the United States Government, Fiscal Year 1986,* p. 5-151.

24. Quoted in Stanfield, "Block Grants Look Fine to States," p. 829.

25. Personal interview, August 18, 1983.

26. Quoted in Dale Tate, "New Federalism No Panacea for State and Local Governments," *Congressional Quarterly Weekly Reports*, April 25, 1981, p. 710.

27. *Elementary and Secondary Education Consolidation Act of 1981*, Hearings before the House Committee on Education and Labor, 97 Cong. 1 sess. (GPO, 1981), pp. 61, 64.

28. Spencer Rich, "Panel Rejects Reagan Plan for Block Grants to States," *Washington Post*, May 15, 1981.

29. Ad Hoc Coalition on Block Grants, "Letter to Rep. Henry Waxman," in *Congressional Record*, June 24, 1981, p. 13785.

30. Testimony of Sandy Solomon, executive director, Coalition on Block Grants and Human Needs, *Block Grant Implementation*, Hearings before the Subcommittee on Intergovernmental Relations of the Senate Committee on Governmental Affairs, 97 Cong. 2 sess. (GPO, 1982), p. 176.

31. Quoted in "The New Federalism: Where Are the Cities?" *The Mayor*, April 15, 1981, p. 2. See also "Reagan's Block Grant Proposal Pits Cities Against the States," *Wall Street Journal*, May 12, 1981.

32. Rochelle L. Stanfield, "Congressional Roadblocks," *National Journal*, June 20, 1981, p. 1126.

33. Quoted in "Congress Stalls Reagan Grant Consolidation Plan," *Public Administration Times*, June 1, 1981, p. 6.

34. Congressman Leon Panetta, quoted in Martin Tolchin, "Reagan Used Legislative Shortcut to Slash Budget," *New York Times*, June 28, 1981.

35. Quoted in Bill Peterson, "Billions in Days: Frenzy on the Hill," *Washington Post*, June 28, 1981.

36. *The Omnibus Budget Reconciliation Act of 1981*, H. Rept. 97-208, 97 Cong. 1 sess. (GPO, 1981).

37. Congressman Robert Michel, *Congressional Record*, June 25, 1981, p. H3381.

38. David A. Stockman, *The Triumph of Politics: Why the Reagan Revolution Failed* (Harper and Row, 1986), pp. 197, 201.

39. *Congressional Quarterly Almanac, 1981*, p. 264.

40. Stockman, *Triumph of Politics*, p. 225.

41. Robert Fulton, "Federal Budget Making in 1981: A Watershed in Federal Domestic Policy," *New England Journal of Human Services*, vol. 1 (Fall 1981), p. 29.

42. Personal interview.

43. Martin Tolchin, "Conferees Decide on $37 Billion in Federal Budget," *New York Times*, July 29, 1981.

44. See *Omnibus Budget Reconciliation Act of 1981*, Conference Report to Accompany H.R. 3982, H. Rpt. 97-208, 97 Cong. 1 sess. (GPO, 1981).

45. Harrison Donnelly, "Scaled-Down Block Grants Near Enactment," *Congressional Quarterly Weekly Reports*, July 4, 1981, p. 1180.

46. Sandra Osbourn, "Block Grants: Inventory and Funding History," Congressional Research Service, November 21, 1986.

47. Linda E. Demkovich, "Feeding the Young—Will the Reagan 'Safety Net' Catch the 'Truly Needy'?" *National Journal*, April 10, 1982, p. 624.

48. George Peterson, "The Block Grants in Perspective," in George Peterson, ed., *The Reagan Block Grants: What Have We Learned?* (Urban Institute Press, 1986), p. 28.

49. Quoted in David S. Broder, "States Offer Reagan a Deal on Aid Cuts," *Washington Post*, August 12, 1981.

50. Quoted in Norman J. Ornstein, "Chipping Away at the Old Blocks," *The Brookings Bulletin*, vol. 18 (Winter–Spring 1982), p. 14.

51. Congressmen Richard Bolling and Barber Conable, quoted in Dale Tate, "Reagan Victory May Bring House Backlash," *Congressional Quarterly Weekly Reports*, July 4, 1981, p. 1168.

52. Quoted in ibid.

53. These and other problems are discussed in U.S. Advisory Commission on Intergovernmental Relations, *Reducing Unemployment: Intergovernmental Dimensions of a National Problem*, A-80 (GPO, 1982), pp. 82–100.

Chapter Nine

1. George E. Peterson, "The State and Local Sector," in John L. Palmer and Isabel V. Sawhill, eds., *The Reagan Experiment* (Washington, D.C.: Urban Institute Press, 1982), p. 168.

2. See, for example Richard A. Musgrave, *The Theory of Public Finance: A Study in Public Economy* (McGraw-Hill, 1959); George Break, *Intergovernmental Fiscal Relations in the United States* (Brookings, 1967), chap. 3; and Wallace Oates, *Fiscal Federalism* (Harcourt Brace Jovanovich, 1972).

3. See Paul E. Peterson, *City Limits* (University of Chicago Press, 1981).

4. U.S. Advisory Commission on Intergovernmental Relations, *State Aid to Local Governments*, A-34 (GPO, 1969), p. 16.

5. ACIR, *Summary and Concluding Observations, The Intergovernmental Grant System: An Assessment and Proposed Policies*, A-62 (GPO, 1978), p. 78; and ACIR, *An Agenda for American Federalism: Restoring Confidence and Competence*, A-86 (GPO, 1981), pp. 111, 112.

6. National Governors' Association, "Agenda for Restoring Balance to the Federal System," *Policy Positions, 1981–82* (Washington, D.C.: NGA, 1981), pp. 15–18.

7. President's Commission for a National Agenda for the Eighties, *A National Agenda for the Eighties* (GPO, 1980), pp. 69–72.

8. ACIR, *State Aid to Local Governments*, pp. 16–18.

9. ACIR, *An Agenda for American Federalism*, p. 101.

10. Ronald Reagan, "Conservative Blueprint for the 1970s," *Congressional Record*, October 1, 1975, pp. 31184–85.

11. *New York Times*, February 24, 1976.

12. Lou Cannon, *Reagan* (Perigee Books, 1982), p. 202.

13. Laurence I. Barrett, *Gambling with History: Reagan in the White House* (Penguin, 1984), p. 342.

14. Rochelle L. Stanfield, "President Reagan's New Federalism . . . A Budget Afterthought," *National Journal*, February 13, 1982, p. 278.

15. David S. Broder, "States Offer Reagan a Deal on Aid Cuts," *Washington Post*, August 11, 1981.

16. David S. Broder and Spencer Rich, "AFDC Shift to States Is Considered," *Washington Post*, August 13, 1981.

17. Linda E. Demkovich, "Political, Budget Pressures Sidetrack Plan for Turning AFDC Over to States," *National Journal*, September 19, p. 1671.

18. Barrett, *Gambling with History*, p. 342.

19. David A. Stockman, *The Triumph of Politics: Why the Reagan Revolution Failed* (Harper and Row, 1986), p. 347.

20. Quoted in Cannon, *Reagan*, p. 348.

21. Quoted in Barrett, *Gambling with History*, p. 342.

22. Ibid., p. 393.

23. Interview with Richard S. Williamson, June 18, 1987.

24. Ibid.

25. Steven R. Weisman, "A Federalism Whose Time Is Now," *New York Times*, January 26, 1982.

26. Interview with senior career official, Office of Management and Budget, February 5, 1986.

27. Barrett, *Gambling with History*, p. 344.

28. Ibid.

29. Ibid., p. 345.

30. "The State of the Union: Address Delivered before a Joint Session of the Congress, January 26, 1982," *Weekly Compilation of Presidential Documents*, February 1, 1982, pp. 79, 80.

31. "Two State Leaders Respond to Reagan's Plan: Cautious, Optimistic, and Loaded with Questions," *State Government News* (March 1982), p. 14; and Bruce Babbitt, "His Plan Deserves a Chance," *Washington Post*, January 28, 1982.

32. Hugh L. Carey, "'New Federalism' Yes, but Reagan's Proposal Needs Major Revision," *New York Times*, March 14, 1982.

33. Reagan, "Conservative Blueprint for the 1970s," p. 31186.

34. "State of the Union: Address," p. 586.

35. Robert B. Carleson, "The Alternatives: True Reform or Federalization," *Commonsense*, vol. 3 (Winter 1980), p. 17.

36. Executive Office of the President, "Fact Sheet: Federalism Initiative," press release, January 27, 1982, p. 7.

37. Quoted in Fred Jordan, "New or 'No Federalism,' It's a Hot Topic in Seattle," *Nation's Cities Weekly*, August 30, 1982, p. 6.

38. Quoted in David S. Broder, "White House Is Warned on Its Federalism Plans," *Washington Post*, July 29, 1982.

39. The State-Local Advisory Group, "Response to the U.S. Treasury Intergovernmental Study," in U.S. Department of the Treasury, Office of State and Local Finance, *Federal-State-Local Fiscal Relations: Report to the President and the Congress* (GPO, 1985), p. 446.

40. Matheson quoted in William Schmidt, "Three Western Governors Seem to Be Potential Allies of 'New Federalism,'" *New York Times*, February 18,

1982; Vasconcellos quoted in Jay Matthews, "States Unable or Unwilling to Shoulder 'Federalism' Burden," *Washington Post,* February 17, 1982.

41. Congressional Budget Office, "AFDC, Food Stamp and Medicaid Exchange," January 29, 1982. See also National Governors' Association and National Conference of State Legislatures, "The President's Federalism Initiative," February 5, 1982, p. 3.

42. Carey, "'New Federalism' Yes," p. E23.

43. For example, one review of opinion surveys on new federalism concluded that it "fit the public's image of the respective roles of the Federal and state governments." "The New Federalism Outlook," Opinion Outlook Briefing Paper, February 12, 1982, p. 6.

44. "The New Old Deal," *New York Times,* January 28, 1982; and Joseph Kraft, "The President Changes the Subject," *Washington Post,* January 28, 1982.

45. AFL-CIO Statement Submitted for the Record, *President's Federalism Initiative,* Hearings before the Senate Committee on Governmental Affairs, 97 Cong. 2 sess. (GPO, 1982), p. 482.

46. Quoted in Neal R. Peirce, "The States Can Do It, but Is There the Will?" *National Journal,* February 27, 1982, p. 377.

47. Quoted in Rochelle L. Stanfield, "A Neatly Wrapped Package with Explosives Inside," *National Journal,* February 27, 1982, p. 360.

48. Richard Brodsky, quoted in Howell Raines, "President Seeking Counties' Support," *New York Times,* July 14, 1982.

49. Richard E. Cohen, "Meanwhile, in Congress, the Long Knives Are Out," *National Journal,* February 27, 1982, p. 381.

50. James R. Thompson, Speech before the Institute for Socioeconomic Studies' Ninth Annual Conference, New York, N.Y., May 10, 1983.

51. Quoted in Broder, "White House Is Warned."

52. Quoted in David Broder and Herbert Denton, "Reagan's Aides Push Program Swap," *Washington Post,* January 29, 1982.

53. *Congressional Insight,* January 29, 1982, p. 1; and Robert Pear, "The Outlook for Reagan's 'New Federalism' Plan," *New York Times,* May 5, 1982.

54. "Despite Opposition to Budget Cuts, Governors Agree to Develop Federalism Proposal," *Governors' Bulletin,* February 22, 1982, pp. 1–3.

55. For a complete list of the members of these negotiating teams, see Richard S. Williamson, "The 1982 New Federalism Negotiations," *Publius,* vol. 13 (Spring 1983), pp. 16, 18.

56. Ibid., p. 16.

57. See Robert Pear, "White House Halts Attempts to Shift Welfare to States," *New York Times,* April 7, 1982.

58. Quoted in Bill Peterson, "White House Agreement on 'New Federalism' Announced by Governors," *Washington Post,* May 6, 1982.

59. "NLC Now Backs Takeover of Welfare by States," *Weekly Bond Buyer,* May 24, 1982, p. 25.

60. Interview with Richard Williamson. See also Williamson, "1982 New Federalism Negotiations," p. 27.

61. David Broder and Dan Balz, "Governors Break with President," *Washington Post*, August 9, 1982.

62. Memorandum, Jim Medas to Steve Farber, "Tentative Administration Decisions on Federalism Initiative," June 22, 1982.

63. Howell Raines, "President Seeking Counties' Support," *New York Times*, July 14, 1982. The new proposal retained food stamps as a federal responsibility along with several controversial programs originally scheduled to be consolidated into the trust fund; required states to pass through to local governments sufficient funds from the federalism trust fund to cover terminated federal-local grants; and replaced the controversial windfall profits tax on oil with more reliable general revenues as a trust fund revenue source. Apart from these concessions, however, the revised plan included federal assumption only of "routine" medical care for the poor and a new block grant for costly long-term care for the elderly. It excluded medicaid coverage for "medically needy" individuals currently covered as a state option. For more details, see Ronald Reagan's "Remarks at the [National Association of Counties] Annual Convention, July 13, 1982," *Weekly Compilation of Presidential Documents*, July 19, 1982, p. 899.

64. Ross Doyen and others, "Report to the NCSL Executive Committee," July 26, 1982, p. 3.

65. Governor Richard Snelling, chairman, National Governors' Association, "The Governors' Federalism Initiative: Report to the Executive Committee," August 8, 1982.

66. David S. Broder, "Governors Relent, to Seek Accord on Federalism with Reagan," *Washington Post*, August 11, 1982.

67. Governors Scott Matheson and Richard Snelling, "Letter to President Reagan," November 19, 1982.

68. "Reagan's Idea of Federalism Called 'Dead,'" *New York Times*, December 12, 1982. See also "Matheson Says Governors Disappointed by Draft Federalism Plan," *Governors' Bulletin*, December 17, 1982, p. 1.

69. Rochelle Stanfield, "Governors, Mayors Turn from Seeking More Power to Fending Off Aid Cuts," *National Journal*, January 22, 1983, p. 167.

70. "Governor Snelling Foresees Reform of Federalism within a Decade," *Washington Report, American Public Welfare Association*, vol. 17 (October 1982), p. 2.

71. Williamson, "1982 New Federalism Negotiations," p. 26.

72. Ibid., p. 31.

73. Ibid., p. 26.

Chapter Ten

1. Executive Office of the President, "The Task Force on Regulatory Relief: Its Impact on Federalism," *Federalism: The First Ten Months, A Report from the President* (GPO, 1981), p. 27.

2. See U.S. Advisory Commission on Intergovernmental Relations, *Regula-*

tory Federalism: Policy, Progress, Impact, and Reform, A-95 (GPO, 1984), chap. 3; and Robert A. Katzmann, *Institutional Disability: The Saga of Transportation Policy for the Disabled* (Brookings, 1986), chap. 2.

3. See Edward I. Koch, "The Mandate Millstone," *Public Interest,* no. 61 (Fall 1980), pp. 42–57.

4. David Stockman, "Avoiding an Economic Dunkirk," reprinted in William Greider, *The Education of David Stockman and Other Americans* (Dutton, 1982), p. 146.

5. For more on the growing intrusiveness of traditional grant requirements during this period, see Donald F. Kettl, *The Regulation of American Federalism* (Louisiana State University Press, 1983); and Paul E. Peterson, Barry G. Rabe, and Kenneth K. Wong, *When Federalism Works* (Brookings, 1986).

6. David R. Beam, "Washington's Regulation of States and Localities: Origins and Issues," *Intergovernmental Perspective,* vol. 7 (Summer 1981), pp. 8–18.

7. Thomas Mueller and Michael Fix, "The Impact of Selected Federal Actions on Municipal Outlays," in *Government Regulations: Achieving Social and Economic Balance,* vol. 5 of *Special Study on Economic Change,* Joint Economic Committee (GPO, 1980), p. 368.

8. ACIR, *Regulatory Federalism,* pp. 174, 175.

9. Ibid., pp. 246, 245.

10. Kettl, *Regulation of American Federalism,* p. xv.

11. See Executive Office of the President, *Federalism,* pp. 2, 7–10.

12. Murray L. Weidenbaum, "Reagan Federalism," *Journal of Contemporary Studies,* vol. 4 (Fall 1981), pp. 74–75.

13. Murray L. Weidenbaum, "Regulatory Reform: Looking Backward and Forward," paper prepared for the Urban Institute Conference on Regulatory Reform, Washington, D.C., June 15, 1983, p. 4.

14. Presidential Task Force on Regulatory Relief, *Reagan Administration Achievements in Regulatory Relief for State and Local Governments: A Progress Report* (Washington, D.C.: Presidential Task Force, August 1982), p. 4.

15. Executive Office of the President, *Federalism,* p. 28.

16. Presidential Task Force, *Reagan Administration Achievements,* pp. ii, i.

17. Michael Fix, "Regulatory Relief: The Real New Federalism," *State Government News,* January 1985, p. 8.

18. Molly Sinclair, "Reagan Helps State, Local Regulators," *Washington Post,* June 27, 1984.

19. Fix, "Regulatory Relief," p. 7.

20. Ibid., p. 8.

21. "The Pitfalls of Defederalization," *Chemical Week,* June 17, 1981, pp. 34–58.

22. Weidenbaum, "Regulatory Reform," p. 5.

23. Richard S. Williamson, "A New Federalism: Proposals and Achievements of President Reagan's First Three Years," *Publius,* vol. 16 (Winter 1986), p. 25.

24. Ibid.

25. Calculated from data in Judith Havemann, "OMB Cracks Whip on Rule-Making," *Washington Post*, June 21, 1987.

26. Erik D. Olson, "The Quiet Shift of Power: Office of Management and Budget Supervision of Environmental Protection Agency Rulemaking under Executive Order 12291," *Virginia Journal of Natural Resources Law*, vol. 4 (1984), pp. 48, 49.

27. Calculated from data in Havemann, "OMB Cracks Whip."

28. See testimony of Daniel Guttman and Gary D. Bass, *Oversight of the Office of Management and Budget Regulatory Review and Planning Process*, Hearing before the Senate Committee on Governmental Affairs, 99 Cong. 2 sess. (GPO, 1986), pp. 249–51, 254–55.

29. Alison Mitchell, "The Silent Shift of Power," *Newsday*, May 4, 1986, p. 24.

30. See Marshall R. Goodman and Margaret T. Wrightson, *Managing Regulatory Reform: The Reagan Strategy and Its Impact* (Praeger, 1987), pp. 106–08.

31. Quoted in ibid., p. 108.

32. Ibid., p. 90.

33. Sandra S. Osbourn, "The Office of Management and Budget and Intergovernmental Management," in Senate Committe on Governmental Affairs, *Office of Management and Budget: Evolving Roles and Future Issues*, 99 Cong. 2 sess. (GPO, 1986), p. 335.

34. See Irene Fraser Rothenberg and George J. Gordon, "'Out with the Old, In with the New': The New Federalism, Intergovernmental Coordination, and Executive Order 12372," *Publius*, vol. 14 (Summer 1984), pp. 31–47.

35. Williamson, "New Federalism," p. 25.

36. Goodman and Wrightson, *Managing Regulatory Reform*, p. 206.

37. Interview with John Purcell, National School Boards Association, May 27, 1983.

38. Weidenbaum, "Reagan Federalism," p. 76. See also C. Boyden Gray, "Regulation and Federalism," *Yale Journal on Regulation*, vol. 1 (1983), pp. 93–110.

39. Quoted in Daniel Gottlieb, "Business Mobilizes as States Begin to Move into the Regulatory Vacuum," *National Journal*, July 31, 1982, p. 1342.

40. Felicity Barringer, "U.S. Preemption: Muscling in on the States," *Washington Post*, October 25, 1982.

41. Alan B. Morrison, "N[e]w Fed[e]ral[i]sm Holes," *New York Times*, September 20, 1982.

42. Alfred R. Light, "Federalism, FERC v. Missippi, and Product Liability Reform," *Publius*, vol 13 (Spring 1983), p. 85.

43. Ibid., p. 96.

44. Gray, "Regulation and Federalism," pp. 96, 97.

45. Caroline Mayer, "Product Liability Dispute Is Settled," *Washington Post*, July 16, 1982.

46. Ernest Holsendolph, "Lewis Offers Plan on Trucks as Exchange for a Tax Rise," *New York Times*, May 5, 1982.

47. Ibid.

48. *Congressional Quarterly Almanac, 1982* (Washington, D.C.: CQ, 1983), p. 317.

49. Barbara Harsha, "DOT Sets Final Routes for Large Trucks," *Nation's Cities Weekly,* June 19, 1984, p. 2.

50. Steven R. Weisman, "Reagan Signs Law Linking Federal Aid to Drinking Age," *New York Times,* July 18, 1984.

51. Douglas Feaver, "Reagan Now Wants 21 as Drinking Age," *Washington Post,* June 14, 1984.

52. Weisman, "Reagan Signs Law."

53. Eric Wiesenthal, "Municipal Affirmative Action Plans Attacked," *Public Administration Times,* June 1, 1985, p. 1.

54. Neal R. Peirce, "Republican Mayor Blasts Reagan on Civil Rights," *County News,* June 3, 1985, p. 18.

55. Herbert Stein, "The Reagan Revolt That Wasn't," *Harpers,* February 1984, p. 48.

Chapter Eleven

1. Interview with *Evening Star* and *Washington Daily News,* November 9, 1982, in "Nixon Goal: A Leaner but Stronger Government," *National Journal,* December 16, 1982, p. 1915.

2. Edwin Harper, deputy staff director, White House Domestic Council, quoted in Timothy B. Clark and others, "New Federalism: Return of Power to States and Cities Looms as Theme of Nixon's Second-Term Domestic Policy," *National Journal,* December 16, 1982, p. 1909.

3. Quoted in A. James Reichley, *Conservatives in an Age of Change: The Nixon and Ford Administrations* (Brookings, 1981), p. 70.

4. William Safire, "Newest Federalism," *New York Times,* January 28, 1982.

5. Theodore J. Lowi, "Ronald Reagan—Revolutionary?" in Lester M. Salamon and Michael S. Lund, eds., *The Reagan Presidency and the Governing of America* (Washington, D.C.: Urban Institute Press, 1984), p. 41.

6. "Economic Report of the President: Annual Message to the Congress, February 10, 1982," *Weekly Compilation of Presidential Documents,* February 15, 1982, p. 164.

7. "Reagan to the Nation's Governors—The Federal Aid Cupboard Is Bare," *National Journal,* November 28, 1981, p. 2110.

8. Quoted in Lester M. Salamon, "Nonprofit Organizations: A Lost Opportunity?" in John L. Palmer and Isabel V. Sawhill, eds., *The Reagan Record* (Urban Institute Press, 1984), p. 261.

9. Ronald Reagan, "Conservative Blueprint for the 1970s," reprinted in *Congressional Record,* October 1, 1975, p. 31184.

10. Ibid., p. 31185.

11. Robert Carleson, quoted in E. Clarke Ross, "Changing Policies and Program Trends in Publicly Financed Services to the Developmentally Disabled," *Word from Washington,* vol. 4 (September 1982), p. 11.

12. Samuel H. Beer, "The Adoption of General Revenue Sharing: A Case Study in Public Sector Politics," *Public Policy*, vol. 24 (Spring 1976), pp. 127–96.

13. Eric M. Uslaner, "The Decline of Comity in Congress," paper prepared for the 1987 annual meeting of the Political Studies Association of the United Kingdom, abstract page.

14. Steven S. Smith, "New Patterns of Decisionmaking in Congress," in John E. Chubb and Paul E. Peterson, eds., *The New Direction in American Politics* (Brookings, 1985), pp. 203–34.

15. Paul E. Peterson, "The Politics of Deficits," in Chubb and Peterson, eds., *New Direction in American Politics*, pp. 365–97.

16. Lloyd Free and Hadley Cantril, *The Political Beliefs of Americans: A Study of Public Opinion* (New Brunswick, N.J.: Rutgers University Press, 1967), p. 180.

17. Seymour Martin Lipset and William Schneider, "The Confidence Gap during the Reagan Years, 1981–1987," *Political Science Quarterly*, vol. 102 (Spring 1987), p. 21.

18. See John E. Chubb, "Federalism and the Bias for Centralization," in Chubb and Peterson, eds., *New Direction in American Politics*, pp. 273–306.

19. Dennis P. Doyle and Terry W. Hartle, "Excellence in Education: The States Respond," paper prepared for the American Enterprise Institute's Public Policy Week, Washington, D.C., December 5, 1984, p. 1.

20. See Rodney Moen, "Midwest Tests New Policies," *State Government News*, vol. 29 (September 1986), pp. 12–13; and "Going to Market: New Aggressiveness in Farm Marketing," *Governor's Weekly Bulletin*, October 17, 1986, pp. 1–2.

21. John Herbers, "The New Federalism: Unplanned, Innovative and Here to Stay," *Governing*, vol. 1 (October 1987), p. 28.

22. This broad pattern of institutional modernization among the states is abundantly documented in U.S. Advisory Commission on Intergovernmental Relations, *The Question of State Government Capability*, A-98 (GPO, 1985); and Mavis Mann Reeves, "Look Again at State Capacity," in Robert Jay Dilger, ed., *American Intergovernmental Relations Today: Perspectives and Controversies* (Englewood Cliffs, N.J.: Prentice Hall, 1986), pp. 143–59.

23. See George Peterson, "The Block Grants in Perspective," in George Peterson, ed., *The Reagan Block Grants* (Urban Institute Press, 1986), pp. 13–16.

24. ACIR, *Significant Features of Fiscal Federalism, 1987 Edition*, M-151 (GPO, 1987), p. 15.

25. See Paul E. Peterson, Barry G. Rabe, and Kenneth K. Wong, *When Federalism Works* (Brookings, 1986); and Martin A. Levin and Barbara Ferman, *The Political Hand: Policy Implementation and Youth Employment Programs* (Pergamon, 1985).

26. Michael Kirst and Richard Jung, "The Utility of a Longitudinal Approach in Assessing Implementation: A Thirteen-Year View of Title I, ESEA," in Walter Williams, ed., *Studying Implementation: Methodological and Administrative Issues* (Chatham, N.J.: Chatham House, 1982), pp. 119–48.

27. Herbers, "New Federalism," p. 34.

28. David B. Walker, "The Condition and Course of the System," in Lewis G. Bender and James A. Stever, eds., *Administering the New Federalism* (Boulder, Colo.: Westview, 1986), p. 344.

29. Laurence H. Tribe, *American Constitutional Law* (Mineola, N.Y.: Foundation Press, 1978), p. 302.

30. See Kenneth C. Wheare, *Federal Government,* 4th ed. (Greenwood Press, 1980); and John Stuart Mill, *Considerations on Representative Government,* ed. Currin V. Shields (Bobbs-Merrill, 1958), chap. 10.

31. See Cynthia Cates Colella, "The United States Supreme Court and Intergovernmental Relations," in Robert Jay Dilger, ed., *American Intergovernmental Relations Today: Perspectives and Controversies* (Prentice Hall, 1986), pp. 30–71.

32. *Garcia v. San Antonio Metropolitan Transit Authority, et al.,* 469 U.S. 528, 552.

33. Martha Derthick, "Preserving Federalism: Congress, the States, and the Supreme Court," *Brookings Review,* vol. 4 (Winter–Spring 1986), p. 32.

34. See Herbert Wechsler, "The Political Safeguards of Federalism: The Role of the States in the Composition and Selection of the National Government," *Columbia Law Review,* April 1954, p. 54.

35. See James McGregor Burns, *The Deadlock of Democracy* (Prentice Hall, 1963); David Price, *Who Makes the Laws? Creativity and Power in Senate Committees* (Cambridge, Mass.: Schenkman, 1972); and Gary Orfield, *Congressional Power: Congress and Social Change* (Harcourt Brace Jovanovich, 1975).

36. Morton Grodzins, *The American System: A New View of Government in the United States,* ed. Daniel Elazar (Rand McNally, 1966), p. 254.

37. ACIR, *The Transformation in American Politics: Implications for Federalism,* A-106 (GPO, 1986), pp. 81–91, 111–22.

38. Leon D. Epstein, "Party Confederations and Political Nationalization," *Publius,* vol. 12 (Fall 1982), p. 100.

39. Robert Huckshorn and John Bibby, "State Parties in an Era of Political Change," in Joel L. Fleishman, ed., *The Future of American Political Parties* (Prentice Hall, 1982), pp. 91–92.

40. By some estimates, the number of interest groups represented in Washington doubled between 1960 and 1980. See Jack L. Walker, "The Origins and Maintenance of Interest Groups in America," *American Political Science Review,* vol. 77 (June 1983), pp. 397–402; and Kay Lehman Schlozman and John T. Tierney, "More of the Same: Washington Pressure Group Activity in a Decade of Change," *Journal of Politics,* vol. 45 (May 1983), p. 356.

41. Interview with Jim Martin, July 28, 1986.

42. Derthick, "Preserving Federalism," p. 36.

43. For more on this important and novel development, see David R. Beam and J. Edwin Benton, "Intergovernmental Relations and Public Policy: Down the Road," in J. Edwin Benton and David R. Morgan, eds., *Intergovernmental Relations and Public Policy* (Greenwood Press, 1986), pp. 209–10.

44. Remarks of Dr. Eugene Summers to the Consortium of Social Science

Associations' seminar on Revitalizing Rural America in an Economically Competitive World, Washington, D.C., April 7, 1987.

45. See Peterson, Rabe, and Wong, *When Federalism Works*, chaps. 6, 7.

46. For a recent example of such continuing interest, see Committee on Federalism and National Purpose, *To Form a More Perfect Union* (Washington, D.C.: National Conference on Social Welfare, 1985).

47. Richard P. Nathan and Fred C. Doolittle, *Reagan and the States* (Princeton University Press, 1987), chap. 15.

48. Samuel H. Beer, "Federalism, Nationalism, and Democracy in America," *American Political Science Review*, vol. 72 (March 1978), pp. 9–21.

49. See Martha Derthick, *New Towns In-Town: Why a Federal Program Failed* (Urban Institute, 1972).

Index